NOV 21 2022

P9-DGK-435

East Meadow Public Library
186 Front Street, East Meadow, NY 11554
(516) 794-2570
www.eastmeadow.info

ALSO BY ANDY GREENBERG

Sandworm

This Machine Kills Secrets

TRACERS
IN
THE
DARK

TRACERS
IN
THE
DARK

The Global Hunt for
the Crime Lords
of Cryptocurrency

ANDY GREENBERG

Doubleday
New York

Copyright © 2022 by Andy Greenberg

All rights reserved. Published in the United States by Doubleday, a division of Penguin Random House LLC, New York, and distributed in Canada by Penguin Random House Canada Limited, Toronto.

www.doubleday.com

DOUBLEDAY and the portrayal of an anchor with a dolphin are registered trademarks of Penguin Random House LLC.

Jacket images: (coins) Image Source; (circuit) Turnervisual / DigitalVision Vectors; (metal texture) Katsumi Murouchi / Moment, all Getty Images
Jacket design: Michael J. Windsor
Book design: Betty Lew

Library of Congress Cataloging-in-Publication Data
Names: Greenberg, Andy, author.
Title: Tracers in the dark: the global hunt for the crime lords of crypto-currency / Andy Greenberg.
Description: First edition. | New York: Doubleday, [2022] | Includes bibliographical references.
Identifiers: LCCN 2022005413 (print) | LCCN 2022005414 (ebook) | ISBN 9780385548090 (hardcover) | ISBN 9780385548106 (ebook)
Subjects: LCSH: Computer crimes. | Commercial crimes. | Cryptocurrencies. | Transnational crime.
Classification: LCC HV6773.G7424 2022 (print) | LCC HV6773 (ebook) | DDC 364.16/8—dc23/eng/20220215
LC record available at https://lccn.loc.gov/2022005413
LC ebook record available at https://lccn.loc.gov/2022005414

MANUFACTURED IN THE UNITED STATES OF AMERICA

10 9 8 7 6 5 4 3 2 1

First Edition

For Bilal and Zayd

"And I beheld, unclouded by doubt, a magnificent vision of all that invisibility might mean to a man—the mystery, the power, the freedom. . . . And after three years of secrecy and exasperation, I found that to complete it was impossible—impossible."

"How?" asked Kemp.

"Money," said the Invisible Man, and went again to stare out of the window.

—H. G. Wells, *The Invisible Man*

CONTENTS

PART III ALPHABAY

PART IV WELCOME TO VIDEO

AUTHOR'S NOTE

The story told here, particularly in the later parts titled "AlphaBay," "Welcome to Video," and "The Next Round," includes references to suicide and self-harm. The part titled "Welcome to Video" also includes references to child abuse, though the abuse is not graphically described.

If you or someone you know needs help, please find it at sites including 988lifeline.org, missingkids.org, and stopitnow.org.

TRACERS
IN
THE
DARK

Proof of Concept

Early one fall morning in 2017, in a middle-class suburb on the outskirts of Atlanta, Chris Janczewski stood alone, inside the doorway of a home that he had not been invited to enter.

Moments earlier, armed Homeland Security Investigations agents in ballistic vests had taken positions around the tidy, two-story brick house, banged on the front door, and, when a member of the family living there opened it, swarmed inside. Janczewski, an Internal Revenue Service criminal investigator, had followed quietly behind them. Now he found himself in the foyer, at the eye of a storm of activity, watching the Homeland Security agents as they searched the premises and seized electronic devices.

They had separated the family, putting the father, an assistant principal at the local high school and the target of their investigation, in one room; his wife in another; the two kids into a third. An agent had switched on a TV and put on the cartoon *Mickey Mouse Clubhouse* in an attempt to distract the children from the invasion of their home and the interrogation of their parents.

Janczewski had come along on this raid only as an observer, a visiting IRS agent flown in from Washington, D.C., to watch and advise the local Homeland Security team as it executed its warrant. But it was Janczewski's investigation that had brought the agents here, to this very average-looking house with its well-kept yard among all the average-looking houses they could have been searching, anywhere in America. He had led them there based on a strange, nascent form of evidence:

Janczewski had followed the strands of Bitcoin's blockchain, pulling on a thread that had ultimately connected this ordinary home to a very dark place on the internet, and then connected that dark place to hundreds more men around the world. All complicit in the same massive network of unspeakable abuse. All now on Janczewski's long list of targets.

Over the previous few years, Janczewski, his partner Tigran Gambaryan, and a small group of law enforcement investigators at a growing roster of three-letter American agencies had used this newfound investigative technique, tracing a cryptocurrency that had once seemed untraceable, to crack one criminal case after another—starting small but ballooning into operations on an unprecedented, epic scale. They'd followed Bitcoin transactions to identify culprits from Baltimore to Moscow to Bangkok. They'd exposed crooked cops stealing millions. They'd tracked down half a billion dollars in stolen funds, the fruits of a multiyear, international heist and money-laundering operation. And they'd pulled off the biggest online narcotics market takedown in history, capturing the market's creator and shutting down his bustling digital bazaar, one that had generated more than $650 million in contraband sales.

But even after all of those journeys into the depths of the cybercriminal underworld, tracing cryptocurrency had never before led them to a case quite like this one. That morning's search in the suburb near Atlanta, as Janczewski would later put it, was "a proof of concept."

From where Janczewski was positioned at the front of the house, he could hear the agents speaking to the father, who responded in a broken, resigned voice. In another room, he could simultaneously hear the Homeland Security agents questioning the man's wife; she was answering that, yes, she'd found certain images on her husband's computer, but he'd told her he'd downloaded them by accident when he was pirating music. And in the third room he could hear the two elementary-school-age children—kids about as old as Janczewski's own—watching TV. They asked for a snack, seemingly oblivious to the tragedy unfolding for their family.

Janczewski remembers the reality of the moment hitting him: This was a high school administrator, a husband, and a father of two. Whether he was guilty or innocent, the accusations this team of law enforcement agents were leveling against him—their mere presence in his home— would almost certainly ruin his life.

He thought again of the extradimensional evidence that had brought them there, a tool like a digital divining rod, one that revealed a hidden layer of illicit connections underlying the visible world. He hoped, not for the last time, that it hadn't led him astray.

PART I

MEN
WITH
NO
NAMES

Eladio Guzman Fuentes

On September 27, 2013, four years before Chris Janczewski stepped into that house in the Atlanta suburbs, someone moved 525 bitcoins. Those coins, worth around $70,000 when they were sent but more than $15 million as of this writing,* traveled from one Bitcoin address identified by a meaningless string of thirty-four characters to another address with an equally long and meaningless identifier. More specifically, 15T7SagsD2JqWUpBsiifcVuvyrQwX3Lq1e sent them to 1AJGTi3i2tPUg3ojwoHndDN1DYhJTWKSAA.

The transaction, like all Bitcoin transactions, happened silently, but not at all secretly. The sender's computer had sent out a message to nearby computers in Bitcoin's global network "announcing" the payment. Within minutes the announcement had been passed to thousands of other machines around the world, all of which confirmed that they'd witnessed it, adding it into their copy of the Bitcoin blockchain, the unforgeable, unchangeable, and altogether public ledger of who owns which bitcoins in the global cryptocurrency economy. In fact, these witnesses noting the transaction in their collective accounting of all bitcoins—agreed to by all of the cryptocurrency's users—represented the only meaningful sense in which the abstract coins could be said to have "moved" at all, or to have even existed in the first place.

---

* Bitcoin's exchange rate is famously volatile, but at the time this book was being finalized in the spring of 2022, its price in dollars was fluctuating around $30,000, so certain descriptions of value in the book roughly reflect that number.

But they did exist, and they did move: You can type one of those long-winded addresses into a search engine today and see the transaction for yourself, on a site like blockchain.com or btc.com. This public, permanent record of someone's five-figure payment cannot be rescinded or erased.

Yet to anyone who looked at the same transaction record at the time, there would be no clue revealing *who* that someone was—neither the sender nor the recipient. Nothing in that record, sitting fully visible on the open internet, would indicate that the money had, in fact, moved from the accounts of the world's first dark web drug lord to the wallet of a federal agent, payment to that agent for acting as a mole inside a global team of investigators working to take down a giant narcotics market.

A month after that payment, the dark web drug lord would be arrested and jailed. But it would take nearly a year longer before an IRS criminal investigator named Tigran Gambaryan laid eyes on the record of that transaction. Sitting in his Hayward, California, home, with his infant daughter in his lap, he would painstakingly click through addresses on Bitcoin's blockchain, "hand tracing" the movement of that dirty money, as he would later describe it. And when he identified its destination, his epiphany would unlock a new era of law enforcement investigation, one in which detectives like Gambaryan could follow the money, digitally, to unfathomable hoards of ill-gotten wealth and to the doorsteps of the criminals who had collected it.

.   .   .

For Gambaryan, the case began with a fake ID.

George Frost, an older, white-haired lawyer, passed the printout to Gambaryan across a conference table, showing a scan of a Maryland driver's license for one "Eladio Guzman Fuentes." The man pictured on the license was middle-aged, with a shaved head, a goatee, and an unreadable look. Frost also pulled out what appeared to be copies of Fuentes's utility bill and his Social Security card. The identifying documents, Frost said, were all part of the package Fuentes had used to open an account on Bitstamp, a cryptocurrency exchange founded in Slovenia where Frost served as general counsel. Bitstamp, like other exchanges around the world, allowed its users to buy bitcoins and other more obscure cryptocurrencies with older forms of legal tender like dollars, euros, and yen—and vice versa, cashing out their crypto coins for those traditional currencies.

The ID documents in front of them, Frost explained, were forgeries. Fuentes's real name was Carl Mark Force IV, and he was an agent with the Drug Enforcement Administration. This man, Frost went on, had cashed out more than $200,000 worth of bitcoins through Bitstamp over the previous six months, and he was trying to extract another $200,000 of the cryptocurrency when Frost had frozen his account for suspicious activity, just days before this meeting.

It was early May 2014, and Frost was sitting in a conference room on the ninth floor of the Department of Justice building, deep within its warren of offices and cubicles in the financial district of San Francisco. Across the table from him sat Gambaryan, a twenty-eight-year-old Armenian American IRS agent with a trim beard, a shaved head, and a compact build; the Eastern Orthodox tattoos on his left arm and right shoulder were hidden under his suit. One of Tigran Gambaryan's colleagues described him as a "short, buff Andre Agassi."

Sitting next to Gambaryan was Kathryn Haun, a prosecutor for the Northern District of California who had asked Frost to come in that day. Until this point in the meeting, Gambaryan and Haun had been questioning Frost about something else entirely. They were building a case against the founders of another start-up, called Ripple, which had issued a cryptocurrency of the same name. Gambaryan and Haun believed Ripple might be acting as an unlicensed money exchanger, letting people buy and sell cryptocurrency while skirting U.S. banking regulations. Frost had once been general counsel for Ripple, and Bitstamp was now being used to trade in Ripple's own form of cryptocurrency, too.

Frost, a former veteran newspaper reporter who now practiced law out of his Berkeley home office, considered himself an ACLU-supporting, lowercase-*l* libertarian. He had no love for the IRS or the Justice Department. But he'd put on a suit, traveled across the bay, subjected himself to the building's security screenings, and then responded to Haun and Gambaryan's interrogation for well over an hour.

Now, after answering those questions, Frost had arrived at his own reason for coming: Didn't they perhaps want to talk about this strange DEA agent, his fake identity, and where the hell his unexplained six-figure hoard of bitcoins had come from?

Haun and Gambaryan suggested he go on.

So Frost showed them Force's fake "Fuentes" ID documents and explained that Bitstamp's staff had rejected them: His Social Security number didn't match any in the databases of personal information they used for checking users' identities. When Bitstamp's staff later spotted Force registering for another account from the same computer, but this time under his own name, it was clear his first round of ID documents had been forgeries—pretty damn good ones, Frost had to admit. Bitstamp had confronted Force about his fraudulent ID and threatened to close his second account, too, based on their legally required know-your-customer rules.

Force had then surprised Frost by revealing that he was a federal agent. "Fuentes" was merely the undercover identity he had used in his DEA investigations, he said.

Bitstamp had noticed, though, that Force was connecting to their website using Tor, a piece of anonymity software that encrypts users' internet connections and routes them through servers around the world to make them as difficult to trace as possible. It seemed an unusual choice for a federal agent using a cryptocurrency exchange in his official work.

"I utilize TOR for privacy," Force had explained in an email to Bitstamp's staff. "Don't particularly want the NSA looking over my shoulder. :)"

All of it left Frost feeling deeply uneasy. Was this DEA agent using Bitstamp's crypto exchange as part of his undercover work to bank dirty drug money? And if so, why would he want to hide his tracks from another U.S. government agency? "The harder we looked at this, the stranger it seemed," Frost recalled.

In subsequent emails, Force changed his story again: He was an early Bitcoin investor, he now said, and the money he was cashing out was his own, not the DEA's. He added that he had learned about Bitcoin in the course of his DEA work, and specifically "through my investigation of DREAD PIRATE ROBERTS and the SILK ROAD."

At Frost's mention of those two bold-faced names, Gambaryan's attention suddenly sharpened. The Silk Road had already become legendary: the sprawling, Bitcoin-based online black market for dark web narcotics sales, created by a pseudonymous figure known as the Dread Pirate Roberts. Just months earlier, the FBI, IRS, and DHS had finally, after a two-and-a-half-year hunt, identified the site's founder as a twenty-nine-year-old Texan with no criminal record, a man by the name of Ross Ulbricht. Agents had swarmed into the science fiction section of a San Francisco library, arrested Ulbricht where he sat running his vast drug empire, grabbed his laptop, and shut down the Silk Road for good.

Stories of the landmark dark web case still reverberated through the law enforcement community. Gambaryan, based in the IRS's Oakland office—just a few miles away, it turned out, from Ross Ulbricht's home—had been asked only to interview a few witnesses in the aftermath of Ulbricht's arrest. The IRS agent had itched to be a bigger part of the investigation.

But if Gambaryan was excited now, he gave no indication. Frost remembers that, typically for a federal agent, the younger man had no visible reaction, instead quietly taking notes on a yellow legal pad. Although Frost knew Haun from other cases, it was his first meeting with Gambaryan. Despite his wariness toward federal law enforcement, Frost found that he liked the agent's open mind and sharp questions, his way of understated probing. It reminded Frost of his own days working as an investigative journalist, early in his career.

Frost continued his story: Something about the DEA agent's answers to Bitstamp's questions had felt off. "There's something wrong with this guy," he told Haun and Gambaryan. "This doesn't pass the smell test."

So Frost had filed a suspicious activity report with the U.S. Treasury's Financial Crimes Enforcement Network, or FinCEN. He'd gotten a call back from a Secret Service agent based in Baltimore, a man named Shaun Bridges.

Frost had worked with Bridges in the past, he explained. The Secret Service agent had helped Frost when hackers associated with the Palestinian militant movement Hamas had targeted Bitstamp users with unusually well-crafted phishing emails designed to hijack their accounts. Despite Frost's antiestablishment leanings, he had found the Secret Service agent conscientious, well connected, and technically adept. When Frost told him about his troubling new Carl Force situation, Bridges assured Frost he'd personally make sure it was taken care of.

But since then, months had passed, with no real update from Bridges. Frost had begun to suspect that he was being stonewalled. Force, meanwhile, was still cashing out hundreds of thousands of dollars' worth of bitcoins through his company's exchange.

Then an agent from the same Baltimore law enforcement team as Force had begun sending Bitstamp emails demanding account information for other users and asking questions about their compliance with money-laundering laws. Frost had gone so far as to call Force to talk about his strange behavior and the Baltimore agent's demands. In the strained phone call, Force had seemed "belligerent," Frost recounted, but had also been brazen enough to suggest that Bitstamp hire him as a chief compliance officer.

To Frost, what had started as merely unwelcome business from a shady customer was starting to seem like a shakedown. And no one was shielding Frost from this bizarre, aberrant DEA agent.

"This guy has a badge. A gun. He can go anywhere. He can tap anybody's phone, including mine," Frost told Gambaryan and Haun. He needed their help.

· · ·

As the meeting ended, Haun warned Frost that there was still no evidence Force had done anything illegal. Opening an investigation into a federal agent was no small matter. But before Frost walked out, she promised that she and Gambaryan would look into it.

Despite his poker face throughout their meeting, Gambaryan shared little of Haun's professed reluctance. He'd been waiting for a case like this for years.

Since he'd become an IRS criminal investigator in 2011, Gambaryan had been fascinated by the budding Bitcoin economy. In this new digital currency, he'd come to see not only an intricate technical novelty but a wild, untamed, and lawless new territory of finance. For an IRS special agent, that frontier represented a vast greenfield of potentially career-making cases. He'd gone so far as to ask for meetings with the staff of any Bitcoin start-up in the Bay Area who would let him visit, just to pick their brains and learn more about this strange new world of digital money.

When he'd gotten wind of the Silk Road's Bitcoin black market, not long after its inception in 2011, he'd suggested to a supervisor that they take on the case. But his superior had answered vaguely that someone else in law enforcement was already handling it. In fact, multiple investigations into the Silk Road were already spinning up from Chicago to Baltimore to New York, and at the time none of them seemed to need the help of a junior IRS agent in Oakland.

When the Silk Road's creator had finally been located and arrested two years later, Gambaryan's bosses were surprised—and perhaps a bit embarrassed—to learn the dark web site had been run in San Francisco, their own backyard. By the time the online black market was taken down in October 2013, the Silk Road had grown into a gargantuan narcotics and money-laundering bazaar unlike any ever seen before in history. And for much of its time online, its founder had been just across the bay, practically under their noses.

Now, six months after the Silk Road bust, Frost's story seemed to hint that some part of the site's mysteries still remained unsolved. For Gambaryan, it was a welcome lead back into a case he'd coveted for years—or rather, a thread, however tenuous, that seemed to trail off from the Silk Road's vast tangle of criminality, into the unknown.

Nob

Gambaryan's first call was to his friend and fellow IRS agent Gary Alford, an unsung hero of the Silk Road investigation. Alford's role in that case, as the agent who had first identified Ross Ulbricht as the suspected creator of the world's largest dark web drug market, was largely untold outside law enforcement circles at the time. From 2011 until 2013, agents had scoured the Silk Road site for clues that could help unmask the site's creator and mastermind, known as the Dread Pirate Roberts, or DPR. But as the Silk Road gained thousands of customers and made tens of millions of dollars in Bitcoin-based narcotics profits, DPR had never shared any identifying details in his communications with his staff or users, and certainly not with the undercover agents trying to pry those details out of him. And because the Silk Road ran on Tor's anonymity network, no one could trace DPR's connection to an IP address, the internet protocol identifier that might reveal his location.

When agents finally swooped in on Ross Ulbricht and handcuffed him in that San Francisco public library in October 2013, it was the FBI who received most of the public credit. But in fact, it had been the IRS's Gary Alford, sitting in his New Jersey home four months earlier, who'd done the meticulous, unglamorous work that had led to the case's first real breakthrough.

Alford had been using Google to dig up the earliest online posts about the Silk Road on drug forums when he'd found a curious artifact: Someone going by the name "altoid" had posted to a site called the Shroomery in January 2011 recommending the Silk Road's just-launched dark web market as a source for drugs. Around the same time, a user with the same handle had also asked for programming help on a coding forum. On that page, altoid had listed his email address: rossulbricht@gmail.com.

Though Ulbricht later managed to delete his email address from the coding forum post, it had been copied into someone's response to the message, indelibly preserving it on the web, where it hid in plain sight for years.

When Alford pointed this out to colleagues, they struggled to believe that Google alone could unveil the world's most mysterious digital drug lord. It had taken more than a month for the FBI, DEA, and DOJ staff assigned to the investigation to even take the IRS agent's lead seriously. Ultimately, his discovery had cracked the case.

To IRS criminal investigators like Gambaryan and Alford, both special agents in the service's Criminal Investigation division, known as IRS-CI, the story was irritatingly typical. While the FBI were made into near superheroes in countless Hollywood films, TV shows, and press conferences, no one seemed to have even heard of IRS-CI agents like them. ("The IRS is the redheaded stepchild of law enforcement," as one judge told me. "They get no respect from anyone.")

The IRS's criminal division agents did shoe-leather detective work, carried guns, executed search warrants, and made arrests, just like their FBI and DEA counterparts. And yet because of the IRS's reputation as pencil pushers—and because of IRS-CI's core focus on following the money—they often found that their fellow agents treated them like accountants. "Don't audit me," their peers from other law enforcement agencies would joke when they were introduced in meetings. Most IRS-CI agents had heard the line enough times that it warranted an instant eye roll.

.　.　.

Gambaryan had a friendly working relationship with Alford. The New York–based agent had been the one to call up Gambaryan after Ulbricht's arrest and ask him to do a few low-stakes witness interviews. Now, as Gambaryan relayed to Alford on the phone what he'd heard from Frost about this seemingly rogue DEA agent named Carl Mark Force, the mere mention of Force's name seemed to set off alarms in Alford's head.

Force, Alford explained, was part of the Baltimore Task Force that had been investigating the Silk Road, separate from the New York team of FBI, Homeland Security, and IRS agents of which Alford was a part. The two teams had clashed early on: In "deconfliction" meetings, they'd jostled for control of the case and parted on unfriendly terms. In the end, each went its own way, essentially racing in parallel in their pursuit of the mysterious dark web mastermind who called himself DPR.

The New York team had prevailed: They'd identified Ulbricht in San Francisco, thanks in no small part to Alford's work; found a way to circumvent the Silk Road's anonymity software to locate its servers, housed in Icelandic and French data centers; and charged Ulbricht with a slew of felonies, from narcotics and money-laundering conspiracies to a "kingpin statute" usually reserved for mob bosses and drug cartel leaders.

The Baltimore investigators, meanwhile, had taken a very different path. Their central focus had been infiltrating the Silk Road undercover: They created the persona of a Puerto Rican drug cartel operative who went by the handle "Nob." Nob had spent countless hours on the Silk Road exchanging messages with DPR to gain his friendship and trust.

The undercover DEA agent playing the role of Nob? None other than Carl Mark Force, assuming the identity of a Puerto Rican man named Eladio Guzman Fuentes—the name that later appeared on the forged documents he gave Bitstamp.

When DPR later came to suspect that one of his Silk Road employees had stolen hundreds of thousands of dollars' worth of Bitcoin from him, it was Nob—Force—whom DPR turned to for help handling the situation. The Silk Road boss asked his associate, with his supposed cartel connections, to track down his thieving staffer and torture him until he returned the money. In a dark turn, DPR later changed the order, asking Nob to kill his wayward worker instead.

Nob agreed. Carl Mark Force, along with other agents from the Baltimore Task Force, had helped to stage fake photos in which they appeared to be waterboarding the Silk Road's rogue staffer, followed by images depicting what appeared to be the man's corpse. He sent them to DPR as proof that he'd done the job.

When the New York team arrested Ulbricht a few months later and unsealed their indictment accusing him of running the Silk Road, the Baltimore team had piled on their own murder-for-hire charge in a separate indictment, based on the fake murder that they themselves had helped Ulbricht to carry out.

In Alford's telling, the Baltimore team's work sounded remarkably messy. There were other rumors about Force, too: that years earlier he'd spent time cooling off in rehab after an undercover narcotics investigation. He'd gotten in too deep, the story went, inhabiting the role of the drug dealer he was playing a bit too fully, maybe losing track of which side he was on.

Now a lawyer for Bitstamp was warning them that this same DEA agent was cashing out mysterious six-figure bitcoin stashes? Carl Mark Force IV, Gambaryan could see, was worthy of his full attention.

. . .

Gambaryan knew there would be a high bar to opening a formal investigation of a federal law enforcement officer. The whiff of impropriety surrounding Force was overwhelming, but was it enough to persuade a prosecutor like Kathryn Haun to launch a criminal case? Haun, for her part, had discussed it with her boss, a veteran U.S. attorney named Will Frentzen who had spent his career taking down Chinatown organized crime bosses and corrupt California politicians. Frentzen was open-minded but unconvinced. "We need to run this down," he told her. "But it's likely a misunderstanding."

Then, just one day after their initial meeting, Haun received an email from Frost. The Bitstamp lawyer forwarded a request that Force had just sent to the cryptocurrency exchange's customer service. "Could you please delete my transaction history to date?" the agent had written. "It is cumbersome to go through records back to November 2013 for my accountant."

Haun and Frentzen saw the email as a shocking red flag. After all of his other suspicious behavior, Force now seemed to be trying to destroy evidence. Any reluctance evaporated. They opened an investigation into Force the same day, with Gambaryan as lead agent.

The twenty-eight-year-old IRS investigator had finally found the meaty cryptocurrency case he'd been looking for. It had put him onto the trail of a fellow federal agent.

CHAPTER 3

The Auditor

Tigran Gambaryan was perhaps destined to be an accountant. His parents were both accountants, and for much of his life he assumed he'd become one, too. He'd also always had the right sort of mind for it, with an attention to detail and a willingness to embrace thorny numerical systems.

But another side of Gambaryan would never be satisfied with merely balancing books. There was a tougher, more combative streak to his personality—a pronounced sense of justice, a fixation on right and wrong, that went beyond the technical correctness of a tax filing. He traces that harder part of himself to his childhood, which he describes as a happy one—until a very specific point.

Gambaryan was born in 1984 in Yerevan, the capital of then-Soviet Armenia, where his parents were both high-level finance officials in Armenia's communist government. His father had been a boxer and a water polo player, accomplished enough to have made the Soviet national team. Despite his elite Soviet credentials, he'd developed a love of Western music like Elvis and the Beatles. When the water polo team was on tour, he had even managed to buy and smuggle home a complete collection of Beatles LPs. The family's TV antenna could pick up Turkish signals from across the western border, and young Tigran loved to watch Rocky and Rambo films, a thrilling taste of another world, even though the movies were dubbed in Turkish and he couldn't understand a word.

Gambaryan remembers happy afternoons playing in the streets of Yerevan with his cousins and friends, surrounded by the city's iconic pastel pink and orange buildings constructed from volcanic tufa stone.

On the weekends, his extended family would gather at his grandfather's dacha in the rolling hills outside the city, with an orchard and a river running along the edge of the property.

"It was a good time," Gambaryan says. "Then the Soviet Union collapsed and it all went to hell."

Of the fifteen independent countries that emerged practically overnight from the shattered U.S.S.R. in the early 1990s, struggling to survive without Moscow's support, perhaps none fared worse than Armenia. War broke out almost immediately with neighboring Azerbaijan, a conflict sparked by Armenia's nearly century-old claim to the disputed territory of Nagorno-Karabakh. Once a fellow Soviet republic, Azerbaijan now imposed an embargo and blockaded the border, cutting off its vast oil supply that had been Armenia's main source of energy.

Soon, Gambaryan's family, like practically every family in Yerevan, had no electricity or heating in their home. When frozen pipes cracked in the winter, they lost running water, too. Gambaryan remembers waiting in line for hours, holding a ticket for bread. Neighbors were drafted and sent east to fight in the war. The forests around Yerevan were leveled as desperate city dwellers chopped down any firewood they could find. Some resorted to pulling up and burning their floorboards. Many Armenians rigged makeshift wood-burning stoves indoors and died of carbon monoxide inhalation. In winter, the schools initially asked students to bring firewood to heat the classrooms, then finally gave up and sent the children home.

In 1993, Gambaryan's family fled to Moscow, where his father held a position with the Armenian government. They moved into a five-story Khrushchev-era apartment building on the outskirts of the capital. For Tigran, then nine years old, it marked a huge lifestyle upgrade: After two years of Armenia's energy crisis, he delighted at how, when he flicked a light switch, the bulb actually lit up.

But he also remembers becoming aware that despite having been just as Soviet as any Russian a few years earlier, he was now considered very different from his Russian neighbors. Many of the real estate listings the family scoured had openly excluded requests from "people of Caucasian ethnicity." Police, too, would hound immigrants from the region, detaining them, demanding to see their papers, threatening them with deportation if they didn't offer a bribe.

Russia was at war with Chechen separatists in the Caucasus, and kids at school taunted Gambaryan, calling him a Chechen. Gambaryan, not one to shrink from confrontation, would toss back insults of his own. Soon he was regularly getting into fistfights and even full-on brawls at school, which he says the Russian teachers accepted as a normal part of Russian boyhood.

Eventually, though, Gambaryan settled into Muscovite life. Many of those Russian kids he'd fought with later became close friends. He would carouse with them around the streets of Moscow, just as he had earlier in the streets of Yerevan. He excelled in school, got perfect scores, and even skipped a grade—the sort of academic success his strict immigrant parents demanded.

But to Gambaryan, life in early-1990s Moscow always felt as though it were perched on the edge of a precipice. He came to recognize the crime and corruption that surrounded him. Mafia and crooked government officials seemed to be running the city. Every block was a gang's territory. Every business paid protection money to racketeers. He saw firsthand the aftermath of shootings and car bombings that resulted from turf wars. At one point, organized criminals kidnapped one of Gambaryan's father's friends and held him for an exorbitant ransom, which Gambaryan's family helped to pay.

That lawlessness left a deep mark on Gambaryan—as well as an almost zealous, black-and-white starkness to his ideas of criminality. Even today he says the sense remains with him that there are real elements of corruption and chaos in every society, that the "law of the land" he witnessed in Moscow lies just beneath the surface, everywhere, ready to emerge whenever people have a sense of impunity from consequences.

"Americans don't know how good they have it," Gambaryan says. "You let it slip, it turns into the chaos that I saw."

· · ·

In 1997, when Gambaryan was thirteen, his family moved again, this time to Fresno, California. Fresno had been a historic Armenian enclave since a flood of refugees had settled there after fleeing the Turkish campaign of genocide against Armenians in 1915. But the move meant Gambaryan was essentially starting over again as an outsider, dropped into American society without knowing more than a few words of English.

Their neighborhood in South Fresno, where the family lived in a three-bedroom apartment in a two-story stucco building, had rough edges. Gambaryan's father had been forced to stay behind in Moscow due to U.S. immigration bureaucracy, and it would take him seven years to join the family in California and obtain a green card. Meanwhile, Gambaryan's mother, an accomplished financier and former government official, was reduced to opening a shoe repair and alteration shop.

Compared with Russia and Armenia, though, life in the United States was easy and uneventful. Gambaryan adapted well to his new American environment, quickly learning the language. To his delight, he got his first computer as a gift from his parents: a Packard Bell desktop PC from Best Buy with a 166-megahertz processor. He left the tower's case open, the better to admire its engineering and fiddle with its components. That machine, and the early internet it unlocked, represented an enormous step up from what he'd experienced in Moscow, where his access to computers had consisted of an old Sega Genesis and messing around on his father's office PC, trying to figure out how to run *Prince of Persia* on a pirated version of DOS.

Gambaryan enrolled in Fresno State and—following in his parents' footsteps—got a degree in accounting, then a finance job in the California state government, followed by another in the California Franchise Tax Board, the state-level equivalent of the IRS. He worked as an auditor, meticulously reviewing the records of potential tax cheats. Gambaryan found he was well suited to the work, motivated in part by his outrage at seeing companies, and even individuals, amassing hundreds of millions of dollars while paying less in taxes than he did himself. Soon after, he joined the IRS and moved to Oakland to work out of the federal office there, auditing major tax fraud cases at the national level.

Still, Gambaryan wasn't entirely satisfied: His section of the IRS brought only civil lawsuits against tax evaders, or else referred them to the criminal division—throwing the cases over a wall and often never even hearing the results.

At orientation on his first day at the IRS in 2008, a public information officer had spoken to the new staff about the IRS Criminal Investigation division. Gambaryan had never heard of IRS-CI before, but it sounded like everything he'd ever wanted to do in his career, without realizing it: travel internationally, serve search warrants, take down criminals firsthand, and see them prosecuted. "I can use my accounting skills and also put away bad guys," Gambaryan remembers thinking. He'd started his application immediately.

After three years of paperwork, background checks, and training, Gambaryan was made an IRS-CI special agent. He threw himself into the job and soon had a full load of mortgage fraud, public corruption, and drug-related money-laundering investigations. But he often found that as a new recruit he was left to work the low-level cases that no other agents had wanted to take. Much of his time was spent busting gangs in East Oakland who had graduated from dealing drugs to filing fraudulent tax returns with stolen identities, a more lucrative crime that threatened them with far less prison time.

Gambaryan pursued the fraudsters, executed the warrants, made the arrests, but he began to realize that if he didn't somehow alter his course, he could easily spend the rest of his career assigned to the IRS equivalent of street crime. These were hardly the white-collar kingpins and international mafia figures he dreamed of taking down.

So after a couple of years, he made a commitment to himself: He'd no longer settle for whatever investigations fell to him. He'd make cases of his own.

. . .

Since he'd gotten that first Packard Bell PC in 1997, Gambaryan had remained a digital hobbyist, building and repairing computers and playing with new technologies whenever he read about them on forums like Reddit or *Slashdot*. In 2010, while still in the process of applying to join IRS-CI, he'd come across a post on one of those sites describing something called Bitcoin.

Bitcoin was a new digital currency, and it used a clever system to track who owned which coins: The Bitcoin network stored thousands of copies of a distributed accounting ledger on computers around the world—a ledger known as the blockchain. Many of Bitcoin's advocates seemed to believe that because no bank or government was necessary for Bitcoin's operation, no institution could control its payments or identify its users. Transactions flowed from one address to another, with none of the names or other personal details that a bank or payment service like PayPal might collect. "Participants can be anonymous," read one line in an email sent to a cryptography mailing list by the currency's mysterious inventor, known as Satoshi Nakamoto.

Bitcoin burrowed into the very center of Gambaryan's mind, at the point where his obsessions with computers and forensic accounting converged. As an IRS investigator tasked with following the money, he considered the notion of anonymous digital cash vaguely foreboding. Who would pay taxes on these "anonymous" transactions? Wouldn't Bitcoin become the perfect money-laundering tool?

But a more basic and skeptical thought immediately struck Gambaryan about this new form of currency. "Participants can be anonymous," he had read. But if this blockchain truly recorded every transaction in the entire Bitcoin economy, then it sounded like the precise opposite of anonymity: a trail of bread crumbs left behind by *every single payment*. A forensic accountant's dream.

Either way, no one seemed to be actually using Bitcoin for much at the time. So Gambaryan dismissed it as a kind of "silly internet money," more technically interesting than practical, and forgot about it.

The next time he would hear about Bitcoin, it would already be anointed as the coin of choice for the dark web's budding black market. And for a young IRS criminal investigator looking for his own vein of cases to mine, the currency would come to represent a mother lode of hidden money flows, demanding to be cracked open and traced to their source.

Cryptoanarchy

One evening in April 2011, just before Tigran Gambaryan was starting his training as an IRS-CI special agent, I visited MtGox.com, a website where I'd been told I could buy these so-called bitcoins. I was working on a story for *Forbes*—the magazine where I covered cybersecurity and cryptography—about a curious new form of virtual coin that somehow, in just the last year, had appreciated remarkably in value, from about half a penny each to just under a dollar. I figured that to understand this weird new currency I was writing about, I should try owning some of it.

So I attempted to place an order on MtGox.com (pronounced "Mount Gox," I was told) for $40 worth of bitcoins. I got no confirmation any transaction had occurred. It wasn't clear if the site, the only Bitcoin exchange I'd ever heard of, had even accepted my money or if it had simply gotten hung up on a bug in its code, like a vending machine spitting back out a perfectly good dollar bill. After a couple of refreshes and retries, I gave up.

Over the years since, I've occasionally looked back on that lack of persistence with regret. A decade later, those $40 worth of bitcoins would be worth $2.6 million.

.   .   .

My interest in Bitcoin had been sparked a few weeks earlier in the spring of 2011, when I stumbled across a YouTube video posted to Twitter, one that showed a software engineer named Gavin Andresen giving a talk at a TED-like event called Ignite, held in Amherst, Massachusetts. Andresen, a kind of baby-faced, central-casting programmer dressed in a blue button-down shirt, was introduced as the head of the "BitCoin Project."

Bitcoin, Andresen explained, was a "new kind of money," one that allowed anyone to spend cash-like currency from their computer while using cryptography to ensure that no one could create counterfeit coins or fraudulently spend someone else's. It had been invented by someone named Satoshi Nakamoto a few years earlier, he said, not long after the 2008 financial crisis, and it had been designed so that anyone could generate these bitcoins, too. They just had to run a so-called mining program on their own computer, performing calculations that entered them into a kind of automated lottery that distributed bitcoins to the winning computer every ten minutes.

This kind of computational effort was the only way anyone could "mine" new bitcoins, and they could do it only at a predefined, globally limited rate. That scarcity made it the perfect currency for anyone suspicious of how governments control money—their ability to print cash willy-nilly, to fund wars, or to hand money to corporate friends. "With the global financial crisis and bank bailouts all over the world, a lot of us are starting to wonder: Can we really trust the people who control our money?" Andresen explained in his Ignite talk. "Satoshi didn't. So he created Bitcoin."

Bitcoin, Andresen conceded, was still a "brand-new baby currency." The sum total of all bitcoins at the time was worth about $3 million. About $30,000 worth of bitcoins were changing hands every day, used to buy everything from alpaca socks to sex toys to dog sweaters.

"I don't know where it's going to go, but there's a small possibility that in fifty years it just might replace the dollar as the world's reserve currency," Andresen said, speaking in the sort of light tone that might have led the audience to believe he was joking. But he was not. "It might happen!" he added, as if to dispel any doubt about his seriousness. Exactly one person in the crowd responded with an enthusiastic whoop.

As radical as Andresen's dreams for Bitcoin's future value might have been, it was something else he said that got my attention: his brief description, almost in passing, of Bitcoin's pseudonymous creator, Satoshi Nakamoto, as "this mysterious guy who was definitely inspired by the cypherpunks."

The cypherpunks were, as I'd been obsessively researching at the time, a group of radical libertarians who had formed in the 1990s, unified around the grand mission of using unbreakable encryption software to take power away from governments and corporations and give it to individuals. When I discovered the YouTube video of Andresen's talk, I was in the midst of writing a book that chronicled the cypherpunk movement. I'd spent countless hours digging through the archives of the Cypherpunks Mailing List, a community of hundreds of programmers, cryptographers, anarchists, and trolls who, for nearly a decade, had shared their innovations, manifestos, and internal squabbles in a torrent of emails.

Julian Assange was an active participant on the Cypherpunks Mailing List, where many of the ideas for WikiLeaks, with its anonymity protections for its sources, were born. The first developers of so-called proxy servers, which offered encrypted and anonymized internet connections—and which would evolve into virtual private networks, or VPNs, in common use today—were core cypherpunk contributors. The creators of the anonymity software Tor, too, were deeply influenced by the discussions they read in the list's archives.

Cypherpunks envisioned a world where free cryptographic programs in the hands of everyday internet users promised total secrecy—from hackers, snoops, law enforcement, and even intelligence agencies. For ideological libertarians who dreamed of a day when governments could no longer control what they said, what they owned, or what they put in their bodies, encryption tools represented a new sort of untouchability: a future in which communications not only were impervious to eavesdropping but could be carried out behind perfectly unidentifiable and untraceable pseudonyms.

And if anonymous and untraceable digital communications were possible, the cypherpunks believed, it followed that anonymous and untraceable online *payments* must be, too—an innovation that was sure to unlock both a new era of financial privacy and a vast, flourishing black market on the internet.

The cypherpunk who most clearly—and darkly—articulated that vision was one of the group's founders, Timothy May. A brilliant and coldly realist former Intel engineer who had retired young to a house in the Santa Cruz mountains, May had imagined a future where encryption tools supercharged a global black market for information. In a semi-satirical essay he posted to the Cypherpunks Mailing List, he proposed what he called BlackNet, a kind of monetized WikiLeaks where classified information and trade secrets could be anonymously sold for untraceable "CryptoCredits."

In his most famous essay, "The Crypto Anarchist Manifesto," May summarized in 1988 the lawless future he both foresaw and, as a kind of absolutist libertarian, largely welcomed. "A specter is haunting the modern world, the specter of crypto anarchy," May wrote forebodingly, imagining a "CryptoNet" of perfectly private communications and payments.

> The State will of course try to slow or halt the spread of [encryption] technology, citing national security concerns, use of the technology by drug dealers and tax evaders, and fears of societal disintegration. Many of these concerns will be valid; crypto anarchy will allow national secrets to be traded freely and will allow illicit and stolen materials to be traded. An anonymous computerized market will even make possible abhorrent markets for assassinations and extortion. Various criminal and foreign elements will be active users of CryptoNet. But this will not halt the spread of crypto anarchy.

. . .

By the time I read May's words, more than two decades later, many elements of his vision had already come true: Encryption had, in fact, enabled secret, uncrackable communication for billions of ordinary people. Tools like Tor had made anonymous communication possible, too, hiding not just the contents of online messages but also their senders and recipients.

Yet Tim May's notion of "CryptoCredits"—that key financial ingredient to true cryptoanarchy—had still not come to fruition. Cryptographers, including some Cypherpunks Mailing List regulars, had invented digital money systems with names like DigiCash, Bit Gold, and B-Money. But all of them had suffered from technical or logistical hang-ups, and none had caught on or gained actual real-world value.

Now, watching Gavin Andresen speak onstage, I heard him name-check Satoshi Nakamoto as the inheritor of the cypherpunk mantle. And even more remarkably, he seemed to be saying that Nakamoto's invention, Bitcoin, was finally that crypto-anarchist holy grail: truly anonymous, untraceable, and practical digital money.

"The cypherpunks have done a lot of cool stuff. They had the idea of creating an anonymous, private money, but they couldn't figure it out," Andresen said in the cheerful tone of his Ignite talk, far removed from Tim May's foreboding vision of cryptoanarchy. "Until Satoshi figured it out about three years ago. Like any good hacker, he wrote the software, and he released it to the world."

Silk Road

I tracked down Gavin Andresen, interviewed him by phone, and, after my ill-fated attempt to buy bitcoins of my own, persuaded my editors to let me publish a one-page article about Bitcoin in an April 2011 issue of *Forbes,* perhaps the most high-profile press the budding cryptocurrency had gotten up to that point.

In the process of reporting that story, I had asked Andresen to pass on a request to Bitcoin's pseudonymous creator, Satoshi Nakamoto, to let me interview them, too. Andresen got back to me a few days later: Satoshi had declined.

I've tried not to take that rejection personally. Satoshi had, in fact, never spoken to a reporter. It would turn out that emailed response Andresen had received, refusing my request for an interview, would be one of Satoshi's last known communications with anyone, to this day. Bitcoin's creator disappeared from the internet less than two weeks after my article appeared, never to return. Their identity remains unknown—one of the greatest mysteries in the history of technology.

Whoever and wherever they may be, Satoshi is likely very, very wealthy. With an estimated million-plus bitcoins they mined in the currency's earliest days—and haven't touched since—the net worth of Bitcoin's creator, as of this writing, has theoretically fluctuated around $30 billion, which would make him or her one of the world's richest people.

But back in the spring of 2011, I had little interest in Bitcoin's potential as an investment, or in identifying Satoshi Nakamoto. As a reporter with a cypherpunks fixation, whose beat was all things malicious or subversive on the internet, I was fascinated by the notion of what Andresen had described as "anonymous, private money." I wanted to see how it was being spent.

. . .

When I'd asked Gavin Andresen for examples of who was actually buying and selling things for bitcoins, his short list had included a site called the Silk Road. The site sold drugs—the illegal kind. Andresen, a strait-laced software engineer who preferred to talk about Bitcoin's economic advantages over centralized banking systems more than its potential as a black-market currency, wasn't a fan. "Illegal stuff will be a niche for Bitcoin," he admitted. "That bothers me, but it's just like any currency. You can't stop dollar bills from being used for the drug trade either. That's an unfortunate feature of any cash-like system."

The Silk Road, I learned, was an e-commerce market on the dark web. In other words, it was one of thousands of specially protected websites that relied on Tor to hide the location of its servers and that could be visited only by someone running Tor on their computer, too. Tor was the dark web's active ingredient, providing a kind of double-blind anonymity. It was designed so that anyone could visit a dark web site who knew the site's address—a long and random-seeming string of characters. But no visitor to that site could see where it was physically hosted, nor could the site identify the location of its visitors. Any third party snooping on their connection could learn nothing about the locations of the computers on either end.

So I fired up Tor and began hunting through dark web directories for this purported Bitcoin drug bazaar. In 2011, this was a painstaking process: There were no real search engines for the dark web, and browsing it was often vexingly slow, given that Tor worked by triple encrypting your web traffic and bouncing it through three random computers around the world.

When I found the Silk Road, I wasn't impressed. At a glance the site did, in fact, seem to have dozens of listings for ecstasy, marijuana, hallucinogenic mushrooms, and even offerings of cocaine and heroin. But looking at its bare-bones design and slow-loading pages, I had a hard time believing it had any real customers. The Silk Road struck me as, at best, a stoner's janky experiment and, at worst, a scam designed to bilk would-be customers out of their bitcoins. After all, even if Bitcoin and Tor didn't reveal the site's users to law enforcement, how could they possibly ship or receive their drugs without volunteering a mailing address? Even Tim May's imaginary BlackNet had only gone so far as to imagine people selling each other *digital* contraband—like classified documents and trade secrets—not putting physical, illegal narcotics in envelopes, dropping them in mailboxes, and hoping for the best.

Then, around six weeks later, I found my Twitter feed blowing up with links to news of a press conference that New York's senator Chuck Schumer had given that morning. Its subject: the Silk Road.

Onstage, the senator had described the Silk Road very differently from how I'd seen it: as a full-blown, unprecedented new threat to any attempt to control illegal narcotics. "It's a certifiable one-stop shop for illegal drugs that represents the most brazen attempt to peddle drugs online that we have ever seen," Schumer told reporters. "It's more brazen than anything else by lightyears."

Like an antagonistic politician out of a cypherpunk libertarian fantasy, Schumer had pointed to both Tor and Bitcoin as dangerous new tools for this anonymous trade. "Literally, it allows buyers and users to sell illegal drugs online, including heroin, cocaine, and meth, and users do sell by hiding their identities through a program that makes them virtually untraceable," Schumer said, referring to Tor. As for Bitcoin, he described it as "an online form of money laundering used to disguise the source of money, and to disguise who's both selling and buying the drug."

Schumer's speech had been inspired by an article on the news site *Gawker,* written by the journalist Adrian Chen. Chen, like me, had stumbled on the Silk Road. But rather than dismiss it, he'd found visitors to the site who had successfully made purchases from it. One satisfied customer, for instance, had paid 50 bitcoins for a hundred micrograms of LSD, which had arrived in an envelope from Canada. "It kind of felt like I was in the future," the source had told Chen. The Silk Road was real, and it worked.

I had missed, it seemed, the story that represented all of the cypherpunks' dreams coming to fruition. Untraceable digital money was being used to buy actual, highly illegal contraband on a cryptographically anonymous e-commerce site. Bitcoin and Tor had, together, unlocked a new phenomenon that Tim May and his 1990s crypto-anarchists could only dream of: a bona fide dark web marketplace.

. . .

Amid the clamor surrounding Adrian Chen's article, I hardly noticed an "update" that appeared shortly after it was posted. Chen had originally described Bitcoin in the piece as an "untraceable digital currency." But in an addendum, he'd noted that Jeff Garzik, a programmer who worked with Gavin Andresen as a core developer of Bitcoin's opensource software, had emailed him to correct a misconception. Garzik pointed out that while Bitcoin senders and receivers are identified only with addresses, all those anonymized transactions are still recorded on the blockchain in public view. Large transactions might attract the attention of investigators who could potentially *de-anonymize* users—those who had published their addresses online, for instance, or who had given identifying information to Bitcoin exchanges. "Attempting major illicit transactions with bitcoin, given existing statistical analysis techniques deployed in the field by law enforcement, is pretty damned dumb," Garzik wrote.

But Garzik's warning could scarcely be heard above the noise created by Schumer's public outcry against Bitcoin and the Silk Road. In a letter he and Senator Joe Manchin sent to the DEA and Attorney General Eric Holder, Schumer demanded that they "take immediate action and shut down the Silk Road network." The letter, running exactly counter to Garzik's warning, described how the "only method of payment for these illegal purchases is an untraceable peer-to-peer currency known as Bitcoins."

Would-be Bitcoin buyers seemed to like what they heard. In the days following Schumer's letter and press conference, they pushed the cryptocurrency's exchange rate on Mt. Gox from less than $10 in early June of that year to a peak of nearly $32 as they scrambled to purchase this purportedly "untraceable"—and newly notorious—coin of the dark web. In attempting to shut down the Bitcoin black market, Schumer had inadvertently given it its best publicity yet.

The Dread Pirate

When the world first took notice of the Silk Road in the summer of 2011, Tigran Gambaryan had yet to graduate from the Federal Law Enforcement Training Center in Brunswick, Georgia. But he saw in the Silk Road's use of Bitcoin a kind of grim confirmation of his initial reaction when he'd first learned about the cryptocurrency: The Silk Road seemed to prove that Bitcoin, with its promise of anonymity, was indeed about to become a tool for criminals and money launderers of every variety.

"This is going to blow up," he remembers thinking to himself. "As soon as I saw Silk Road, I knew Pandora's box had been opened. There was no going back."

Sure enough, after the *Gawker* article and Chuck Schumer's press conference, the Silk Road exploded. Its number of user accounts, by some estimates, swelled immediately from mere hundreds to more than ten thousand as curious drug buyers downloaded Tor and swarmed onto the dark web to learn more about the anonymous black market that Schumer had so dramatically condemned.

The new marketplace at times buckled under the weight of so many new visitors, running slowly and even dropping off-line for periods as long as a week, as its enigmatic administrator struggled to manage a dark web site with more traffic than any other before in history. But the users kept coming back in greater numbers. After all, the Silk Road was offering something that wasn't available anywhere else on the internet. Soon the basic selection I had seen on my first visit there had expanded into an array of products that included rare hallucinogens, bespoke marijuana strains, MDMA, and a growing selection of harder drugs like methamphetamine, heroin, and cocaine, as well as other contraband like fake IDs and pirated software. And because the Silk Road functioned as an eBay-style community of third-party vendors signing up to sell their wares on the site rather than a centralized Amazon-style market, the diversity of its illegal inventory was growing as fast as its customer base.

As the Silk Road grappled with the challenges of truly anonymous online sales, it began to come up with impressive innovations to solve them: Ratings and reviews allowed customers to trust the purity of the potentially dangerous substances ordered over the internet from faceless sellers. A growing number of professional moderators patrolled the site, settling disputes and helping users with technical issues. After a buyer paid a dealer, a clever escrow system kept their bitcoins locked in a kind of holding pen until they received their drugs in the mail and released the money, preventing scams. And since Bitcoin was subject to wild swings in price, the Silk Road even offered dealers a hedging feature, promising to cover the difference if a payment lost value while it sat in escrow. And for all those services, it charged a commission, which ran along an inverse sliding scale, from 10 percent for small orders to 1.5 percent for those above $1,000.

"Silk Road doesn't really sell drugs, it sells insurance and financial products," the Carnegie Mellon computer engineering professor Nicolas Christin put it at the time, expressing his amazement at the Silk Road's smooth management of online transactions in an entirely new, anonymous medium. "It doesn't really matter whether you're selling T-shirts or cocaine. The business model is to commoditize security."

. . .

It was months later, in February 2012, when the Silk Road went beyond being a faceless marketplace and began to develop a personality. Or rather, a persona. "Silk Road has matured, and I need an identity separate from the site," the site's anonymous administrator wrote. "I am Silk Road, the market, the person, the enterprise, everything. But I need a name." He revealed the one he'd chosen: "Dread Pirate Roberts."

That handle, taken from the book and film *The Princess Bride*, was carefully selected for a specific purpose, it would later turn out: The Dread Pirate Roberts, in the original story, is a fear-inspiring title, handed down from one pirate leader to the next, generation after generation. This dark web pirate hoped to invoke the same idea of an inherited pseudonym, and in doing so, to muddy the question of which actual person had created the Silk Road or run it at any particular time, should law enforcement ever get onto his trail.

But the creation of the new handle wasn't merely intended for obfuscation. The Silk Road's leader, whom customers and vendors more commonly came to know as DPR, quickly became an outspoken, outsized character on the site. He posted more and more to the Silk Road forums he'd created for users, using a black-masked pirate as his avatar. And he seemed to be at least as interested in the libertarian potential of the site as its swelling profits.

In early posts, DPR began referring to the Silk Road as a "community" and the vendors on the site as "heroes," not mere drug dealers in a loose criminal network. The Silk Road, he wrote in one early screed on the forums, was a "dream" that without their help would be "swallowed by the nightmare reality of an ever-expanding, all-powerful global oligarchy."

He explained that the Silk Road's true goal was to keep the "thieving murderous mitts" of "the State" out of the private lives of people around the world who should have the freedom to buy and sell and ingest whatever substance they chose. In another long manifesto posted a month later, he revealed more of his grand vision: a kind of radically libertarian cryptoanarchy that resembled Tim May's cypherpunk philosophy, but flush with idealism and possibility. Unlike Tim May, DPR seemed to believe that cryptoanarchy was not in fact an inevitability, but only achievable through the great struggle of the Silk Road and its users—an ultra-libertarian Lenin to Tim May's Marx.

"Some day, we could be a shining beacon of hope for the oppressed people of the world just as so many oppressed and violated souls have found refuge here already," the Dread Pirate Roberts wrote. "Now it is profitable to throw off one's chains, with amazing crypto technology reducing the risk of doing so dramatically. How many niches have yet to be filled in the world of anonymous online markets? The opportunity to prosper and take part in a revolution of epic proportions is at our fingertips!"

Soon, DPR was regularly posting antigovernment political musings and love letters to his faithful buyers and vendors. He even created a Dread Pirate Roberts Book Club, where he moderated discussions on authors from the Austrian school of free-market economics. On the Silk Road, it was becoming clear, the Dread Pirate Roberts was more than a digital drug dealer or a black-market website administrator. He was, as various users wrote in forum posts, "our own Che Guevara," a "job creator," and, as one fan put it, a figure that would be remembered "among the greatest men and women in history as a soldier of justice and freedom."

· · ·

I was, by late 2012, obsessed with the Dread Pirate Roberts. Here was someone making millions of dollars in highly illegal narcotics sales—a study by Carnegie Mellon's Christin earlier that year had estimated that the Silk Road was moving $15 million in narcotics annually—while evading every global law enforcement agency. All of this after the DEA and Justice Department had been explicitly ordered by two U.S. senators to hunt him down and take his market off-line. The fact that he remained free more than a year after Schumer's press conference seemed to testify to the very real power and impunity granted by encryption tools like Tor and Bitcoin. And DPR was publicly flaunting that impunity in the face of the most powerful government on the planet.

In the fall of that year, I had started writing private messages to DPR every few weeks on the Silk Road's forums, trying to persuade him to answer my questions for his first on-the-record, in-depth interview. He initially demurred, saying he wasn't ready. I offered to meet him in a foreign country and to keep his identity a secret. "Meeting in person is out of the question," he responded. "I don't meet with even my closest advisers."

When I sent him an unsolicited list of questions that included, unwisely, queries about his location, gender, and age, he responded saying he would never answer anything remotely so private. Clearly spooked, he clammed up for months.

But as DPR's star rose, the appeal of appearing on the cover of *Forbes* magazine seemed to grow in his mind. (He eventually suggested that the cover might show an anonymous silhouette of a pirate, along with the headline "How a Pirate Won the Drug War.") After eight months, he finally agreed to talk to me at length through the Silk Road's Tor-protected messaging system, upgrading my account to the status of a drug dealer on the site to make it easier for us to exchange messages. On

July 4, 2013, as we sat at our computers for five hours—me in a studio office in Brooklyn ignoring my friends' Independence Day barbecue on the rooftop outside, him at some unidentified location, somewhere across the dark web—I interviewed the Dread Pirate Roberts for the article that would introduce him to the world.

.   .   .

DPR's answer to my very first question, it now appears with a decade of hindsight, was a lie.

"What inspired you to start the Silk Road?" I asked, lobbing him an open-ended prompt.

"I didn't start the Silk Road, my predecessor did," DPR answered, to my surprise. He described how, early in the Silk Road's history, he had discovered a vulnerability in the site that would have allowed a hacker to de-anonymize the site's Bitcoin wallet. When he brought it to the Silk Road founder's attention, they became friendly, and eventually the original administrator of the site suggested "passing the torch" in the form of a hefty buyout. (All of this, I'd later learn—in part from reading Ross Ulbricht's own secret journal—seems to have been part of the "Dread Pirate Roberts" myth that Ulbricht was spinning to cover his tracks should he ever be found out.)

After that initial misdirection, DPR began to answer my questions more honestly. He hinted at real ambitions for the Silk Road's future, including expansion into encrypted communications tools and a Silk Road–branded Bitcoin exchange that would compete with Mt. Gox— the leading Bitcoin exchange that was now beginning to demand users' identifying information to create an account.

On that note, I asked him how the Silk Road dealt with the problem of Bitcoin's traceability. After all, I'd read Jeff Garzik's warning in response to the *Gawker* article on the Silk Road, by now two years earlier. Weren't the Silk Road's transactions, even if they were only between pseudonymous addresses, visible on Bitcoin's blockchain?

DPR answered, somewhat vaguely, that the Silk Road had a built-in "tumbler" system that shuffled users' payments so that when a user put bitcoins into their Silk Road wallet and made a purchase, and the money was withdrawn by the vendor, the chain that linked their transactions would be deliberately broken, its forensic trail tangled up in a mass of other Silk Road payments. "This makes it impossible to link your deposits and withdrawals," DPR wrote, "and makes it really hard to even tell that your withdrawals came from Silk Road."

Rather than press him on the details of that system, I moved on to other subjects, such as the extent of his ultra-libertarian politics ("How can you go too far liberating people from bondage?" he asked) and his stratospheric-bordering-on-absurd financial goals for the Silk Road ("At this point I wouldn't sell out for less than 10 figures, maybe 11"), along with the barest glimpse of his personal life ("I love a bowl of sticky indica buds at the end of a long day"). He described a modest standard of living, spending very little of his millions of dollars in profits in order to stay under the radar—a claim that would prove to be entirely true.

When I questioned the morality of his booming business, DPR laid out a strict, if somewhat oversimplified, code of ethics: "We don't allow the sale of anything that's main purpose is to harm innocent people, or that it was necessary to harm innocent people to bring it to market." That meant no violent services like hit men or extortion, no child porn, not even counterfeit coupons. The Silk Road had at one point briefly allowed the sale of firearms—DPR argued guns could be used in self-defense—but his code of conduct forbade weapons "that are designed to be used on crowds of people or whole populations."

None of those self-imposed rules, of course, made the Silk Road any less of a target for the panoply of law enforcement agencies now hunting the Dread Pirate Roberts. Was he actually confident that his crypto tools would let him continue to evade them? "I am, unless they have cracked the modern encryption algorithms, which I highly doubt," DPR wrote. "There are a multitude of security measures we take to secure the infrastructure that powers Silk Road."

Before our interview, I had thought that DPR might credit Tor as the most fundamental technology that had enabled that security. But he quickly made clear that it was Bitcoin that he saw as the key that had unlocked the anonymous financial potential of the dark web. "We've won the State's War on Drugs because of Bitcoin, and this is just the beginning," DPR wrote. "Sector by sector the state is being cut out of the equation and power is being returned to the individual. I don't think anyone can comprehend the magnitude of the revolution we are in. I think it will be looked back on as an epoch in the evolution of mankind."

The Puzzle

In early 2013, the shelves of a windowless storage room in a building of the University of California began to fill up with strange, seemingly random objects. A Casio calculator. A pair of alpaca wool socks. A small stack of Magic: The Gathering cards. A *Super Mario Bros. 3* cartridge for the original Nintendo. A plastic Guy Fawkes mask of the kind popularized by the hacker group Anonymous. An album by the classic rock band Boston on CD.

Periodically, the door would open, the light would turn on, and a petite, dark-haired graduate student named Sarah Meiklejohn would enter the room and add to the growing piles of miscellaneous artifacts. Then Meiklejohn would walk back out the door, down the hall, up the stairs, and into an office she shared with other graduate students at the UC San Diego computer science department. One wall of the room was almost entirely glass, and it looked out onto the sunbaked vista of Sorrento Valley and the rolling hills beyond. But Meiklejohn's desk faced away from that expanse. She was wholly focused on the screen of her laptop, where she was quickly becoming one of the strangest, most hyperactive Bitcoin users in the world.

Meiklejohn had personally purchased every one of the dozens of items in the bizarre, growing collection in the UCSD closet using Bitcoin, buying each one almost at random from a different vendor who accepted the cryptocurrency. And between those e-commerce orders and trips to the storage room, she was performing practically every other task that a person could carry out with Bitcoin, all at once, like a kind of cryptocurrency fanatic having a manic episode.

She moved money into and out of ten different Bitcoin wallet services and converted dollars to bitcoins on more than two dozen exchanges such as Bitstamp, Mt. Gox, and Coinbase. She wagered those coins on thirteen different online gambling services, with names like Satoshi Dice and Bitcoin Kamikaze. She contributed her computer's mining power to eleven different mining "pools," groups that collected users' computing power for mining bitcoins and then paid them a share of the profits. And, again and again, she moved bitcoins into and then out of accounts on the Silk Road, without ever actually buying any drugs.

In all, Meiklejohn carried out 344 cryptocurrency transactions over the course of a few weeks. With each one, she carefully noted on a spreadsheet the amount, the Bitcoin address she had used for it, and then, after digging up the transaction on the Bitcoin blockchain and examining the public record of the payment, the address of the recipient or sender.

Meiklejohn's hundreds of purchases, bets, and seemingly meaningless movements of money were not, in fact, signs of a psychotic break. Each was a tiny experiment, adding up to a study of a kind that had never been attempted before. After years of claims about Bitcoin's anonymity—or lack thereof—made by its users, its developers, and even its creator, Meiklejohn was finally putting its privacy properties to the test.

All of her meticulous, manual transactions were time-consuming and tedious. But Meiklejohn had time to kill: As she was carrying them out and recording the results, her computer was simultaneously running queries on a massive database stored on a server that she and her fellow UCSD researchers had set up, algorithms that sometimes took as long as twelve hours to spit out results. The database represented the entire Bitcoin blockchain, the roughly sixteen million transactions that had occurred across the entire Bitcoin economy since its creation four years earlier. For weeks on end, Meiklejohn combed through those transactions while simultaneously tagging the vendors, services, markets, and other recipients on the other end of her hundreds of test transactions.

When she had started that process of probing the Bitcoin ecosystem, Meiklejohn had seen her work almost as anthropology: What were people doing with Bitcoin? How many of them were saving the cryptocurrency versus spending it? But as her initial findings began to unfold, she had started to develop a much more specific goal, one that ran exactly counter to the Dread Pirate Roberts's crypto-anarchist, idealized notion of Bitcoin: She aimed to prove, beyond any doubt, that Bitcoin transactions could very often be traced. Even—or, in fact, especially—when the people involved thought they were anonymous.

. . .

As Meiklejohn painstakingly fiddled with bitcoins and watched the digital trails they created, she found herself having flashbacks to a particular day, decades earlier, in her mother's downtown Manhattan office. That morning, Meiklejohn and her mother had taken the subway together, all the way from their Upper West Side apartment near the American Museum of Natural History to the federal building at Foley Square, across from the city's intimidating, stone-columned courthouses.

Meiklejohn was still in elementary school, but it was take-your-daughter-to-work day, and Meiklejohn's mother was a federal prosecutor. Over the years that followed, the elder Meiklejohn would make her career taking on contractors who were bilking the city government out of tax dollars—bribing government staffers to choose overpriced school food or street-paving services—or else banks colluding to sell low-performing investments to the city's financiers. Many of her targets in those corruption probes would be sentenced to years in prison.

That day in the Justice Department's New York office, Sarah Meiklejohn, not yet ten years old, was put to work. She was assigned to comb through a pile of paper checks, searching for clues of a corrupt kickback scheme in one of her mother's investigations.

It was that feeling, the drive to manually assemble tiny data points that built into a larger picture, that would give Meiklejohn a kind of déjà vu twenty years later as she studied the Bitcoin blockchain, even before she consciously knew what she was doing.

"Somewhere in the back of my mind was this idea," says Meiklejohn, "the idea of following the money."

As a child, Meiklejohn loved puzzles—the more complex, the better. On road trips, in airports, or any other time the small-for-her-age, hyper-inquisitive girl needed to be distracted, her mother would hand her a book of puzzles. One of the first websites Meiklejohn remembers visiting on the nascent World Wide Web was a GeoCities page devoted to deciphering the *Kryptos* sculpture on the campus of the CIA, whose copper, ribbonlike surface contained four coded messages that even the cryptanalysts at Langley hadn't been able to crack. By the age of fourteen she would finish the *New York Times* crossword puzzle every day of the week.

On a vacation to London Meiklejohn's family visited the British Museum, and Meiklejohn became fixated on the Rosetta stone, along with the broader notion of ancient languages—the remnants of entire cultures—that could be deciphered if the puzzler simply found the right key. Soon she was reading about Linear A and Linear B, a pair of written scripts used by the Minoan civilization on Crete until roughly 1500 BC. Linear B had been deciphered only in the 1950s, thanks in large part to a classicist at Brooklyn College named Alice Kober who labored in obscurity over samples of the Bronze Age language for twenty years, writing her notes on 180,000 index cards.

Meiklejohn became so obsessed with Linear A and B that she persuaded a teacher at her middle school to organize an evening seminar on the subject (only she and one friend attended). More tantalizing than even the story of Alice Kober's work on Linear B, for Meiklejohn, was the fact that *no one* had been able to decipher Linear A, even after a century of study. The best puzzles of all were the ones that had no answer key—the ones for which no one even knew if a solution existed.

When Meiklejohn started college at Brown in 2004, she discovered cryptography. This branch of computer science appealed directly to her puzzle addiction—what was an encryption system, after all, but another secret language demanding to be deciphered?

There was a maxim in cryptography, often referred to as Schneier's law after the cryptographer Bruce Schneier. It asserted that anyone can develop an encryption system clever enough that they can't themselves think of a way to break it. Yet, like all the best conundrums and mysteries that had fascinated Meiklejohn since childhood, another person with a different way of approaching a cipher could look at that "unbreakable" system and immediately see a way to crack it and unspool a whole world of decrypted revelations.

Studying the science of ciphers, Meiklejohn began to recognize the importance of privacy and the need for surveillance-resistant communications. She was not quite a cypherpunk: The intellectual appeal of building and breaking codes drove her more than any ideological drive to defeat surveillance. But like many cryptographers, she nonetheless came to believe in the need for truly unbreakable encryption, technologies that could carve out a space for sensitive communications—whether dissidents organizing against a repressive government or whistleblowers sharing secrets with journalists—where no snoop could reach. She credited her intuitive acceptance of that principle to her years as a teenager who kept to herself, trying to maintain her own privacy in a Manhattan apartment, with a federal prosecutor for a mother.

. . .

Meiklejohn showed real talent as a cryptographer and soon became an undergraduate teaching assistant to Anna Lysyanskaya, a brilliant and highly accomplished computer scientist. Lysyanskaya had herself studied under the legendary Ron Rivest, whose name was represented by the R in the RSA algorithm that formed the basis for most modern encryption, used everywhere from web browsers to encrypted email to instant messaging protocols. RSA was one of the few fundamental encryption protocols that had not succumbed to Schneier's law in more than thirty years.

Lysyanskaya was at the time working on a pre-Bitcoin cryptocurrency called eCash, first developed in the 1990s by David Chaum, a cryptographer whose groundbreaking work on anonymity systems had made possible technologies from VPNs to Tor. After finishing her undergraduate degree, Meiklejohn began a master's degree at Brown under Lysyanskaya's wing, researching methods to make Chaum's eCash, a truly anonymous payment system, more scalable and efficient.

The cryptocurrency scheme they were laboring to optimize was, Meiklejohn admits in hindsight, difficult to imagine working in practice. Unlike Bitcoin, it had a serious problem: An anonymous spender of eCash could essentially forge a coin and pass it off to an unsuspecting recipient. When that recipient deposited the coin at a kind of eCash bank, the bank could perform a check that would reveal the coin to be a forgery and the fraudster's anonymity protections could be stripped away to reveal the identity of the bad actor. But by then, the fraudster might have already run off with their ill-gotten goods.

Still, eCash had a unique advantage that made it a fascinating system to work on: The anonymity it offered was truly uncrackable. In fact, eCash was based on a mathematical technique called zero-knowledge proofs, which could establish the validity of a payment without the bank or recipient learning anything else at all about the spender or their money. That mathematical sleight of hand meant that eCash was *provably* secure. Schneier's law did not apply: No amount of cleverness or computing power would ever be able to undo its anonymity.

When Meiklejohn first heard about Bitcoin in 2011, she had started her PhD studies at UCSD but was spending the summer as a researcher at Microsoft. A friend at the University of Washington had mentioned to her that there was a new digital payment system that people were using to buy drugs on sites like the Silk Road. Meiklejohn had moved on from her eCash studies by then; she was busy with other research—systems that would allow people to pay road tolls without revealing their personal movements, for instance, and a thermal camera technique that revealed PIN codes typed into an ATM by looking for heat remnants on the keypad. So, with heads-down focus, she filed Bitcoin's existence away in her brain, barely considering it again for the next year.

Then, one day on a UCSD computer science department group hike in late 2012, a young UCSD research scientist named Kirill Levchenko suggested to Meiklejohn that perhaps they should start looking into this burgeoning Bitcoin phenomenon. Levchenko was fascinated, he explained as they trekked around the jagged landscape of the Anza-Borrego Desert State Park, by Bitcoin's unique proof-of-work system. That system demanded that anyone who wanted to mine the currency expend enormous computing resources performing calculations—essentially a vast, automated puzzle-solving competition—whose results were then copied into transactions on the blockchain. By then, ambitious bitcoiners were already developing custom mining microprocessors just for generating this strange new form of money, and Bitcoin's ingenious system meant that any single bad actor who might want to write a false transaction into the blockchain would have to use a collection of computers that possessed more computational power than all those many thousands of miners. It was a brilliant approach that added up to a secure currency with no central authority.

Considering Bitcoin's mechanics for the first time, Meiklejohn was intrigued. But when she got home from the hike and began poring over Satoshi Nakamoto's Bitcoin white paper, it immediately became clear to her that Bitcoin's trade-offs were the exact opposite of the eCash system she knew so well. Fraud was prevented not by a kind of after-the-fact forgery analysis carried out by a bank authority but with an instantaneous check of the blockchain, the unforgeable public record of who possessed every single bitcoin.

But that blockchain ledger system came at an enormous privacy cost: In Bitcoin, for good and for ill, everyone was a witness to every payment.

Yes, identities behind those payments were obscured by pseudonymous addresses, long strings of between twenty-six and thirty-five characters. But to Meiklejohn, this seemed like an inherently dangerous sort of fig leaf to hide behind. Unlike eCash, whose privacy protections offered snoops no hint of revealing information to latch onto, Bitcoin offered an enormous collection of data to analyze. Who could say what sorts of patterns might give away users who thought they were cleverer than those watching them?

"You could never prove anything about the privacy properties of this system," Meiklejohn remembers thinking. "And so as a cryptographer, the natural question was, if you can't prove it's private, then what attacks are possible? If you don't get privacy, what do you get?"

The temptation was more than Meiklejohn could resist. The blockchain, like a massive, undeciphered corpus of an ancient language, hid a wealth of secrets in plain view.

Men with No Names

When Meiklejohn began digging into the blockchain in late 2012, she started with a very simple question: How many people were using Bitcoin?

That number was much harder to pin down than it might seem. After downloading the entire blockchain onto a UCSD server and organizing it into a database that she could query, like a gargantuan, searchable spreadsheet, she could see that there were more than twelve million distinct Bitcoin addresses, among which there had been nearly sixteen million transactions. But even amid all that activity, there were plenty of recognizable events in Bitcoin's history visible to the naked eye. Spenders and recipients might have been hidden behind pseudonymous addresses, but some transactions were unmistakable, like distinctive pieces of furniture hidden under thin sheets in someone's attic.

She could see, for instance, the nearly 1 million bitcoins that were mined by Satoshi in the early days of the cryptocurrency, before others started using it, as well as the first transaction ever made when Satoshi sent 10 coins as a test to the early Bitcoin developer Hal Finney in January 2009. She spotted, too, the first payment with real value, when a programmer named Laszlo Hanyecz famously sold a friend two pizzas for 10,000 bitcoins in May 2010 (as of this writing worth hundreds of millions of dollars).

Plenty of other addresses and transactions had been recognized and widely discussed on forums like Bitcointalk, and Meiklejohn spent hours cutting and pasting long strings of characters into Google to see if someone had already claimed credit for an address or if other Bitcoin users had been gossiping about certain high-value transactions. By the time Meiklejohn began to look, anyone with enough interest and patience to wade through a sea of garbled addresses could see money transfers between mysterious parties just beneath the surface of the blockchain's obfuscation that, even at the time, were often worth small fortunes.

Getting beyond that obfuscation, however, was the real challenge. Sure, Meiklejohn could see transactions between addresses. But the problem was drilling down further, definitively drawing a boundary around the Bitcoin hoard of any single person or organization. A user could have as many addresses as they chose to create with one of the many wallet programs that managed their coins—like a bank that allows you to spread your wealth across as many accounts as you liked, creating new ones with a mouse click. Plenty of those programs even automatically generated new addresses every time the user received a Bitcoin payment, adding to the confusion.

Still, Meiklejohn was sure that searching for patterns in the mess of transactions would allow her to untangle at least some of them. In Satoshi Nakamoto's own original white paper, Meiklejohn recalled that he had briefly alluded to a technique that could be used to collapse some addresses into single identities. Often, a single Bitcoin transaction has multiple "inputs" from different addresses. If someone wants to pay a friend 10 bitcoins but holds those coins at two different addresses of 5 coins each, the spender's wallet software creates a single transaction that lists the two 5-coin addresses as inputs and the address receiving 10 coins as the output. To make the payment possible, the payer would need to possess both of the so-called secret keys that allow the 5 coins at each address to be spent. That means anyone looking at the transaction on the blockchain can reasonably identify both of the input addresses as belonging to the same person or organization.

Satoshi had hinted at the privacy dangers this introduced. "Some linking is still unavoidable with multi-input transactions, which necessarily reveal that their inputs were owned by the same owner," Satoshi wrote. "The risk is that if the owner of a key is revealed, linking could reveal other transactions that belonged to the same owner."

So, as Meiklejohn's first step, she simply tried the technique Satoshi had inadvertently suggested—across every Bitcoin payment ever carried out. She scanned her blockchain database for every multi-input transaction, linking all of those double, triple, or even hundredfold inputs to single identities. The result immediately reduced the number of potential Bitcoin users from twelve million to date to around five million, slicing away more than half of the problem.

Only after that initial step—practically a freebie—did Meiklejohn switch her brain into true puzzle-solving mode. Like a twentieth-century archaeologist scanning hieroglyphics for identifiable words or phrases that might help to decipher a passage of text, she began to hunt through Bitcoin's transactions for other clues that might reveal identifying information. Messing around with Bitcoin wallets—making test payments to herself and her colleagues—she began to understand a quirk of the cryptocurrency. Many Bitcoin wallets only allowed spenders to pay the entire amount of coins sitting at a certain address. Each address was like a piggy bank that has to be smashed open to spend the coins inside. Spend less than the whole amount in that piggy bank and the leftovers have to be stored in a newly created piggy bank.

This second piggy bank, in Bitcoin's system, is called a "change" address: When you pay someone 6 bitcoins from a 10-coin address, 6 coins go to their address. Your change, 4 coins, is stored at a new address, which your wallet software creates for you. The challenge, when looking at that transaction on the blockchain as a sleuthing observer, is that the recipient's address and the change address are both simply listed as outputs, with no label to tell them apart.

But sometimes, Meiklejohn realized, spotting the difference between the change address and the recipient address was easy: If one address had been used before and the other hadn't, the second, totally fresh address could only be the change address—a piggy bank that had materialized on the spot to receive leftover coins from the one that had just been shattered. And that meant these two piggy banks—the spender's address and the change address—must belong to the same person.

Meiklejohn began to apply that change-making lens, looking for instances where she could link spenders and the remainders of their payments. She began to see how powerful the simple act of tracking Bitcoin change could be: In instances where she couldn't distinguish a recipient address from a change address, she would be stuck at a fork in the road with no signposts. But if she could link change addresses to the addresses they had split off from, she could make her own signposts. She could follow the money despite its branching paths.

The result was that Meiklejohn could now link together entire *chains* of transactions that had previously been unlinked: A single sum of coins would move from change address to change address as the spender paid fractions of the total pile of coins in one small payment after another. The remainder of the pile might move to a fresh address with each payment, but those addresses must all represent the transactions of a single spender.

She'd come to refer to those chains of transactions as "peeling chains" (or sometimes just "peel chains"). She thought of them like someone peeling bills off a roll of dollar bills: Though the roll of bills might be put back in a different pocket after a bill was peeled off and spent, it was still fundamentally one wad of cash with a consistent owner. Following these peeling chains opened avenues to trace the digital money's movements like never before.*

Meiklejohn now had two clever techniques, both of which were capable of linking multiple Bitcoin addresses to a single person or organization, what she came to call "clustering." What had initially looked like disparate addresses could now be connected into clusters that encompassed hundreds or, in some cases, even thousands of addresses.

Already, she was tracing bitcoins in ways that many of the cryptocurrency's users wouldn't have believed possible. But following coins didn't necessarily mean understanding who owned them. The identities behind those coins remained a mystery, and each of her clusters remained just as

---

* Meiklejohn would discover during her research that several other research groups had previously attempted the same sort of examination of Bitcoin's anonymity and privacy as she and her UCSD colleagues were undertaking, including a group of Swiss and German researchers, an Israeli team at the Weizmann Institute of Science in Israel, and a team from University College Dublin in Ireland. But while they all used the first clustering method suggested in Satoshi's original Bitcoin white paper, only the Irish team had briefly suggested the change-making method in its 2012 study and, unlike the UCSD team, didn't actually implement that technique. Meiklejohn says she wasn't in fact aware of the Irish team's mention of change-based clustering at the time she was working on the technique.

pseudonymous as the single, disconnected addresses had been originally. To put a name to those clusters, she began to realize, she'd have to take a much more hands-on approach: not simply observing the artifacts of the Bitcoin economy after the fact like an archaeologist, but becoming a player in it herself—in some cases, an undercover one.

.   .   .

Searching for guidance in her budding Bitcoin research, Meiklejohn turned to Stefan Savage, a UCSD professor who was on the other end of the spectrum from the deeply mathematical cryptography research Meiklejohn had spent years on. Savage was a hands-on, empirical researcher, more interested in real-world experiments with real-world results than abstractions. He had been one of the lead advisers of a now-legendary team of researchers who had first shown it was possible to hack a car over the internet, demonstrating to General Motors in 2011 that his team could remotely take over a Chevy Impala's steering and brakes via the cellular radio in its OnStar system, a shocking feat of hacker wizardry.

More recently, Savage had helped lead a group that included Kirill Levchenko—the scientist who'd introduced Meiklejohn to Bitcoin on their desert hike—working on a massively ambitious project to track the spam email ecosystem. In that research, as with the earlier car-hacking breakthrough, Savage's team hadn't been afraid to get their hands dirty: They'd collected hundreds of millions of web links in junk marketing emails, mostly ones intended to sell real and fake pharmaceuticals. Then, as Savage describes it, they acted out the role of "the world's most gullible person," using bots to click through on every one of those links to see where they led and spending more than $50,000 on the products the spammers were hawking—all while working with a cooperative credit card issuer to trace the funds and see which banks the money ended up at.

Several of those shady banks were ultimately shut down as a result of the researchers' tracing work. As another UCSD professor working on the project, Geoffrey Voelker, described it at the time, "Our secret weapon is shopping."

So when Meiklejohn began talking over her Bitcoin tracking project with Savage, the two agreed she should take the same approach: She would manually identify Bitcoin addresses one by one by doing transactions with them herself, like a cop on the narcotics beat carrying out buy-and-busts. To decipher the blockchain, they'd again make shopping their secret weapon.

That's how Meiklejohn found herself in the early weeks of 2013 ordering coffee, cupcakes, trading cards, mugs, baseball hats, silver coins, socks, and a closet's worth of other truly random objects from online vendors who accepted Bitcoin; joining more than a dozen mining collectives; fiendishly gambling bitcoins at every online crypto casino she could find; and moving bitcoins into and out of accounts on practically every existing Bitcoin exchange—and the Silk Road—again and again.

The hundreds of addresses Meiklejohn identified and tagged manually with those 344 transactions represented only the tiniest fraction of the overall Bitcoin landscape. But when she combined that address tagging with her chaining and clustering techniques, many of those tags suddenly identified not just a single address but an enormous cluster belonging to the same owner. With just a few hundred tags, she had put an identity to more than a million of Bitcoin's once-pseudonymous addresses.

With just the 30 addresses she had identified by moving coins into and out of Mt. Gox, for instance, she could now link more than 500,000 addresses to the exchange. And based on just four deposits and seven withdrawals into wallets on the Silk Road, she was able to identify nearly 300,000 of the black market's addresses. This breakthrough didn't mean Meiklejohn could identify any actual users of the Silk Road by name, nor could she unmask, of course, the mysterious Dread Pirate Roberts overseeing all of it. But it would directly contradict DPR's claims to me that his Bitcoin "tumbler" system could prevent observers from even seeing when users moved cryptocurrency into and out of their Silk Road accounts.

When Meiklejohn brought her results back to Savage, her adviser was impressed. But as they began to plan to publish a paper on her findings, he wanted a concrete demonstration for readers, not a bunch of arcane statistics. "We need to show people," Meiklejohn remembers him saying, "what these techniques can actually do."

So Meiklejohn went a step further: She began to look for specific Bitcoin transactions she could track—particularly criminal ones.

. . .

As Meiklejohn had trawled cryptocurrency forums for discussions of interesting addresses worth scrutinizing, one mysterious mountain of money in particular stood out: This single address had, over the course of 2012, accumulated 613,326 bitcoins—5 percent of all the coins in circulation. It represented around $7.5 million at the time, a figure nowhere near the billions it would represent today, but a heady sum nonetheless. Rumors among Bitcoin users suggested that the hoard was possibly a Silk Road wallet, or perhaps the result of an unrelated, notorious Bitcoin Ponzi scheme carried out by a user known as pirate@40.

Meiklejohn couldn't say which of the two rumors might be correct. But with her clustering techniques, she could now follow that giant sum of cryptocurrency. She saw that after conspicuously gathering at one address, the pile of money had been broken up in late 2012 and sent on forking paths around the blockchain. Meiklejohn's understanding of peel chains meant she could now trace those sums of hundreds of thousands of bitcoins as they split, distinguishing the amount that remained in the control of the initial owner from the smaller sums that were peeled off in subsequent payments. Eventually, several of those peel chains led to exchanges like Mt. Gox and Bitstamp, where they seemed to be cashed out for traditional currency. For an academic researcher, this was a dead end. But anyone with the subpoena power of law enforcement, Meiklejohn realized, could very likely force those exchanges to hand over information about the accounts behind those transactions and solve the mystery of the $7.5 million stash.

Looking for more coins to hunt, Meiklejohn turned her focus to another sort of dirty money: Large-scale cryptocurrency heists were, in early 2013, a growing epidemic. After all, Bitcoin was like cash or gold. Anyone who stole a Bitcoin address's secret key could empty out that address like a digital safe. Unlike with credit cards or other digital payment systems, there was no overseer who could stop or reverse the money's movement. That had made every Bitcoin business and its stash of crypto revenue a ripe target for hackers, especially if the holders of those funds made the mistake of storing their secret keys on internet-connected computers—the equivalent of carrying six- or seven-figure sums of cash in their pockets while strolling through a dangerous neighborhood.

Meiklejohn found a thread on Bitcointalk that listed addresses of many of the biggest, most conspicuous crypto thefts in recent memory, and she began to follow the money. Looking at a robbery of 3,171 coins from an early Bitcoin gambling site, she immediately found she could trace the stolen funds across no fewer than ten hops, from address to address, before different branches of the money were cashed out at exchanges. Another theft of 18,500 bitcoins from the exchange Bitcoinica similarly led her along a winding series of peel chains that ended at three other exchanges, where the robbers were no doubt cashing in their ill-gotten gains. Sitting in front of Meiklejohn, on her screen, was a bonanza of leads, each just waiting for any actual criminal investigator with a handful of subpoenas to follow them.

Now, when Meiklejohn showed Savage her results, he agreed: They were ready to publish.

In the final draft of the paper Meiklejohn and her co-authors put together, they definitively stated conclusions—based for the first time on solid, empirical evidence—that flew in the face of what many Bitcoin users believed at the time: Far from being untraceable, they wrote, the blockchain was an open book that could identify vast swaths of transactions between people, many of whom thought they were acting anonymously.

"Even our relatively small experiment demonstrates that this approach can shed considerable light on the structure of the Bitcoin economy, how it is used, and those organizations who are party to it," the paper read. "We demonstrate that an agency with subpoena power would be well placed to identify who is paying money to whom. Indeed, we argue that the increasing dominance of a small number of Bitcoin institutions (most notably services that perform currency exchange), coupled with the public nature of transactions and our ability to label monetary flows to major institutions, ultimately makes Bitcoin unattractive today for high-volume illicit use such as money laundering."

Having set down those words, and blowing a gaping hole in the myth of Bitcoin's inherent untraceability, Meiklejohn, Savage, and her other adviser Geoffrey Voelker started brainstorming a clever title. In an homage to the wild west of the economy they were chronicling—and her advisers' mutual love of spaghetti Westerns—they started with the phrase "A Fistful of Bitcoins," an allusion to the 1960s Clint Eastwood classic *A Fistful of Dollars*. They settled on a subtitle that evoked both Eastwood's most famous cowboy vigilante and the world of shadowy figures their nascent techniques could unmask. When the UCSD paper hit the internet in August 2013, it was introduced with a description that, to those involved, had come to seem inevitable: "A Fistful of Bitcoins: Characterizing Payments Among Men with No Names."

Cyber Narc

In late July 2013, an independent security journalist named Brian Krebs found an unwelcome, if not entirely unexpected, gift in the mail.

Inside a thin envelope postmarked from Chicago was a copy of *Chicago Confidential,* the weekly magazine insert distributed to subscribers of the *Chicago Tribune.* Taped to a jewelry ad on the back of the magazine were a baker's dozen of small plastic bags, covered in a pattern of black and gold skulls. Each one contained a teaspoon or so of fine white powder: heroin.

Krebs, who had a well-earned reputation for identifying pseudonymous cybercriminals and disrupting their operations, was being framed—but not very effectively. A couple of weeks earlier, he had spotted a post on an exclusive criminal forum written by one of the Russian hackers who considered Krebs his nemesis. The hacker, known as Flycracker, was taking up a collection of bitcoins to make a purchase of Silk Road heroin to send to Krebs, soon to be followed by a phone call to Krebs's local police station reporting him as a drug dealer.

After translating the Russian-language post, Krebs had promptly called the local police station himself and warned them that someone was trying to set him up. A friendly officer made a note. Then, after the package of Silk Road heroin arrived at his door, Krebs turned to a computer science postdoctoral researcher he knew at UCSD, one with whom he'd collaborated on spam investigations and who had mentioned to him that his group at the university was now doing some work on tracing bitcoins. The UCSD postdoc directed Krebs to one of his graduate students. And that's how Sarah Meiklejohn got her first real-world request to trace a criminal cryptocurrency transaction.

Flycracker had made it easy. By posting a Bitcoin address to the cyber-criminal forum, he'd given Meiklejohn a starting point. She simply copied the thirty-four-character string into her blockchain software and looked at the transactions at that address. After collecting 2 bitcoins in donations at the address he'd posted, worth around $200 at the time, a little over three-quarters of the money had been sent to another address, with a third collecting the change.

At a glance, Meiklejohn immediately identified the change address and checked the money's destination against her database. Sure enough, the address was one of the nearly 300,000 she had already tagged as belonging to the Silk Road. Meiklejohn had just connected Flycracker's address directly to the source of the heroin he'd tried to use to frame Krebs.

Meiklejohn couldn't identify Flycracker or the heroin seller. But by following the money from Flycracker's crowdsourced donations to a drug buy, she'd offered another solid piece of evidence exonerating an investigative journalist. "It felt really cool," Meiklejohn remembers, "to just put the address in the database, see Silk Road pop up, and realize just how possible this was."

. . .

Around the same time, I was receiving some Silk Road drug deliveries of my own—voluntary ones, admittedly. As a sidebar to my interview with the Dread Pirate Roberts, I'd proposed to *Forbes*'s editors that we actually buy a few grams of marijuana off the dark web ourselves as an experiment. By the time the editor in chief concluded that illegal drug purchases were too edgy for the pages of *Forbes* magazine—*Vice* might have been more appropriate—three grams of weed were already in the mail headed to our Fifth Avenue headquarters.

By then, in the late summer of 2013, the Dread Pirate Roberts had competition. Two other dark web bazaars called Black Market Reloaded and Atlantis had appeared, modeling themselves on the Silk Road and attracting their own, smaller collections of drug dealers and customers. ("I like having them nipping at my heels," DPR had told me derisively in our interview. "Keeps me motivated.")

I'd ordered one gram of pot from each of the three markets as a test. Two days later I opened up a triple-vacuum-sealed package that contained a single perfect bud of White Kush, shipped by a dealer called Adventure Time on the Atlantis market. A few days later, a few small buds of a strain called Grape God arrived from a Silk Road dealer called the DOPE Man. My pre-rolled joints from Black Market Reloaded never arrived, perhaps caught by customs, given that the dealer was based in the Netherlands. (Alas, no one at *Forbes* could attest to the quality of the two other varieties. The magazine's in-house lawyer insisted we flush our dark web merchandise down a toilet at the end of a video we published online about the experiment.)

Just weeks later, UCSD released its "Men with No Names" paper, ahead of a conference that fall where the research had been accepted for more formal publication. Immediately, Meiklejohn's findings were covered in publications like *Wired, Vice*'s *Motherboard* tech news site, *The Economist,* and *Bloomberg Businessweek*. Meiklejohn was careful not to overstate her findings: Not every Bitcoin transaction could necessarily be tracked. If bitcoins were spent carefully, it might still be possible to elude her tracing techniques. But that description of Bitcoin's privacy properties was still a far cry from what many of its users believed. Like a kind of crypto-Cassandra warning of a crackdown to come, she found herself telling one reporter after another that Bitcoin's much-hyped anonymity promises weren't what they seemed.

So I wrote an email to Meiklejohn to see if she'd be willing to try out her techniques on me: I asked her to trace my three dark web market drug buys. She wrote back right away, gamely agreeing to give it a shot.

To start, I gave Meiklejohn the seven addresses I could see listed in my account on Coinbase, the exchange where I'd paid for a few bitcoins on *Forbes*'s expense account for my drug-buying experiment. That might, in retrospect, sound like giving Meiklejohn an unfair advantage. But in fact, I wanted her to have the same data she'd have if she were a law enforcement agent with subpoena power—or even just a snooping staffer at Coinbase.

A few days later, she wrote me a long email annotating in meticulous detail every move the money in my Coinbase account had made, eleven transactions in total, going so far as to include hyperlinks to the pages on the website Blockchain.info that showed each one. Meiklejohn had identified my deposits into all three dark web markets, as well as the withdrawals of leftover bitcoins from each. She'd distinguished those transactions from others where Coinbase had moved my money from one of its addresses to another for its own housekeeping. She'd even spotted half a bitcoin I'd sent to my fellow *Forbes* writer Kashmir Hill, who was carrying out her own journalistic experiment in trying to live on solely Bitcoin for a full week.

Meiklejohn's assessments of the payments I'd made to the drug markets Atlantis and Black Market Reloaded, she admitted in an email, were partly guesses. She hadn't done enough test transactions on those sites to be totally sure of her answers (though they were both correct).

For my two deposits—0.2 and 0.3 bitcoins—into the Silk Road wallet I used for my pot buy, on the other hand, there was no guesswork needed. Both payments had initially gone into a single address Meiklejohn had never seen before. But then the blockchain had shown the money at that address being combined with two hundred other small sums of bitcoin and swept into a larger, 40-bitcoin pool at a new address, all in one, big multi-input transaction.

Thanks to her test payments and clustering techniques, Meiklejohn had already identified a handful of the other input addresses in that transaction. She could say with confidence they were among the hundreds of thousands of addresses associated with the Silk Road. And as Satoshi himself had pointed out, the same person always has control of the keys for all the input addresses in a multi-input transaction. This was, after all, the first rule of thumb that had guided Meiklejohn's research.

Meiklejohn could see that I'd sent my 0.2- and 0.3-bitcoin payments, indisputably, to someone on the Silk Road, clear evidence of my illegal dealings.

As complex as her process might sound to the rest of us, Meiklejohn had, by the time she was explaining this to me on the phone in September 2013, completely internalized those bitcoin-tracing techniques. To her, outing my online drug deal was utterly intuitive.

"The transactions were just completely right there," she said to me. "It couldn't have been easier."

. . .

Within a few months of publishing her "Men with No Names" paper, however, Meiklejohn began to realize that not everyone in the Bitcoin community entirely appreciated her work.

At a cryptocurrency conference in Princeton where she'd been invited to speak in the spring of 2014, Meiklejohn sat down to breakfast in the hotel dining area next to one programmer and cryptography expert who had worked on Bitcoin privacy issues. She began chatting with him about their respective philosophies around cryptocurrency, privacy, and its limits. They both agreed that privacy should be a fundamental human right. Since the previous summer, Meiklejohn had read the coverage of Edward Snowden's bombshell leaks of classified documents from the National Security Agency about mass surveillance, and it had bolstered her innate sense of the importance of cryptography to protect spaces for all sorts of human expression. The two cryptographers started discussing how Bitcoin or its wallet programs could be altered to protect its users from the sort of blockchain analysis Meiklejohn had proved was possible, to achieve that sort of privacy for people's finances, too, and what the trade-offs might be.

The cryptographer made a simple argument: that those privacy protections should be universal and absolute—even if they enabled criminal or dangerous behavior.

"Oh, I'm not sure about that," Meiklejohn remembers saying.

"Then you eat babies," the cryptographer told her without hesitation.

Meiklejohn was slightly stunned. She laughed off the bizarre comment—though there was no sign it was a joke—and finished her breakfast. She was, after all, accustomed to the social eccentricities of computer scientists.

Later that morning, Meiklejohn was sitting in the audience of a panel discussion of cryptocurrency luminaries at the Princeton conference. A few minutes in, a well-known Bitcoin programmer named Gregory Maxwell with a long brown ponytail and a scraggly red beard made some opening remarks about the role of "the research community" in the Bitcoin world.

"There have been a number of papers doing research on Bitcoin privacy and on user anonymity, and many of these papers have done direct analysis that has effectively de-anonymized Bitcoin users," Maxwell told the small crowd, "and in fact have even gone as far as claiming they were involved in criminal activity.

"This is something some of my friends that do work in sociology and computational analytics would see as actual *interventions*," Maxwell continued, "where we're disclosing something that could have a real impact on people. And I think there's a need for some dialogue about what standards of conduct are appropriate for privacy-related stuff." As Maxwell delivered that admonition to Bitcoin researchers, Meiklejohn remembers him catching her gaze with a meaningful look.

She was shocked. Was Maxwell talking about *her*? Meiklejohn felt she had just been called out—publicly, if not by name—in front of her academic peers. (Later in the day she says Maxwell, who'd seen her look of dismay, privately apologized to her.)

But just as she was starting to feel pushback from the Bitcoin community, Meiklejohn was feeling pulled in the other direction. She and her co-authors Stefan Savage and Damon McCoy were invited to a meeting at a government agency (she declined to say which) to talk about how their work might be used to identify criminal suspects who were using cryptocurrency. She had gone into the meeting with an open mind. After all, she and the other researchers on the team had explicitly suggested in their paper that a law enforcement agency with subpoena authorities could easily identify criminal activity on the blockchain.

But she was turned off by the aggressive tone of the agents in the room: They began describing the anonymity software Tor simplistically, as a haven of crime and abuse that prevented them from catching bad actors. Meiklejohn saw Tor as an essential privacy tool. She knew, for instance, that it was used by millions of people around the world, often living under repressive regimes, to attain a modicum of free and unsurveilled access to the internet. She was personally friendly with Tor's creators and developers, whom she'd met at cryptography conferences, and she'd found them to be likable, principled people. She left the meeting deeply disillusioned with any notion of cooperating with federal law enforcement.

At one point during her bitcoin-tracing pursuits, Meiklejohn's adviser Savage had quipped that she was becoming a "cyber narc." After that government agency encounter, the epithet rolled around in her head. The more she considered the phrase, the less she liked the sound of it.

Glen Park

Just a few weeks after I asked Meiklejohn to trace my pot purchases, on October 1, 2013, a handsome, tousle-haired, and wiry twenty-nine-year-old named Ross Ulbricht walked down Diamond Street in the Glen Park neighborhood of San Francisco. He entered a small café called Bello Coffee and Tea, carrying his Samsung 700Z laptop in his backpack. This was one of Ulbricht's preferred spots to sit and work on his start-up. From this modest coffee shop, he operated the world's largest online black market as the Dread Pirate Roberts, the facilitator of hundreds of millions of dollars' worth of narcotics deals.

He looked around the crowded café briefly for a good spot. When he saw that no power outlets were available, he walked out and continued down the street toward the Glen Park Public Library—the setting for a scene that, in the years since, has become an almost legendary moment in the lore of the dark web.

Ulbricht climbed the stairs and found a seat at a circular table in the science fiction section, with a nice view out the window. After setting up, he immediately spotted an encrypted message from one of his moderators on the Silk Road's staff, an employee who went by the name "Cirrus," asking him to check out a situation on the Silk Road that needed his attention, ASAP. He logged in to the site under a "mastermind" account that gave him a full display of the site's activities.

Just at that moment, a disheveled couple behind Ulbricht shuffled into his peripheral vision. "Fuck you!" the woman shouted, when she was just behind his chair. Ulbricht turned as the man grabbed the woman's shirt and raised a fist.

At that exact moment, another young woman across the table from Ulbricht grabbed his laptop without hesitation, gingerly whisked it away, and handed it to a man who had suddenly appeared behind her, seemingly out of nowhere. Ulbricht lunged for the machine but found that he was caught in a bear hug. Everyone involved, on all sides of Ulbricht, was in fact an FBI agent. Before he was even aware of what had happened, Ulbricht was being cuffed.

As it turned out, even the Silk Road moderator he'd been chatting with had been an undercover agent: A Homeland Security Investigations official named Jared Der-Yeghiayan had quietly arrested a real moderator months earlier and then taken over her account, and was now sending Ulbricht messages from a bench just across the street from the library.

This elaborate, highly orchestrated arrest had been overseen by the New York field office of the FBI and designed around one critical goal: to catch Ulbricht with his laptop open and logged in to the Silk Road. Grabbing the machine in an open state was not merely a matter of catching Ulbricht red-handed. He used an encryption program on his laptop that would automatically transform the entire contents of his hard drive into an uncrackable cipher the instant the lid was shut, concealing its secrets from investigators forever.

On the live PC, swept out of Ulbricht's hands, the FBI found a vast smorgasbord of evidence, the kind that only a criminal with far too much confidence in his laptop's encryption would dare to keep: Ulbricht had, amazingly, maintained a diary, a logbook, a spreadsheet of his net worth, and even comprehensive records of his chats with the Silk Road's entire staff.

The next day, the Silk Road's dark web site was replaced with a banner displaying the words "THIS HIDDEN SITE HAS BEEN SEIZED" surrounded by various law enforcement agency badges.

On the Silk Road's forums, users reeled as they came to learn that their seemingly untouchable black market, reliant on untraceable currency, was no more. "Jesus christ this is TERRIBLE!!" lamented one user. Others quickly put the blame on Ulbricht, whose hubris had led to the downfall of their underground free-market Eden. "Sorry, but when he gave the fucking Forbes interview I imagined this would be coming," wrote one user. "Should have kept all this shit on the down low rather than publicly bragging about it."

In fact, it would turn out that when I was interviewing the Dread Pirate Roberts just three months earlier, Ulbricht had already been identified as a suspect—thanks to the IRS agent Gary Alford's web sleuthing. The FBI, meanwhile, had tracked down the Silk Road's servers in Iceland and France.* As Ulbricht was being cuffed in San Francisco, other agents were simultaneously taking over the Silk Road's infrastructure and preparing to transfer more than 144,000 bitcoins held on Ulbricht's servers and laptop.

In other words, even as the Dread Pirate Roberts was telling me, that Fourth of July, about the revolutionary future that his work would usher in for all mankind, spinning a dream of a new era of lawless online liberty, his role in that dream was already coming to an end.

---

* The FBI has described that cybersurveillance coup as the result of a misconfiguration in the site's use of the Tor anonymity software but has been reluctant to ever officially explain that error in a courtroom. Some cybersecurity experts have speculated some other secret technique actually allowed the bureau to break or bypass Tor's anonymity protections. The Department of Justice would ultimately argue that because the server was located abroad, the Fourth Amendment privacy protections against warrantless searches—including potentially hacking it—didn't apply.

11

The Double Agent

Six months after the fall of the Silk Road, Tigran Gambaryan opened a file on Carl Mark Force, the DEA agent who had investigated the dark web market but whose undercover hijinks—impersonating a Puerto Rican drug lord, staging a murder—ultimately had no role in the site's demise. Based on his attempted withdrawals from Bitstamp, it would seem that Force had lucked into a massive cryptocurrency windfall. Now it was time for Gambaryan to determine its provenance.

Working in his office on an upper floor of the Ronald V. Dellums Federal Building in downtown Oakland, Gambaryan began the familiar process of subpoenaing and then poring over Force's financial records. He found that Force had, in late 2013, paid off his home's entire mortgage, an outstanding loan of $130,000. He'd repaid, too, a $22,000 loan he'd taken out against his federal retirement account. He'd even made a gift of tens of thousands of dollars to his local church, the sort of largesse that, Gambaryan knew all too well, was tough to afford on a federal agent's salary.

The numbers only got shadier from there: Gambaryan found records of real estate investments in which Force had listed his net worth as more than $1 million. That wealth was almost entirely due, it became clear, to a massive influx of liquidated bitcoins from cryptocurrency exchanges like Bitstamp and CampBX that had flowed into Force's bank accounts. The payments totaled $776,000 beyond his $150,000 annual DEA salary over the two prior years that he'd worked on the Silk Road case. With that ample financial padding, Force had then retired from the DEA, just days before Gambaryan began to look into his records.

As they dug into the former agent's pile of money, Gambaryan and the prosecutor on the case, Kathryn Haun, arranged a call with Shaun Bridges, the Baltimore-based Secret Service agent whom Bitstamp's lawyer George Frost had consulted with. Gambaryan knew that Bridges had been on the same Baltimore-based team investigating the Silk Road as Force, but he and Haun weren't interested in their work together—just that Bridges had been the first to respond to the suspicious activity report that Frost had filed about Force with the U.S. Treasury. Bridges, after all, was still listed as the law enforcement contact on that report.

When they reached Bridges on the phone, however, he was immediately, inexplicably hostile. "What is a federal prosecutor in San Francisco doing investigating anything going on in Baltimore?" Haun remembers him asking. "Why do you have any jurisdiction here?" Gambaryan and Haun, taken slightly aback by Bridges's tone, explained they'd learned about Force's suspicious behavior from George Frost.

Bridges responded, as Gambaryan remembers it, with defensive posturing and non sequiturs. He bragged that in addition to his Secret Service role, he was the Baltimore Task Force's liaison to the NSA and an expert on Tor and cryptocurrency, implying that he, Shaun Bridges, was best qualified to deal with the Force case. He made it clear to Gambaryan and Haun that Baltimore—and in particular anything related to Carl Force—was his territory and he wasn't going to share that turf with them.

After the Secret Service agent hung up the phone, Gambaryan and Haun gave each other a look. Their shared reaction: "What the hell was that?"

· · ·

Gambaryan and Haun could see they weren't going to get any help from Baltimore. But there was another team of investigators who held a wealth of Carl Force's communications records: the coalition of FBI, DHS, and IRS agents, led by New York prosecutors, who had successfully taken down the Silk Road. After all, the server they had seized, along with Ulbricht's laptop, contained the logs of all of the administrator's conversations with Silk Road buyers, sellers, and staff—including those with Force's alter ego Nob.

Gambaryan had inroads with that New York–based team of investigators: First, of course, there was his IRS colleague Gary Alford. And separately, he'd befriended Jared Der-Yeghiayan, the DHS agent who'd gone undercover as a Silk Road moderator and who had been messaging Ulbricht at the moment of his arrest. After an earlier conference call with agents in Chicago, where Der-Yeghiayan was based, Gambaryan and Der-Yeghiayan had recognized each other's Armenian names. In a follow-up conversation they'd bonded over their shared connection to the old country.

As a result, within a few days Gambaryan had access to all the collected evidence in the Silk Road case, including all of DPR's recorded communications. He immediately began digging through more than eighteen months of Carl Force's conversations with the Dread Pirate—ones in which Force had used his Nob drug cartel persona—poring over the documentation of the undercover narcotics agent's day-to-day work. He found, in that mountain of chat logs, the entire evolution of Nob and DPR's relationship.

Force had first approached DPR as Nob in April 2012, brashly offering to buy the Silk Road outright. When those buyout negotiations fizzled—DPR asked for no less than $1 billion—Nob spent the next months ingratiating himself as a friend and mentor, a more experienced *narcotraficante* who could help this budding digital drug runner learn the ropes.

In early 2013, the messages showed that Force had gotten more serious about tightening the net around DPR. Nob had suggested to the Dread Pirate that he wanted to off-load a kilo of cocaine—did DPR have a buyer? DPR, seeming to sense an opportunity to profit a bit more directly from the Silk Road's burgeoning drug sales, ponied up $27,000 in Bitcoin and gave Nob the address of a Silk Road moderator who had agreed to serve as a middleman: a man named Curtis Clark Green, who lived in Spanish Fork, Utah.

Then, just days later in the chats, DPR came back to Nob with a very different request, of a much more violent variety: Green, the very moderator DPR had trusted enough to receive a $27,000 drug shipment, now appeared to have turned on him and stolen a substantial sum of the Silk Road's bitcoins. Over the previous days, Green's moderator account seemed to have reset the passwords on high-value Silk Road dealer and buyer accounts, one by one, then logged in and emptied out their Bitcoin savings. In total, $350,000 worth of cryptocurrency had been stolen, and DPR now had to make the angry users whole.

DPR wanted Green taught a lesson. He wanted to pay Nob, his supposed cartel contact, to make it happen. "do you want him beat up, shot, just paid a visit?"* Force had written as Nob, playing the cold-blooded killer.

The Silk Road's boss had initially asked only that Green be coerced to give back the money. But then he dug up public court records showing that Green had recently been arrested for cocaine possession. Now DPR feared that his employee had been flipped—that he'd turned informant. Green didn't actually know his boss's real identity, naturally, but the possibility of a mole on his staff was more than DPR could risk. He wrote to Nob, asking him to "change the order to execute."

They negotiated a price of $80,000 for the hit. A week later, Nob shared a photograph of Green's body, with what looked like vomit dribbling out of his mouth. He said that the deed was done, the body destroyed.

Like any good mentor figure, Nob asked DPR how he felt about the outcome. "A little disturbed, but I'm ok," DPR had responded. "I'm new to this kind of thing is all."

Reading those messages—and reading between the lines, based on what he'd learned about the Baltimore Task Force's investigation of the Silk Road and the separate, murder-for-hire indictment of Ulbricht that had resulted—Gambaryan marveled at the dramatic irony. Green's arrest for drug possession had been arranged by Carl Force himself, the very agent who had sent the drugs to Green's address, in a sting operation. Then, when Green had apparently gone rogue, stealing hundreds of thousands of dollars' worth of bitcoins from Silk Road coffers, DPR had turned to none other than Force, under the guise of Nob, to carry out Green's "murder," staged for DPR's benefit. (The vomit dribbling out of Green's mouth in the photo was, in fact, Campbell's Chicken & Stars Soup.) Shakespeare himself couldn't have written the misunderstandings and coincidences more tidily.

But amid all the faux-grisly drama, there was an untidy element that

---

* Throughout this book, text-based messages have been reproduced in their original state, including grammatical errors and typos.

still nagged at Gambaryan: If Green had been in the custody of the Baltimore Task Force during the time between his arrest and his staged death, how had he managed to steal the Silk Road's $350,000?

. . .

Gambaryan didn't dwell on the mystery of that theft for long—in part because he was looking at another series of messages, deep within Nob's chat log with DPR, that began to point toward Force's unexpected Bitcoin riches: In the early summer of 2013, Gambaryan was surprised to learn, Nob had offered to start selling DPR a stream of intelligence about the federal manhunt targeting him.

After gaining DPR's trust through the elaborate murder-for-hire ruse, Nob had made DPR a business offer: He had a friend at a federal agency, he claimed, a man he suggested they call "Kevin." For a price, Kevin was ready to act as a source inside law enforcement, selling counterintelligence back to the Dread Pirate. DPR initially agreed to pay 400 bitcoins for a sample of whatever intel Kevin had to offer, a sum worth about $45,000 at the time.

Gambaryan reviewed Force's official DEA reports and saw that the agent had at first documented those conversations, giving the impression that they were just another ruse to bring Force closer to his prey. He had eventually moved those 400 bitcoins to an official DEA account.

Not long after that initial payment from DPR, however, Gambaryan began to see that the messages between DPR and Nob on the Silk Road server had shifted into indecipherable passages of random-looking characters. At Nob's suggestion, he and the Silk Road boss had started to use PGP, or Pretty Good Privacy, a free and widely trusted encryption program, which Nob suggested could give them an added layer of protection from surveillance.

It also prevented Force's supervisors at the DEA—and now Gambaryan—from reading their messages. What's more, Force's DEA reports had no record of the decrypted text of these conversations.

That subterfuge made Gambaryan deeply suspicious: Underneath this added layer of encryption, was Force still an undercover agent on the Silk Road working for law enforcement and merely pretending to have a mole inside the feds? Or was he using his position to act as a double agent, working for DPR as an *actual* mole, selling his own DEA intel to DPR? The layers of deception were dizzying.

Just what information Nob sold DPR has never been revealed. Given that Force's Baltimore investigation was entirely walled off from the rival New York–based investigation that was closing in on Ulbricht, it was unlikely to have included anything of real substance. But whatever it might have been, it was interesting enough to the Dread Pirate that he was willing to pay for more. DPR offered Nob another 525 bitcoins, then worth roughly $70,000, for a second installment of Kevin's intel.

"Please keep me posted and you have my word that no one else knows anything about this," the Dread Pirate wrote. "I'm sorry I didn't know how much to send before. I was afraid of offending if I sent too little and looking foolish if I sent too much." It concluded, in the typical insecure style of the Dread Pirate's communications with Nob, "I hope I didn't make things difficult for you."

Amid the garbled, encrypted conversations between Nob and DPR, Gambaryan was able to read that one message. The Dread Pirate Roberts had made a critical slipup: He'd forgotten to encrypt that single text with PGP. Nob's message in response was again encrypted and unreadable for Gambaryan. But its subject line was legible. It read, "Use PGP!"

Nob's scolding came too late. Gambaryan could plainly see that the Dread Pirate Roberts had made a 525-bitcoin payment to Nob. Force not only had left a key piece of the conversation out of his official report but now seemed to be trying to cover it up. He'd written in his DEA report, without explanation, "AGENT'S NOTE: DPR made no such payment."

But the Dread Pirate Roberts had, in his fateful, unencrypted message, documented the money transfer—one that even the undercover agent's overseers didn't know about. And now that evidence was in Tigran Gambaryan's hands.

CHAPTER 12

Receipts

Gambaryan felt they were ready to confront Force—to hear him try to explain these discussions of payments between DPR and Nob—and the prosecutors agreed.

Kathryn Haun, her boss, the U.S. attorney Will Frentzen, and Gambaryan set up a video connection from San Francisco to Baltimore, where Force appeared with a lawyer he'd hired after learning that he was under investigation. Face-to-face for the first time, on opposite sides of the country, Gambaryan recognized the same bald, goateed figure he'd seen on the "Eladio Guzman Fuentes" driver's license that Force had given to Bitstamp.

They asked Force about the payments he'd received from DPR and the origins of his newfound personal crypto wealth. Force answered their questions in a confident, almost arrogant tone, neither friendly nor explicitly resistant, Frentzen remembers. But the unspoken answer to their line of interrogation, as Frentzen describes it, was a dismissive "get the fuck out of here."

Yes, Force conceded, he'd temporarily put the 400 bitcoins from DPR into a personal account. But that was just because of the novelty of dealing with cryptocurrency as evidence, he argued. He'd put it into a DEA account soon after, hadn't he? He pointed out that the money had actually gained value during the time he'd held on to it, thanks to Bitcoin's price swings. He'd practically done the government a favor, in other words.

As for the second message about a 525-bitcoin payment from DPR, that required no explanation. As he'd written in his DEA report, it never happened: "DPR made no such payment."

When Haun asked about the source of his gains of the better part of a million dollars in a few short years, Force explained that he'd been lucky enough to learn about Bitcoin early thanks to his Silk Road assignment—the same explanation he'd given George Frost when Bitstamp had raised red flags. Force had made some wise investments, he said. The hundreds of thousands of dollars he'd earned as a result were all thanks to the savvy Bitcoin buys he'd carried out in a personal capacity. Now he just wanted to move on, enjoy his retirement from law enforcement, and perhaps put his new expertise to use in some other job in the burgeoning crypto economy.

Force gave no visual cues that he was lying, Gambaryan remembers. But he knew that this gruff, old-school law enforcement agent also had years of experience undercover. Despite Force's story, Gambaryan was sure that his money was dirty. But no one was going to indict Carl Force based on Gambaryan's gut alone.

• • •

Sitting in his office, Gambaryan stared at the Dread Pirate Roberts's message, in which he stated unequivocally that he had paid Nob 525 bitcoins. It amounted to written evidence of a roughly $50,000 payment that had almost certainly landed in Force's pockets. But Gambaryan was a forensic accountant. He knew that a conversation about a payment was very different from proof that it had actually occurred.

Gambaryan needed receipts. And Bitcoin had become the chosen currency of crypto-anarchists and criminals precisely because there was no one to provide them.

The prevailing wisdom in law enforcement agencies at the time still held that lawbreakers and libertarians were correct about Bitcoin—that it presented a serious problem for any agent who sought to trace dirty money movements. An unclassified FBI report published in 2012 had been titled "Bitcoin Virtual Currency: Unique Features Present Distinct Challenges for Deterring Illicit Activity." The report had flatly stated that "since Bitcoin does not have a centralized authority, law enforcement faces difficulty detecting suspicious activity, identifying users, and obtaining transaction records." The report noted that Bitcoin exchanges that demanded identification from traders might help identify Bitcoin users. But two years had passed since the report had been written, and U.S. law enforcement hadn't actually managed to prosecute anybody based on those records, even as Bitcoin black markets like the Silk Road had flourished in plain view.

Still, Gambaryan had always had his doubts about Bitcoin's untraceability. From the very first time he'd read about Bitcoin, back in 2010, his accountant's brain had wondered how it could truly provide anonymity when the records of every transaction were shared with so many thousands of machines around the world—even if those transactions were to addresses rather than names. At one point early in his tenure as an IRS-CI agent, watching the Silk Road's unchecked growth, he had even gone so far as to suggest to a fellow agent that they try tracing bitcoins on the blockchain. His colleague had laughed at him. "Oh, so we're going to bring in Satoshi Nakamoto to introduce the blockchain as evidence in court?" the agent had joked.

But Gambaryan had read the news coverage on the heels of UCSD's "Men with No Names" research in late 2013, and it had only reinforced what he'd suspected all along: Despite the prevailing belief of both cops and criminals, cryptocurrency *was* traceable.

So, why not use the blockchain as evidence? If a cryptographically unforgeable, giant ledger displaying every Bitcoin transaction was good enough to prove who owned millions of dollars within Bitcoin's economy, Gambaryan thought, it ought to be good enough to use as evidence in a criminal indictment, too.

Gambaryan wasn't at all sure of how to trace bitcoins himself. But he had no choice but to try. "I had a case in front of me," he says. "I had to figure out how to solve it."

· · ·

It was late afternoon on a fall day in 2014 when Gambaryan got to work tracing Force's money on the blockchain. Despite having read Meiklejohn's paper, he possessed none of the data that she'd assembled over months of clustering Bitcoin addresses and identifying them with test transactions. So he simply started copying Bitcoin addresses from Carl Force's account records—the ones he'd gotten from exchanges such as

CampBX and Bitstamp—and pasting them into the search field on Blockchain.info, which displayed the entire blockchain on the web.

At first, the collections of garbled character strings seemed meaningless to Gambaryan. But almost immediately, he could see he was onto something. On September 27, 2013, just a few days before Ross Ulbricht's arrest, Gambaryan saw with a jolt of recognition that one of Force's CampBX addresses had received a 525-bitcoin payment— the magic number that DPR had mentioned in his conveniently unencrypted message.

The blockchain entry showed that the coins, by then worth $66,000 thanks to a bump in Bitcoin's price, had moved to Force's address as one solitary payment from another single address. So Gambaryan clicked on that second address on Blockchain.info, working backward through time, only to find that the money had moved to that second link in the chain a few weeks earlier, on September 1, again as a single collection of coins.

When Gambaryan looked for the source of the coins at that second address, however, the picture became vastly more complicated: Ten addresses had combined their coins there. If he was going to follow the bitcoins any further, he'd have to trace back all ten paths.

So Gambaryan began patiently clicking through them, one by one. Each of the ten tributary streams of money that had flowed into Force's 525-bitcoin pool had its own individual sources, and Gambaryan had no idea if tracing them back would lead to anything remotely recognizable. He was feeling around in the dark, finding his way through an entirely abstract maze of digits. But as a tax auditor, he'd dealt with long, winding trails of numbers plenty of times before. So as that fall afternoon turned to evening, he continued painstakingly clicking through the transactions, even as the IRS office closed and his colleagues began filing out of the building.

Gambaryan drove home at dusk with his laptop, ate dinner with his wife and baby daughter, then got back to work at the desk in the living room of their two-bedroom, single-story house in the Oakland suburb of Hayward. Gambaryan's wife, Yuki, remembers seeing him that night, glued to his screen, sifting through a sea of inscrutable figures.

Their baby would periodically crawl under Gambaryan's desk to get his attention. That night Gambaryan propped her up in his lap as he continued clicking through the dozens of branching addresses. He was still combing through them when Yuki picked up their daughter and put her to sleep and then went to bed herself, leaving Gambaryan alone. He sat in the silent, darkening living room as he followed Force's 525 bitcoins to their origin.

. . .

By around 11:00 p.m., Gambaryan had traced the money's movements back to early August—nearly a month earlier than when it had landed in Force's CampBX account. Gambaryan had now assembled a nearly complete, though very messy, picture. Working backward, he could see how the money had split out into the ten streams and then, several transactions back in each individual stream, begun to converge again into a smaller number of addresses. Those branching and converging money flows, he thought, looked familiar: They struck Gambaryan as the typical, contrived complexity of someone splitting up and reassembling their illicit funds in the hopes of throwing an auditor off their trail.

Following the money at each of the remaining addresses back one more step, he now saw the coins had originally come from just four sources. Each of those addresses had received their funds on the same day: August 4, 2013—the exact date when the Dread Pirate Roberts had told Nob he'd paid him. Gambaryan mentally recorded the payments: They were for 127, 61, 134, and 203 bitcoins. He added the numbers in his head. They summed up to 525 bitcoins.

Sitting alone in his living room, he knew he had just found DPR's payment to Nob in the unfailingly honest record of the blockchain—the payment Force had written in an official report never took place.

Gambaryan spent the rest of the night checking and rechecking his work, then reconstructing it in a clean Excel spreadsheet of transactions and Bitcoin addresses that he could share with prosecutors. His mind buzzing with sleep deprivation and adrenaline, he wrote an email to Kathryn Haun and Will Frentzen that night, telling them he believed he had done what so many in the law enforcement world considered impossible: He had traced Carl Force's dirty cryptocurrency.

The next morning, after a few hours' sleep, Gambaryan began texting his DHS contact Jared Der-Yeghiayan, the Armenian American agent in Chicago whom he'd befriended. He needed to check the four addresses he'd found with someone who had access to the Dread Pirate Roberts's Bitcoin wallet. As a member of the Silk Road investigation team, Der-Yeghiayan still had access to all the site's server data, including its Bitcoin addresses. Der-Yeghiayan called Gambaryan back a few hours later and confirmed what Gambaryan already knew: Each of the four addresses belonged to DPR.

For a moment, Gambaryan and Der-Yeghiayan sat on the phone in silence. Gambaryan had just, for the very first time in a U.S. criminal investigation, traced cryptocurrency payments to prove someone's guilt.

"Oh, shit," Gambaryan remembers thinking. "We broke Bitcoin."

FrenchMaid, DeathFromAbove

Gambaryan now had proof: Carl Force had lied.

But one payment of $70,000 in bitcoins didn't explain the $700,000 worth of bitcoins that had shown up in Force's accounts. If Force had been willing to turn his alter ego Nob into a double agent, what else was he capable of?

Bolstered by his bitcoin-tracing coup, Gambaryan was now determined to look through every scrap of evidence that might reveal the full extent of Force's misbehavior. Slowly he began to see that Force hadn't merely tried on the role of a rogue agent but had come to inhabit it with almost ludicrous abandon.

Gambaryan had once observed a curious entry in Ross Ulbricht's Silk Road log from September 13, 2013. It noted that Ulbricht had offered $100,000 not to Nob but to another supposed informant with the handle "FrenchMaid," looking for intel about one of the names law enforcement had suspected might be DPR.

With his newfound sense of the scale of Force's ambitions, Gambaryan searched the Silk Road server's log for messages from French-Maid. He found a series of them sent to DPR. Force had played the role of one of DPR's counterintelligence sources, Gambaryan thought. Could he have played the role of another?

Most of FrenchMaid's messages were encrypted with PGP. But encrypting a message to someone with PGP requires possessing the person's "public key," a long string of characters that scrambles messages such that only that particular recipient and no one else can unscramble them. The first message from FrenchMaid had been left unencrypted by necessity. "I have received important information that you need to know asap," it read. "Please provide me with your public key for PGP."

It was signed, Gambaryan saw with astonishment, "Carl."

Gambaryan could hardly believe what he was seeing. Amid the multiple personas Carl Force was juggling, he seemed to slip up and sign a message to DPR with *his own name.*

Gambaryan could see Force's attempt to undo the damage four hours later. DPR had received another message from the same account titled "Whoops!" The message read, "I am sorry about that. My name is Carla Sophia and I have many boyfriends and girlfriends on the market place. DPR will want to hear what I have to say;) xoxoxo."

. . .

Gambaryan could now see that Force was wearing not one mask in his interactions with the Dread Pirate but at least two. So he began to search for more.

As part of the standard practice of documenting his undercover work, Force had periodically used a screen recording program called Camtasia to make first-person videos of his sessions as Nob. Gambaryan watched hours and hours of the videos, painstakingly replaying Force's online performances in real time.

Sure enough, for one brief moment in those videos, Gambaryan saw that Force was no longer logged in as Nob. Instead, on the top right of his screen, he saw the username "DeathFromAbove."

The message Force had written was addressed, as usual, to the Dread Pirate Roberts. "I know that you had something to do with Curtis' disappearance and death," it began, a reference to the Silk Road moderator whose staged murder Force himself had helped to arrange. "Just wanted to let you know that I am coming for you," DeathFromAbove wrote. "You are a dead man. Don't think you can elude me."

It was signed "De Oppresso Liber," Latin for "from oppressed to free." A quick Google search revealed that phrase to be the motto of the Green Berets.

Gambaryan switched over to the Dread Pirate Roberts's messages on the Silk Road server, and he could see that DeathFromAbove had gone on to repeatedly threaten DPR, playing the part of a Green Beret who knew Curtis Green and was out for revenge.

DPR had blown him off. "Your threats and all of the other psychos aren't going to deter me," he'd responded to the DeathFromAbove account. "stop messaging me and go find something else to do."

So Force had tried a different approach with his Green Beret character. He claimed to have access to top secret classified information and to know the Dread Pirate Roberts's real identity. He even ventured a guess, accusing DPR of being one of the names on the Baltimore Task Force's list of suspects. "$250,000 in U.S. cash/bank transfer and I won't give your identity to law enforcement," he wrote. "Consider it punitive damages."

Force had apparently guessed the wrong name. DPR never responded to DeathFromAbove again.

· · ·

Nob. Eladio Guzman Fuentes. FrenchMaid. Carla Sophia. DeathFromAbove. Force had been living not merely a double life, it was now clear to Gambaryan, but a whole myriad of them, as if the promise of anonymity offered by the dark web and Bitcoin had splintered his psyche.

DPR seems never to have suspected any relationship among those personas (or, for that matter, that a federal agent might be behind them all). Yes, there was the Carla Sophia blunder. But the Silk Road's boss had presumably never heard the name Carl Force, so he couldn't make the connection. And besides, he had no reason to doubt his informants.

In the log that Ulbricht kept on his laptop, Gambaryan did find an entry in which Ulbricht noted that he still hadn't gotten a response from FrenchMaid, four days after his $100,000 payment for intel, about who the government suspected might be DPR. It's not clear if Ulbricht ever got a name in return for his money.

For Gambaryan, though, that FrenchMaid transaction represented another toehold in his investigation: another payment that he could trace on the blockchain.

Once again, Gambaryan called his friend Jared Der-Yeghiayan. While they were on the phone, Gambaryan began clicking through Bitcoin addresses on Blockchain.info. Looking at Force's CampBX account addresses, he saw that they had received large payments from four addresses. Tracing those sums across hops through two more addresses each, he eventually found a single address from which they'd all originated.

The blockchain's ledger showed that on September 15, just two days after the payment DPR had recorded, 770 bitcoins had been sent out to those four addresses. Their value: $100,000 at that day's exchange rate.

Der-Yeghiayan checked DPR's Bitcoin addresses again and confirmed it: The $100,000 had come from one of the Silk Road boss's wallets. This time tracing Force's money had taken Gambaryan just minutes. And with every transaction he followed, the lasso tightened around his target.*

. . .

By late 2014, Haun and Frentzen could see the end of their investigation on the horizon: They had more than enough evidence to indict Force for extortion, money laundering, and obstruction of justice. But for all of Gambaryan's blockchain-tracing breakthroughs, there was still the mystery of the $350,000 that had been stolen from the Silk Road, the money that Curtis Green had purportedly filched from the market's high rollers just after his arrest.

None of the investigators now believed that Curtis Green, the Silk Road moderator whom the Dread Pirate had ordered murdered for the theft, would have dared to take the money in the midst of his questioning by the Baltimore Task Force. It would have been too brazen, even

---

* Even after the Nob and FrenchMaid payments, there was still another huge swath of Force's ill-gotten riches for Gambaryan to track down. In late 2013, Force had tried to get a job moonlighting as the "chief compliance officer" of a Bitcoin exchange called CoinMKT and then had used his DEA authority to seize nearly $300,000 worth of cryptocurrency from an account holder there.

The unlucky owner of those funds was an actor in California whom Force accused of money laundering, without real evidence. Force had put the actor's confiscated six-figure fund directly into his own Bitstamp account. Just as Bitstamp's George Frost had originally feared, it seemed Force was abusing his DEA powers not only to extort, defraud, and sell counterintelligence to the Dread Pirate Roberts but also to shake down cryptocurrency exchanges on the thinnest pretenses of criminal suspicion.

if Green had somehow managed to get access to his account between interrogations.

Besides, there was now a much more obvious suspect.

After all, it was Carl Force's undercover work as Nob that had helped set up the sting that led to Green's arrest. Force had been there in Utah when Green was arrested and questioned and had his murder staged, not to mention when Green's computer, with moderator access to the Silk Road, was seized. Force had shown himself to be capable of stealing any bitcoins, dirty or clean, that were even vaguely within his reach.

Still, for all the arrows pointing at Force, Tigran Gambaryan alone harbored doubts. By late 2014, the young IRS agent was gaining a new fluency in reading Bitcoin's ledger of transactions. To Gambaryan, the theft just didn't *look* like the work of Carl Force. The $350,000 worth of bitcoins was broken into more chunks than Force had typically bothered with, and they had moved through more hops on the blockchain, to addresses that Gambaryan couldn't find in any of Force's accounts on any exchange.

"It didn't fit the pattern," Gambaryan remembers. "It was almost like I'd gotten used to the way that Carl was using the blockchain. This was different."

He'd come to a conclusion that seemed highly improbable to the prosecutors on the case, and yet he was sure of it. "It's not Carl," Gambaryan told Haun and Frentzen. "I don't know who it is, but it's not Carl." Another thief of the Silk Road's bitcoins was still out there.

The Trial

On a freezing mid-January day in lower Manhattan in 2015, I walked up the stairs of the Southern District of New York's federal courthouse— across the street from the government building where Sarah Meiklejohn had once searched through checks on behalf of her prosecutor mother. I rode an elevator to the fifteenth floor and stepped into a stately court-room with a view of the Brooklyn Bridge out the window behind the judge's bench. A few minutes later, a slim, square-jawed thirty-year-old entered that courtroom, accompanied by his team of lawyers. Ross Ulbricht, wearing a gray suit, looked over the crowded gallery and flashed a smile to his mother. His trial was about to begin.

In the defense's opening statement, Ulbricht's lead attorney, Joshua Dratel, began with a shocking admission: Yes, Ross Ulbricht had created the Silk Road.

But then Dratel, a renowned national security lawyer, launched into the rest of the defense's version of events: The young, idealistic Ulbricht had intended his marketplace to be only a kind of harmless "economic experiment." As it began to grow into a full-blown black market, Ulbricht had sold it off to the *real* Dread Pirate Roberts, who had presided over its years of booming Bitcoin-based narcotics sales. Only when that actual DPR—seemingly unidentified and at large—and his henchmen began to sense law enforcement closing in did they somehow trick Ulbricht into returning and logging in to the Silk Road the day he was caught at San Francisco's Glen Park Public Library.

"At the end, he was lured back by those operators," Dratel told the jury, "to take the fall for the people running the website." Aside from a small fraction of the Silk Road's earnings in its earliest days, the site's bit-coins weren't even Ulbricht's, Dratel claimed. As for the 144,000 coins found on his laptop, the defense made an argument along the lines of Carl Force's: Those were the fruits of Ulbricht's early Bitcoin invest-ments. "Ross was not a drug dealer," Dratel said. "He was not a kingpin."

Sitting in the courtroom, I was immediately struck by the fact that this had been the story DPR told me eighteen months earlier: that he had merely inherited the site from its creator. If it was a cover story, I had to give its author credit for consistency.

But a few hours later, the Berkeley computer scientist Nick Weaver woke up on the other side of the country, read Dratel's words in news reports from the trial, and had a far more visceral reaction: He got angry. *This* was going to be Ross Ulbricht's argument? Weaver was so "offended by the gross stupidity of the defense," as he'd later put it, that he took an unusual step for an academic researcher: He looked up the email addresses of the prosecutors in court documents and wrote them a mes-sage, offering to help them disprove Ulbricht's cover story.

Weaver, who worked at Berkeley's International Computer Science Institute, was among the still-small group of university researchers who had real experience tracing bitcoins. His team often collaborated with Sarah Meiklejohn's at UCSD; they had even co-authored another paper on the subject the previous year. Now Weaver wrote to the prosecutors in his email that he was sure the blockchain could prove that Ulbricht's bitcoins had in fact come not from savvy investments but from the Silk Road.

Weaver's email to the prosecution pointed to 16,000 bitcoins that he could see directly flowing from the Silk Road server to Ulbricht's personal wallet. After all, the FBI had seized the server and Ulbricht's laptop, then pulled the bitcoins off both machines, documenting the two confiscations in public forfeiture notices that Weaver and others in the Bitcoin community could then match up with transactions on the blockchain.

After that seizure announcement months earlier, Weaver had traced nearly 10 percent of the total fortune found on Ulbricht's machine with just a few clicks. A few days later, he'd used one of Meiklejohn's clustering tricks to identify more Silk Road addresses and found another 13,000 coins that had followed the same path from server to laptop. The 29,000 coins together were worth roughly $3 million at the time. As Weaver's emails laid out, he could see some of those Silk Road coins arriving in Ulbricht's coffers as early as July 2013, nearly three months before the defense claimed he was "lured" back to the Silk Road to serve as a patsy.

One of the Silk Road prosecutors followed up with Weaver by phone, and the Berkeley researcher explained exactly how he suggested the Justice Department, with the actual server and laptop in their custody, could indisputably prove the origins of Ulbricht's riches.

A little more than a week later, on the ninth day of Ulbricht's trial, the prosecutor Timothy Howard called to the stand a former FBI agent named Ilhwan Yum. Yum presented a bombshell revelation to the court: He and a cryptologist consultant had together traced on the blockchain no fewer than 700,000 bitcoins from the Silk Road server to Ulbricht's wallet, stretching back as early as September 2012, worth a total of $13.4 million at the time of the transfers.

In fact, one of the Silk Road prosecutors would later tell me, they were a step ahead of Weaver. By the time they spoke to the Berkeley researcher, they had already been planning to track Ulbricht's coins on the blockchain, an idea that had come to them as soon as the defense tried to disavow the money's connections to the Silk Road.

On the stand, Yum went even further than Weaver had: He pointed to a 3,000-bitcoin payment that flowed out of Ulbricht's wallet in April 2013, totaling roughly $500,000. This payment matched up with another shocking piece of evidence revealed in the trial: An encrypted chat transcript recovered from the Silk Road server captured DPR negotiating another *five* murders. A would-be contract killer named redandwhite, who'd claimed to the Dread Pirate Roberts to be part of the Hells Angels motorcycle gang, had written to DPR and offered to take out an assortment of DPR's enemies: a blackmailer, a thief, and even a group of three of the thief's housemates. DPR had agreed to the half-million-dollar job.

Ulbricht hadn't been charged with these murders for hire in the New York trial. By all accounts, no such murders took place, staged or otherwise; redandwhite appears to have been a scam artist. But as Yum demonstrated to the jury, Ulbricht's intent to pay his would-be assassins remained—and remains today—burned into Bitcoin's permanent ledger.

Five days later, the jury returned from just a few hours' deliberation and read out their verdict: Ross Ulbricht was guilty on all counts.

Ulbricht likely never had a chance of acquittal: The evidence stacked against him—long before his bitcoins were traced—had included chat logs with his employees, a journal and logbook of his daily work running the Silk Road, even the testimony of a college friend to whom he'd confessed to running the site.

But the day when the prosecution found the incontrovertible, public, and unerasable proof of Ulbricht's Silk Road millions, argues Nick Weaver, remains a milestone in the history of cryptocurrency and crime. "That is the date," Weaver says, "that you can state unequivocally that law enforcement learned that the blockchain is forever."

. . .

Three months later, Ulbricht reappeared in court for his sentencing. After tearful testimony from the parents of two people who had overdosed and died as a result of drugs purchased on the Silk Road, Ulbricht read his own short statement to the court. He apologized to the families of the dead and expressed his regret that he had, in creating the Silk Road, destroyed his own life, too.

But he also defended his motivations in inventing the notion of the dark web black market. "I remember clearly why I created the Silk Road," he said. "I wanted to empower people to be able to make choices in their lives for themselves and to have privacy and anonymity. I am not saying that because I want to justify anything that has happened, because it doesn't. I just want to try to set the record straight, because from my point of view I am not a self-centered sociopathic person that was trying to express some, like, inner badness. I just made some very serious mistakes."

When Ulbricht had finished, Judge Katherine Forrest read her sentencing speech, speaking quickly in a cool and measured voice. "What is clear is that people are very, very complex, and you are one of them," she read. "There is good in Mr. Ulbricht, I have no doubt, but there is also bad, and what you did in connection with Silk Road was terribly destructive to our social fabric."

She read from his chat logs in which he dismissed the dangers of drug overdoses and ordered killings. These threats of violence, she explained, were not directly charged as attempted murders in his trial but would nonetheless contribute to his sentence. She also spoke about the need for deterrence: to dissuade future would-be kingpins of the dark web from following his lead. "For those considering stepping into your shoes, carrying some misguided flag, they need to understand very clearly and without equivocation that if you break the law this way there will be very, very severe consequences," Forrest said.

The Silk Road, Forrest continued, "was a carefully planned life's work. It was your opus," she said to Ulbricht. "You wanted it to be your legacy. And it is."

Then she sentenced Ulbricht to two life sentences in prison without the possibility of parole.

A silence fell over the courtroom. Even the prosecutors were surprised by the immensity of the punishment Forrest had set down, which was beyond even what they'd asked for in a letter to the judge.

All of Ulbricht's appeals for a new trial or a decreased sentence have since failed. As of this writing—perhaps until the day of his death—he remains in a maximum-security prison in Arizona.

Ulbricht's extreme sentence would hardly have the deterrent effect that Judge Forrest intended. But she was right about his legacy. Today the Dread Pirate Roberts is remembered as the pioneer of a Bitcoin-fueled black market that would, in the years to come, grow immensely beyond the scale of the Silk Road—the first of his kind, but far from the last.

PART II

TRACER FOR HIRE

Collapse

On a rainy fall day in Tokyo near the end of November 2014, a bald, blue-eyed, and cheerful forty-four-year-old Dane named Michael Gronager found himself inside a conference room walled with dark, polished wood panels in a high-rise tower, agreeing to track down half a billion dollars' worth of stolen bitcoins.

Entering the room along with two former colleagues from Kraken, the Bitcoin exchange that he'd helped to run as chief operating officer until two months earlier, Gronager had found a scene that resembled a Japanese megacorp in a cyberpunk sci-fi novel: Surrounding the long conference table, set with small bottles of green tea, were no fewer than twenty-five Japanese executives—all men, all wearing dark suits—whom Gronager bowed to one by one despite possessing no clue who most of them were.

Gronager and his friend Jesse Powell, Kraken's CEO, had come to Tokyo to offer their services to the Japanese law firm acting as the trustees for Mt. Gox, the Bitcoin exchange that had once been the most dominant business in the cryptocurrency world and was now a bankrupt ruin. In the early months of 2014, Mt. Gox had abruptly collapsed, announcing that all of the bitcoins it had stored had been stolen by hackers. It had lost 750,000 of its users' coins, plus 100,000 of its own, totaling to a value of more than $530 million at the exchange rate when the money disappeared.

This was by far the largest trove of bitcoins ever stolen. Among all the scams and heists that had plagued the cryptocurrency world, nothing could match this catastrophic loss: Fully 7 percent of all bitcoins in existence had been taken.

Kraken's management, in a pro bono attempt to help rescue the cryptocurrency ecosystem from the rippling shock of Mt. Gox's failure—and the collapse in Bitcoin's price that followed—had agreed to help distribute any remaining bitcoins that could be found to Mt. Gox's thousands upon thousands of angry creditors.

Michael Gronager, for his part, had taken on a far more uncertain task. He'd agreed to find the missing coins.

By all appearances, this was not a rational decision. The Danish entrepreneur had left his relatively comfortable position as the COO of Kraken to found a new start-up whose sole client, for the moment, was this roomful of Japanese bankruptcy lawyers asking him to track down Mt. Gox's gigantic, wayward fortune. Even calling them a client would be a stretch: He would receive no fee, and no portion of the recovered funds, if he could manage to find any.

Gronager, an unflappable optimist, remembers that he did appreciate the tea served at the meeting. It was cold and unsweetened, just how he preferred it.

After a few more minutes of translated formalities passed across the conference table, Gronager and Powell agreed to the terms and timing of their proposed contract, then flipped to the back page and inked their signatures on lines that identified each of the companies they represented. Powell signed on behalf of Kraken. Gronager signed on behalf of a company that practically no one in the world had heard of at the time, one that would be devoted entirely to tracing cryptocurrency and identifying the players in its shadow-strewn economy: Chainalysis.

. . .

On a winter's day nine months earlier, as Gronager sat in Kraken's rented co-working space in central Copenhagen, he stared at the screen of his laptop and knew that he was watching Mt. Gox die.

The signs of illness had been accumulating for months. The previous summer, Bitcoin's biggest exchange, responsible for close to 70 percent of all cryptocurrency trades, had begun delaying withdrawals of users' funds in dollars. Among skeptics, the move had given rise to rumors that Mt. Gox was out of cash, but Gronager and other optimists had figured it was simply due to problems with the company's U.S. bank account. The Japan-based exchange kept running afoul of American money-laundering laws: In May and June 2013, the Department of Homeland Security had seized a total of $5 million from the company for lying on a regulatory form and for acting as an unlicensed money transmitter.

Meanwhile, a jilted partner company called CoinLab was suing Mt. Gox for $75 million. Insiders were beginning to leak to the press claims of inept leadership. As the crises mounted, some reports said that Mark Karpelès, Mt. Gox's geeky and enigmatic French CEO, was spending his time deep in the weeds of code while also obsessively building a Bitcoin-friendly coffee shop in the company's Tokyo headquarters—indulging his nerd whims, in other words, even as his company burned.

Then, in early February 2014, this stumbling giant of the Bitcoin world had suddenly taken a hard fall. Mt. Gox announced that it was now suspending *all* withdrawals—not just in dollars, but in bitcoins. This time there could be no other explanation: The exchange was insolvent. It would be another week before Mt. Gox would reveal that it had been hacked, and weeks longer before it admitted that the hackers had taken *everything*—that it was bankrupt. But angry account holders were already swarming onto forums to express their outrage that Mt. Gox wouldn't hand over thousands or even millions of dollars' worth of cryptocurrency that was rightfully theirs.

The price of buying a bitcoin on Mt. Gox had fallen hundreds of dollars lower than on other exchanges, reflecting the diminishing probability that any coins bought there could ever be retrieved. One aggrieved Mt. Gox user, a London programmer, had flown all the way to Tokyo and staged a one-man protest, standing in the falling snow outside the company's office, holding a "MT GOX WHERE IS OUR MONEY" sign. A YouTube video of Karpelès dodging the protester to get into the building—the CEO looking flustered and chubby, wearing just a black T-shirt despite the winter weather, and carrying a whipped-cream-topped ice coffee drink—had gone viral among the ever-angrier mob of bitcoiners to whom Mt. Gox owed money.

That February day in Copenhagen, Gronager was browsing through forums filled with the posts of desperate Mt. Gox account holders offering to sell their accounts at steep discounts in the hopes of recouping at least some of their losses. It was around 5:00 p.m. when Gronager's phone rang. He was patched into a conference call with Jesse Powell and the rest of Kraken's small team, to plan how to deal with an inevitable fact: The giant was dead.

The call with Kraken's staff, mostly based in San Francisco, was tense. A central pillar of the Bitcoin economy had collapsed. They had always believed it would, sooner or later; Mt. Gox's management had never inspired confidence. Even the name—based on the "mtgox" web address it inherited from a previous project called "Magic: The Gathering Online Exchange" devoted to trading game cards—was a holdover from an era when Bitcoin was treated as a digital plaything rather than real money. But Mt. Gox's failure, like the cryptocurrency equivalent of Lehman Brothers' 2008 bankruptcy, threatened to pull the entire Bitcoin economy into its implosion. Bitcoin had never even existed as real money *without* Mt. Gox.

Gronager, however, held on to his unshakably sunny outlook. Even though he himself had lost about 100 bitcoins in Mt. Gox's bankruptcy— worth more than $60,000 at the time—he viewed its death as a huge opportunity for Kraken. It could take on some of its predecessor's market share, growing and helping to replace an ailing column of Bitcoin's structure with a newer, far more efficient and stable one.

Beyond even that business opportunity, Gronager had faith in the technology. As he would describe it years later, he saw the fall of the house of Gox as "just another piece of noise" contributing to the ever-present chaos of the cryptocurrency world. The signal amid that noise had always been Bitcoin's underlying mechanics. Those features, Gronager assured himself, remained as elegantly crafted and resilient as ever. The noise would eventually quiet. The signal would persist.

. . .

Gronager had always been the sort of engineering-minded person whose ideas about technology came not from how other people thought about it or used it but from what he'd learned taking a machine apart or putting it together with his own hands. Even as a twelve-year-old in the small Danish town of Roskilde, twenty miles from Copenhagen, he'd tinkered in the workshop maintained by his father, a bank employee who'd never finished high school. As a child in the early 1980s, Gronager built from parts a light switch dimmer for his parents, then an automatic garage-door opener complete with an optical sensor for safety. He even sent design sketches of a kind of rotary engine to his local patent office; to his disappointment, it had already been invented a few decades earlier.

Around those same preteen years, Gronager discovered programming. A bookshop on the main square of Roskilde displayed a new Sinclair ZX81 personal computer. When Gronager found the store owner didn't object to his playing with it, he copied lines of code from a book into its clunky keyboard, making its screen flash colors in a thrilling, perfectly logical pattern. When his parents saw his interest in the machine and bought him a Commodore 64, his life was transformed.

Soon, frustrated by the inelegant way the machine displayed text on the screen, he was coding his own word processor. The Commodore didn't have a real compiler, the software that turns human-readable computer commands in a language like BASIC into machine-readable instructions. Instead, it interpreted the commands in his program one by one as it ran, which Gronager found far too slow and inefficient. Undaunted—and unaware that he was taking on an absurdly technical challenge for a self-taught middle schooler—Gronager began writing his programs directly in Assembly, the near-native language of the Commodore's processor, the better to get his hands as close as possible to the computer's real mechanics.

His interest in his father's workshop waned as his programming obsession grew. "I could see that with code you could build way more with way less," he remembers. "You write something and it *becomes* something. That's coding. It's magic."

By the time he was in college at the Technical University of Denmark half a decade later, Gronager was writing code to solve quantum mechanics problems on supercomputers. But access to the university's high-performance machines was always limited, and programming them required using an obscure coding language. So instead, he began using a distributed computing system that allowed him to split the job over the school's plentiful Linux PCs. That drive to create a kind of hive-mind calculator of epic proportions—how to efficiently split problems of gargantuan complexity between dozens, hundreds, or thousands of normal computers—carried him through a PhD and into a career working on quantum physics visualizations and early virtual reality demonstrations. By the time he was forty, he was managing a group of computer scientists who worked with the European Organization for Nuclear Research—also known as CERN—tasked with storing and interpreting the petabytes of results from the Large Hadron Collider's search for the Higgs boson, which produced hundreds of times as much data as the entire collection of the Library of Congress every year.

Gronager was now building computer systems to grapple with some of the most massive data sets in the world. But he wasn't particularly interested in solving the mysteries of the universe's subatomic composition. His obsession lay in the digital challenge those mysteries provided, the need they created to push computing machinery to its limits.

It was in 2010 that Gronager read a post about Bitcoin on the forum *Slashdot* that would alter the course of his life yet again. Soon he was delving into Satoshi Nakamoto's white paper and code, marveling at how it solved the problem of creating truly scarce, uncopiable digital coins with thousands of mining computers spread across the globe, each one rewarded for its part in collectively hammering out the unforgeable blockchain. Within a few months, it was clear to him that this new cryptocurrency—created and funded by neither the academic nor the government institutions to which he'd devoted most of his life—was the most interesting distributed computing project in the world.

. . .

Gronager began obsessively attending Bitcoin conferences from New York to London to Prague. He fiddled with every Bitcoin service he could find to understand how it worked, a doppelgänger of Sarah Meiklejohn's hyperactive Bitcoin user carrying out test transactions, but driven entirely by a tinkerer's curiosity. Soon he'd designed his own Bitcoin wallets for the iPhone and as a browser plug-in, coming up with a clever way of splitting the blockchain between a phone or PC and a server to optimize its performance. He began talking with a like-minded Bitcoin technologist from the United States he'd met at those conferences, Jesse Powell, about creating their own Bitcoin exchange—what would eventually become Kraken. By the end of 2011, he had quit his job and thrown himself fully into cryptocurrency.

Gronager's attraction to Bitcoin, he remembers, was a pure, technological fascination, like his first experience coding on that Sinclair ZX81 in the shop in Roskilde. Here was a means for anyone to hand anyone else a cash payment from anywhere across the global internet, with no intermediary, no sign-up, no proof of a legal identity—something that had simply never existed before. He had no real preconceptions at the time of what the practical results of this new form of money might be, he says. But he knew that it would create an entire new industry, and he wanted to be a part of it.

At the same conferences where Gronager was making business partnerships and chatting with fellow engineers about blockchain compression schemes, meanwhile, a more ideological side of Bitcoin's community was coalescing. The 2011 Prague conference was keynoted, for instance, by Rick Falkvinge, the founder of the privacy- and information-freedom-focused Swedish Pirate Party, and a British anarchist programmer named Amir Taaki, who would later smuggle himself into Syria to fight ISIS alongside Kurdish revolutionaries. A London Bitcoin conference the next year featured a talk by the Texas radical libertarian Cody Wilson, who had used Bitcoin to fund his invention of the world's first fully 3-D printable firearm, a futuristic symbol of the futility of gun control. At the follow-up event in late 2013, just weeks after the takedown of the Silk Road, Wilson gave another talk, this time a full-throated, defiant defense of the dark web's drug trade. "If Bitcoin means anything, it means a thousand Silk Roads," Wilson intoned to a swell of applause in the back room of a Brick Lane pub. "It means, fuck your law!"

Gronager, a clean-cut computer scientist turned entrepreneur, often found himself standing shoulder to shoulder at conferences with these political extremists, wondering if he was in the right room. As a generally liberal Scandinavian, he wasn't exactly opposed to ideas like drug legalization. But the extent of his personal drug use was a time in his youth when he'd eaten some marijuana-infused pancakes and gotten a little too stoned for his enjoyment. The only occasion when he'd ever fired a gun was skeet shooting with friends on a trip to Norway.

"I found this a little bit embarrassing or weird," he remembers of the crypto-anarchist scenes at those conferences, "and also slightly tangential to what is actually happening."

Gronager had never been convinced that Bitcoin was meant to serve as a tool for untraceable, lawless payments. He'd intuitively understood from the start that the blockchain made Bitcoin a uniquely *transparent* form of money and saw its transparency as a feature, not a bug. When

Meiklejohn's "Men with No Names" paper appeared, he read it as a wel-come confirmation of his belief that any use of Bitcoin as a tool for cryp-toanarchy or crime was a misguided sideshow.

Looking back, he describes all the revolutionary political ambitions and libertarian manifestos surrounding Bitcoin the same way he'd later see the decline and fall of Mt. Gox: as a temporary clamor obscuring this new cryptocurrency's inevitable drive toward mainstream adoption.

"Technology here will prevail," he remembers thinking of those con-ference scenes. "All the other parts of this will be noise."

Dirty Money

Gronager's optimism about the fall of Mt. Gox wasn't entirely misplaced: Bitcoin didn't die. It just crashed, and stayed down long enough that it could have easily been confused for dead.

In the months after Mt. Gox declared bankruptcy in early 2014, Bitcoin's exchange rate plummeted from its late-2013 height of more than $1,100 per coin to less than $300. Investors, many of whom were attracted by a gold rush notion that Bitcoin would gain value indefinitely, lost millions.

For Gronager and his Kraken colleagues, meanwhile, capitalizing on the power vacuum left in Mt. Gox's wake turned out to be harder than it had seemed. Gronager approached one bank after another around the world, hoping to find partners that would let his European exchange expand into vast new markets like the United States and Japan. But he found, again and again, that there was now a growing, invisible resistance to Bitcoin in the world of finance. Banks would inexplicably decline to meet with him. In other cases, he'd make his partnership pitch to an enthusiastic room, only to be told a few days later that the bank's execs had talked to their compliance department and were backing out.

On the few occasions Gronager was able to pin a banker down and have a frank conversation, he'd hear a growing refrain: Bitcoin was the currency of the Silk Road and Mt. Gox. In other words, it was made for crime, prone to theft, and certainly nothing that a respectable bank wanted to be associated with. Wherever he went, Gronager says, cryptocurrency's shady reputation preceded him.

Bitcoin's price, meanwhile, remained stagnant in the low hundreds.

"No one believes in this anymore," Gronager remembers thinking. "The winter had started, and we didn't know if there was another spring day around the corner."

Law enforcement's apparent inability to figure out who had emptied Mt. Gox's coffers only contributed to the cloud of unease hanging over the cryptocurrency world. Had it truly been hacked? Or was it Mark Karpelès himself, or some other embezzler inside the company? The mystery gave more credence to the view that Bitcoin's unregulated economy was awash with dirty money that bad actors would be seeking to launder. Some banks spelled it out for Gronager: If they were going to do business with Kraken, they would need to know the source of all of the funds that passed through his exchange.

In a cab in San Francisco in the late summer of 2014, Gronager and Kraken's deputy general counsel debriefed after their latest abortive meeting: Yet another bank had demanded a kind of detailed transaction monitoring that Kraken couldn't provide. It's funny, Gronager remarked. These banks seemed to believe that Bitcoin's untraceability made it an untouchable liability. But in fact, Bitcoin's technology ought to make transaction monitoring even *easier* than with dollars or yen. After all, he mused, everything was laid out on the blockchain, wasn't it?

Kraken's lawyer, sitting in the car with him, was struck by the observation. If that's possible, Gronager remembers her saying, any service that offered this sort of blockchain analysis would be incredibly valuable.

"Yes," Gronager thought to himself. "It probably would be."

· · ·

The idea rolled around Gronager's head until it became a fixation and then a plan. On another business trip to San Francisco in mid-October 2014, Gronager told Kraken's management that he was leaving the company to pursue a new start-up. He began coding the first prototype that would become Chainalysis's bitcoin-tracing tool on the long flight back from San Francisco to Copenhagen. He had most of it written, he says, before the plane landed.

As a programmer who had spent an entire career optimizing code to deftly manipulate enormous, unwieldy mountains of data, Gronager found that parsing the blockchain came naturally. He was familiar with the clustering techniques Meiklejohn had pioneered—with a year of hindsight, he considered them practically intuitive features of the blockchain—and his prototype integrated both tricks. But unlike UCSD's clunky process of querying a massive database on a server, Gronager exploited a newer database technology called SQLite to interact with a more lightweight version of the blockchain on his laptop. The same queries that sometimes took Meiklejohn as long as twelve hours of processing time took just seventeen seconds in Gronager's proof-of-concept program—a delay that he still considered intolerably slow. And Gronager didn't need to carry out the hundreds of test transactions that Meiklejohn had spent weeks on. His voracious experimentation with every service in the Bitcoin economy over the past several years meant he already had, in his own records, most of the test transactions he needed to identify the collections of addresses his program clustered together.

A few days after Gronager returned to Copenhagen, a friend and fellow Danish Bitcoin programmer named Jan Møller suggested they meet up for a beer. Years earlier, Møller had built an Android Bitcoin wallet and had seen the one Gronager built as a browser plug-in. They'd admired each other's code and even taken a similar approach to splitting the blockchain between the user's device and a server. Møller was looking for a job. Gronager told him that he didn't exactly have one to offer; he'd just left his own job behind, quite suddenly, at the exchange he'd co-founded.

He described to Møller what he was building now: not simply a tool for tracing bitcoins, but a kind of trusted data source that could extract global patterns and money flows from the blockchain, a service that cryptocurrency exchanges would pay for to know more about their customers—including, perhaps, what side of the law they were on. Møller was intrigued and suggested they consider working together. Later they'd look back on that day, October 24, as the birthday of their company, Chainalysis.

Soon, Gronager and Møller were obsessively talking on the phone for two hours a day, charting their start-up's future. Møller suggested that they spend a solid week together in his family's cabin in Jutland, the largely rural mainland of Denmark a few hours away from Copenhagen. At Møller's house in the woods, a brick-walled building with a sod-and-grass roof in the old Scandinavian style, they spent hours drawing mock-ups of their software's interface on sheets of paper clipped to a plywood easel. On other days they hashed out their product's mechanics on long walks through the pine forests and across the seaweed-strewn, windy beaches of western Denmark. "All of our best ideas we had while walking," Møller says.

Even as he took on the challenge of building a company from scratch, Gronager still faced another looming task. Kraken's management had, by then, agreed to work with Mt. Gox's bankruptcy trustees to help Mt. Gox's creditors distribute any remaining bitcoins—a move designed to both show that Kraken was a trustworthy brand in contrast to Mt. Gox and perhaps win over some of their defunct competitor's customers. Even as Gronager split off from Kraken, he had asked his old partner, Kraken's CEO, Jesse Powell, to let him retain his role in that Mt. Gox bankruptcy process. Gronager wanted, in fact, to take sole responsibility for the most challenging part of tying up Mt. Gox's loose ends: He would find Mt. Gox's missing coins.

This promise was hugely ambitious—not least because Gronager had barely coded a working prototype of Chainalysis's software. But there would be no better motivation to perfect it, he figured, than taking on the biggest unsolved criminal case in the history of cryptocurrency.

Noise

In early 2015, a few months after Gronager had met with the Mt. Gox trustees in Japan and committed his new company to trace the exchange's stolen funds, the Chainalysis co-founder was back in Tokyo, this time at the scene of the crime: Mt. Gox's headquarters, where he had an appointment to meet with the bankrupt company's CEO himself, Mark Karpelès.

On a quiet street in Tokyo's Shibuya district, Gronager walked through the front doors of the exchange's empty offices, through the abandoned remains of the Bitcoin Café that Karpelès had dreamed of building on its ground floor, and into a conference room where he met the erstwhile CEO face-to-face for the first time, along with a representative from the Japanese trustee firm.

Mt. Gox had, by the time of that meeting, been bankrupt for nearly a year—a year that Karpelès had spent under investigation by Japanese police while also being accused of gross incompetence and even outright theft by hordes of angry Bitcoin users. Gronager remembers that the Frenchman seemed mildly disheveled, in need of a haircut, and somewhat broken in spirit—"on hold," as Gronager put it, resigned to yet another meeting in the seemingly endless cycle of meetings that had become his life, all as a result of his company's epic downfall.

Weeks before, Gronager had received an envelope in the mail from Mt. Gox's trustees containing a single encrypted USB thumb drive. The drive was supposed to contain all of Mt. Gox's financial data, including records of every trade made on the exchange in its four-year history. But when he decrypted it, Gronager found it was mysteriously incomplete.

Many records of trades were missing the "counterparty"—the buyer or seller on the other side of the deal—and many more entries seem to have been deleted altogether.

When Gronager asked Karpelès about those missing entries, Karpelès told him a strange story in his slightly clumsy, French-accented English. In early 2014, he said, around the time of the hacker breach that had stolen Mt. Gox's entire treasury of bitcoins, someone had physically broken into the exchange's server room and accessed its computers. The company hadn't been able to determine who the intruder was, but Karpelès suggested the break-in was related to the theft and believed it had allowed the burglar to delete the data that Gronager had found missing.

And, Gronager asked incredulously, didn't the company have a backup of that data? Karpelès said no, that the backup system hadn't worked either.

Gronager could see that Karpelès was almost certainly withholding something, if not outright lying. But he avoided calling him out on this unlikely and seemingly unfounded explanation. Gronager wasn't a cop, after all; he didn't have any legal authority to compel Karpelès to speak honestly, or to punish him if he didn't; this was meant to be a friendly fact-finding meeting.

In fact, Gronager already had an idea of at least one sort of misbehavior Karpelès might be covering up with this data burglary tale. There had long been rumors that some of the trades on Mt. Gox were actually run by automated programs controlled by the exchange itself—that it used these bots to create trades at artificially high prices. Since Mt. Gox was secretly playing the role of both buyer and seller in these trades, they hadn't cost the exchange anything. But the trades would create a false sense of bustling activity, bolstering Bitcoin's exchange rate and making Mt. Gox seem more dominant in the Bitcoin economy than it truly was.

The fake trades would have almost certainly been illegal. Many in the Bitcoin world suspected they were also somehow related to Mt. Gox's missing money. A report from the Japanese newspaper *Yomiuri Shimbun* in December 2014 had even cited the bots in an article that claimed Japanese police had come to believe Mt. Gox had indeed been emptied out by insider fraud, not by hackers.

But by the time of his Tokyo meeting with Gronager, Karpelès had come up with what seemed like an extraordinary token of good faith.

Mt. Gox's CEO had discovered one of the company's forgotten Bitcoin wallets that still contained no fewer than 200,000 untouched coins—the equivalent of finding about $50 million between the couch cushions—and he had willingly offered these up to his creditors. This windfall reduced the total amount of Mt. Gox's missing funds to 650,000 bitcoins.

A cynic might have seen this as an unsubtle attempt to deflect blame—to hand over part of the loot while concealing the rest. But as convenient as the discovery might have been, Gronager was inclined to believe it was genuine. Karpelès's offering, to Gronager, felt like the behavior not so much of a criminal mastermind as of a bumbling businessman. Quizzing him that day in Tokyo, Gronager came to the conclusion that Mt. Gox had simply never kept a careful accounting of its assets or reconciled its funds with the trades the exchange was carrying out every day—that, over the years, Karpelès had gotten in over his head, treating Bitcoin as the digital Monopoly money it had seemed to be when the company was founded and never quite adapting to a world in which the cryptocurrency had become truly valuable.

Gronager left Tokyo convinced that Karpelès was not the thief of Mt. Gox's millions. But the exchange's database still contained enormous holes, and the weird, hapless CEO he was investigating clearly wasn't about to help him fill in those gaps—even if that lack of evidence left Karpelès himself under a cloud of suspicion. If Gronager was going to vindicate him, he'd need to find a new prime suspect.

. . .

As he began to delve into the Mt. Gox mystery, Gronager was also honing the software that he hoped would be his most powerful investigative tool to decipher it.

By early March, he and Møller had figured out another optimization trick to vastly speed up their queries of the blockchain. On one of their pine-forest walks, Møller had realized that labeling every transaction with their own chronological identifiers rather than Bitcoin's native transaction IDs would reduce the size of the data their software needed to analyze by as much as 90 percent. That meant they could store the database of all the blockchain's transactions entirely in a PC's memory, rather than on its hard drive. The result was that the program could now implement clustering techniques across the entire blockchain in just 1.8 seconds, and queries about specific addresses or clusters took just fractions of a second—the sort of instantaneous feedback that they knew would be necessary if the product were going to be adopted by real customers. To create a graphical interface for future non-geek users, Gronager and Møller commissioned two front-end coding firms, pitting them against each other to create a slick control panel for their block-chain analysis tool, then hired the one they preferred as a contractor.

But while Gronager and Møller were sharpening Chainalysis's block-chain scanning techniques, Møller was independently working on a separate project. Møller wanted to see if he could track how Bitcoin was being used by following an entirely different—and ultimately more controversial—trail of the data that its users left behind.

When someone moves a sum of bitcoins, their wallet software broad-casts the transaction over the internet to Bitcoin's network of "nodes," the thousands of servers around the world that store copies of the block-chain. Whichever node first receives the announcement of the new transaction then passes it on to other nodes, which in turn broadcast it out further, so that the record of the payment is confirmed and copied into the blockchain's global ledger of all transactions. The system is a bit like a crowd of people who each whisper a rumor to their immediate neighbors, so that the information spreads virally through the crowd in ripples—but at digital speeds designed to inform the entire network in minutes or even seconds.

This broadcasting happens, of course, over the internet. But a cru-cial feature of Bitcoin's privacy properties had always been that the blockchain doesn't store any information about internet protocol, or IP, addresses. After all, those computer identifiers, which allow internet data to be routed around the globe to the right machine, can reveal a user's physical location, precisely the kind of personal data Bitcoin was meant to obscure.

Møller and Gronager had realized, however, that there might be a way to pinpoint the IP address associated with any given transaction. A node that receives a Bitcoin transaction announcement can see the IP address of the computer that sent it. Even putting aside the blockchain analysis that was Chainalysis's central focus, that meant Bitcoin nodes would possess a powerful, specific scrap of identifying information about whichever user had originated a money transfer.

In Bitcoin's fully decentralized system, anyone can set up a node. So Møller and Gronager had the idea of setting up hundreds of their own nodes, ones that would sit on the Bitcoin network, receive transaction orders, and collect the IP addresses of the users who had sent them—a kind of vast, global sensor array.

Soon, Møller had created 250 of these Chainalysis nodes on servers around the world. His goal was not to identify any specific user's location but to assemble data in aggregate, to use IP addresses to create a world map of Bitcoin's broad geographic trends. Chainalysis, he and Gronager figured, could then publish that map in a blog post as a demonstration of their start-up's capabilities.

Then, one morning in mid-March 2015, Gronager woke up to find that Chainalysis's little experiment had been discovered. And Bitcoin's users, it turned out, didn't appreciate being experimented on.

. . .

The scandal had begun to unfold days earlier, when a few users complained in a thread on the forum Bitcointalk that a collection of suspicious Bitcoin nodes had essentially broken the wallet programs they used. Their software had repeatedly connected to these strange nodes, and—thanks to what would turn out to be a bug in Møller's code—the transactions weren't being relayed to the rest of the network. The forum's commenters immediately began to suspect that the nodes were up to something nefarious: Gregory Maxwell, the Bitcoin developer who had once chastised cryptocurrency researchers like Sarah Meiklejohn for privacy violations, weighed in on the forum, writing that someone appeared to be carrying out a "Sybil attack," in which a malicious actor tries to take over a distributed system by overwhelming it with impostor machines.

A few days later, another user named Cryptowatch wrote that they'd scanned the nodes that were disrupting the network and then tried to connect to those servers' IP addresses with a web browser. The result had been a message asking for their "Chainalysis API key." When they googled the name "Chainalysis," they found the company's brand-new website, where it advertised "sophisticated in-depth real-time transaction analysis to determine unique entities within the blockchain."

Cryptowatch wasn't pleased to have discovered a corporate snoop in their midst. "This is akin to spying to be honest," Cryptowatch wrote.

"And it is exactly that we're wanting to get away from with all the monitoring that goes on in the traditional financial system. If Joe pays Alice
10 bucks, it's no one's damn business how, where and what relates to
that payment."

When Gronager belatedly discovered the thread on Bitcointalk about
their experiment gone awry, he tried to head off criticisms. He jumped
into the conversation to apologize, to say that Chainalysis had immediately shut down its nodes upon learning about the problems they'd
caused, and to explain that the intention had only been to create an IP-
based map, not to identify anyone. But his message did little to placate a
growing, angry crowd. "Idiot . . . the bitcoin network is not your personal
playground to just do whatever the hell you want," read the first response
to his message. "Have some respect for what others have done and keep
your retarded experiment off the damn network."

Ending Chainalysis's IP-address tracking hardly helped put out the
fire; the argument quickly went beyond the question of gathering those
addresses, turning into a full-blown debate about the ethics of the company's core mission of tracking payments across the blockchain. "It's
about mass surveillance and controlling the population," wrote Cryptowatch. "If you believe in bitcoin, and want to help the community,
perhaps now would be a good time to shut down the Chainalysis enterprise, and work with the core devs to prevent others from doing the same
as you've been doing."

The debate escalated, and Gronager decided to lay his cards on the
table, fully describing his political perspective. "I believe that bitcoin is
a great technology enabling online cash," he wrote. "It should hence be
regulated and integrated into the existing financial system. I do sympa-
thize with some libertarian views, but I am Danish, I don't believe in
revolutions. I believe in the little change every day, and I truly believe
we get a little bit better world if you can buy and sell bitcoin in your
normal bank."

The crowd was unmoved. "As I see it you are worse than Gox," one
person responded, turning an abbreviation for Mt. Gox into what was,
on Bitcointalk, a scalding insult. "My message to you, in summary, is
simple: Go fuck yourselves."

For cooler-headed bitcoiners, however, the incident was taken less
as a revelation of unethical spying than as a warning about Bitcoin's po-

tential privacy vulnerabilities. They responded with admonishments to block suspicious nodes and to run Bitcoin wallets over Tor to obscure IP addresses so that Chainalysis's IP-mapping trick would become impossible.

In the years that followed, privacy improvements to Bitcoin's protocol would make extracting IP addresses from transactions significantly more difficult. For Chainalysis, meanwhile, the mapping project had served as a very abrupt and hostile coming-out party.

Still, Gronager wasn't one to let a few nasty comments derail his vision.

"Nothing really came out of that except some conversation and blah, blah," he would say dismissively, years later. He says he learned to approach the Bitcoin community more discreetly and understood better how some of its most privacy-conscious users would disdain Chainalysis's work. But he ultimately described the fracas the same way he'd characterized every other temporary impediment to the fully transparent Bitcoin he had always believed was inevitable: "That was some noise."

CHAPTER 18

The Second Agent

Around the same time as Chainalysis's Bitcointalk blowup, an undeterred Michael Gronager flew back to San Francisco, this time to pitch
his new blockchain-tracing software to Bitcoin exchanges. Chainalysis's
fledgling application was quick and powerful now, though still unpol-
ished. In his sales pitches, Gronager couldn't even save the results from
his queries of the blockchain; he had to reenter them every time he
opened the program.

The exchanges he visited in his meetings were intrigued by the notion
of a software tool that would allow them to monitor the sources of transactions without piles of regulatory paperwork. But Gronager found they
were still reluctant to pull out their checkbooks.

Then, one morning a couple of days into his trip, Gronager walked
over to San Francisco's Ferry Building to buy a cup of coffee. He ran
into an old friend, one who had previously worked at the cryptocurrency exchange Coinbase. As they caught up, Gronager explained his
new start-up, and the friend asked if he had tried pitching Chainalysis
to law enforcement agencies. After all, the former Coinbase staffer figured, cybercrime-focused detectives would be at least as interested as any
Bitcoin exchange in following cryptocurrency trails.

Gronager confessed he didn't actually know anyone in law
enforcement—other than the agencies in Japan investigating Mt. Gox.
He came from the spheres of tech, science, and academia; he had no clue
how to penetrate the world of federal investigators and prosecutors. So
the former Coinbase staffer did him a favor and sent an email on the

spot, introducing Gronager to one cryptocurrency-focused prosecutor he was sure would be interested: Kathryn Haun.

To Gronager's surprise, Haun responded to the email immediately. She invited the Danish CEO to visit her at the Justice Department's office that very afternoon—advising him to dress casually because the San Francisco Department of Justice office observed "casual Thursdays."

Just a few hours later, Gronager arrived at the same building where George Frost had come to warn Haun about Carl Force almost a year earlier. Like Frost, Gronager was ushered up to the ninth floor and into a conference room. Seated at the conference table was a silent young man in a T-shirt and a baseball cap with a compact build, a trim beard, a tough expression, and tattoos running up one of his muscular arms.

Gronager tried to hide his uncertainty. He had by now forgotten about Haun's "casual Thursday" warning. As the straitlaced Danish CEO silently took a seat, a thought crossed his mind: Had there been a mistake? Had he been put into a room with a criminal suspect?

A few moments later, Kathryn Haun walked in with a friendly smile and introduced Gronager to the mystery man, Tigran Gambaryan, explaining that he was an IRS special agent who'd be joining them for their meeting.

As Gronager recovered from his confusion, Gambaryan got to the business at hand, asking if they could get Gronager's take on a case they were working on. Gambaryan stood up and began writing Bitcoin addresses on a whiteboard, drawing connections between them. The flowchart he sketched on the board began with an address that had been associated with the Silk Road and at one point held 20,073 bitcoins. It ended with 2,430 of those bitcoins at another address, one that Gambaryan believed had been controlled by Mt. Gox. He asked Gronager if he could confirm that trail of funds across the blockchain.

Gronager gamely pulled out his laptop and began typing the addresses into his Chainalysis software. Sure enough, he could see all the same hops that the coins had taken from the Silk Road to Mt. Gox, just as Gambaryan had. And because Gronager happened to have stored on the same PC's hard drive the Mt. Gox database of user account information he'd been given by the bankruptcy trustees, he offered to go a step further and look at the recipient's account information, too. He wasn't sure if he was supposed to freely share personal details from that Mt. Gox user database with U.S. law enforcement. But he went ahead and gave Haun and Gambaryan an IP address. It placed the account holder in Maryland.

Gambaryan and Haun exchanged a look, seeming satisfied. It struck Gronager that nothing he'd said had surprised this canny prosecutor and IRS agent; they were using him not to glean new information but to double-check their own work.

Gronager was right: Haun and Gambaryan had wanted an extra pair of expert eyes on Gambaryan's blockchain analysis. They already knew the name associated with that Maryland IP address—the name of the person who had used Mt. Gox to cash out a total of 20,073 bitcoins— about $350,000 at the time it had been stolen from the Silk Road.

That name was Shaun Bridges.

. . .

A few months earlier, near the end of 2014, the San Francisco–based team investigating Carl Force had been ready to bring charges against the former DEA agent and wrap up the case. Haun and her boss, Will Frentzen, still suspected that Force had stolen the bitcoins that had initially been pinned on Curtis Green. But they couldn't find any proof of this additional $350,000 bitcoin theft, and they didn't want to delay indicting Force any longer for his repeated acts of extortion and money laundering.

Only Gambaryan, staring at the cryptic fingerprints on the block-chain, still believed that a second culprit was involved—one who would walk free if they simply charged Force and let the trail go cold.

It was Gary Alford, the New York–based IRS special agent who had cracked the Silk Road case, who finally found the telltale message that proved Gambaryan right. Alford had spotted an email from Carl Force to Shaun Bridges in late January 2013, just two days before Baltimore's Silk Road task force would together question Curtis Green in a Utah hotel room and when Green's computer was mysteriously used to siphon that six-figure sum out of the Silk Road.

Force's email had asked Bridges to send some bitcoins to one of Force's Silk Road accounts, a routine transfer of petty cash so that Force could continue his undercover work as yet another of his faceless alter egos on the site. Bridges had complied, sending the money to Force's Silk Road wallet, the site's server logs showed, from an account Bridges controlled called Number 13.

Just two days after that money transfer, the night after the Baltimore Task Force's interrogation of Curtis Green, someone with access to Green's moderator account had repeatedly reset the backup PIN for high-value accounts on the Silk Road, taking control of them one by one, and then emptied out their bitcoins. Gambaryan could see in the Silk Road's server logs, with Alford's help, that the very first payment of those stolen accounts' funds had been dumped into that Number 13 wallet, along with 900 bitcoins from Curtis Green's own account. The blockchain showed that the money had then been siphoned out from Number 13 to an even fatter wallet, one that held 20,073 stolen bitcoins.

Whoever controlled that Number 13 account was almost certainly the thief, in other words. And the email Alford had dug up seemed to show that just two days before the heist, Number 13 had belonged to Shaun Bridges.

No wonder Bridges had been so hostile on their fact-finding call about Force, Gambaryan marveled. The very Secret Service agent whom Bitstamp's lawyer George Frost had turned to for help with his Carl Force problem had apparently pulled off a massive cryptocurrency theft of his own.

Again, Gambaryan turned to the blockchain to find the smoking gun. This time, rather than trace the money unaided, clicking through addresses on Blockchain.info as he had with Force's coins, Gambaryan used a free tool he'd found online called WalletExplorer, created by a Czech programmer named Aleš Janda. In creating WalletExplorer, Janda had done much of the same work as Meiklejohn and Gronager, implementing clustering techniques and labeling known entities on the blockchain. The tool made it relatively easy for Gambaryan to follow the bitcoins that flowed out of the Number 13 account on January 25, trace them through multiple obfuscating hops, and then finally into an address that was labeled in WalletExplorer as part of the Mt. Gox cluster.

From there, Gambaryan turned to the tedious but familiar paperwork of more traditional follow-the-money investigations: He wrote to the owners and trustees of Mt. Gox—which had declared bankruptcy months earlier—asking the defunct exchange to turn over the records associated with the suspected account based on a mutual legal assistance treaty between the United States and Japan. Mt. Gox's trustees agreed, and the resulting documents showed that the liquidated bitcoins, traded for dollars, had been sent by money transfer to a Fidelity account held by an entity called Quantum International Investments LLC. Gambaryan subpoenaed Fidelity, which immediately revealed Quantum International Investments' owner: Shaun Bridges. Bridges had created a shell company using his very own name and home address in Maryland.

It was late December by the time Gambaryan's feverish money tracing had reached its end. Will Frentzen remembers receiving a call from Gambaryan late at night, surprised to see the IRS agent's name appear on his cell phone during their Christmas vacation. Gambaryan explained what he'd found. The veteran prosecutor says he felt the hairs stand up on the back of his neck.

"Holy shit," Frentzen remembers thinking. "There's two of them."

· · ·

In early 2015, Frentzen and Gambaryan flew out to Utah to meet with Curtis Green, the Silk Road moderator who had found himself so roughly exploited by practically every player in the Silk Road drama. Talking to Green and interviewing other Baltimore agents who had been present for the Baltimore Task Force's interrogation of Green on January 25, 2013, they began to piece together how Shaun Bridges had, that evening, retreated to his hotel room with Curtis Green's laptop and spent the night using Green's access to frantically hijack and pillage Silk Road accounts.

The day after that interrogation, Frentzen and Gambaryan learned, Bridges had flown back to Baltimore early, rather than join his team for the second day of questioning Green. The Secret Service agent had claimed he had to be back east to compete in a judo tournament. Just hours later, the rest of the Baltimore agents learned that Green's account had been locked after the Dread Pirate Roberts had discovered the massive spree of thefts from his market. The Baltimore team, including Carl Force, were shocked to find that the Silk Road insider they'd so carefully flipped had now become practically useless to them.

Most surprising of all, two years later, as the San Francisco team investigating Bridges's theft searched through the Baltimore Task Force's correspondence, they found no evidence that Bridges and Force had collaborated in their schemes. By all appearances, Frentzen says, the two men didn't even particularly like each other. Amazingly, each seems to not have been aware of the other's crimes, like a pair of robbers quietly burglarizing different rooms of the same house without ever crossing paths.

"That blew my mind," says Frentzen. "It was unbelievable to us that there were two crooked federal agents on the same task force and that they weren't working together." In fact, if it hadn't been for Force's entirely separate, even more reckless acts of criminality, Bridges's theft might have gone entirely undetected.

. . .

Force and Bridges both had enough experience as law enforcement investigators to know when they'd been caught. A team of agents arrested Force without incident at his home, though Gambaryan himself was too busy with the paperwork for the Bridges investigation to fly out and join them. Confronted with the evidence Gambaryan and the San Francisco prosecutors had assembled, Bridges confessed to taking the Silk Road's bitcoins and turned himself in.

In late March 2015, Gambaryan signed his name to a ninety-four-page affidavit in a combined criminal complaint against the two former federal agents. It concluded, in three pages of attached exhibits, with Gambaryan's charts of Force's and Bridges's Bitcoin movements on the blockchain, the first time such evidence had ever been introduced in a criminal complaint.

When Gambaryan had traced Force's bitcoins, he had been too stunned that his blockchain analysis had actually worked to think of its larger implications. But when he used the technique again to follow Bridges's stolen loot, a revelation was cemented in his mind: The blockchain wasn't merely a cornucopia of evidence—one that would reveal crimes that went far beyond those of two crooked agents. It was a permanent record of often-traceable payments that had served as the perfect honeypot, a trap for anyone seeking financial anonymity online in order to commit crime. And it had persisted for *years*. Now that enormous wealth of evidence lay spread before Gambaryan, or any other law enforcement agent willing to spend the time to retroactively crack it.

"This opens up a whole new world," Gambaryan remembers thinking with awe. "Right now, we can go back and solve a million different crimes."

Will Frentzen would later describe Force and Bridges's double corruption case as "lightning striking twice." But looking again at the temptation of cryptocurrency as Gambaryan had come to see it—a black hole of seemingly consequence-free financial corruption—perhaps it's no surprise that more than one agent had succumbed. The two men, like the Dread Pirate Roberts they were hunting, had been seduced by the same siren song: the false promise of untraceable money.

A Hole in the Vault

The day after Michael Gronager met with Gambaryan and Haun, he was back at work at a café on Montgomery Street in San Francisco's financial district, a loftlike space that he used as a makeshift office. He liked the spot: how you paid a few dollars an hour for a work space and could order coffee and avocado toast from the iPad at each table. Gronager still had no clue that his friendly conversation at the Justice Department just across the neighborhood had helped the IRS to finally pin down a thieving Secret Service agent.

Whenever he had a stretch of time between the meetings where he was pitching his blockchain analysis application, Gronager would return to the café and to his work as that tool's first power user, trying to leverage it to solve the Mt. Gox mystery.

Mt. Gox's database of money movements into and out of the exchange's coffers was still full of unexplained holes. But Gronager knew that the blockchain represented a separate and complete record of those money flows. Perhaps he could compare those two ledgers to fill in the gaps, like an archaeologist overlaying an old etching onto the eroded face of a stone tablet.

So that afternoon, Gronager began trying out database queries that might match up the addresses included in Mt. Gox's transaction records with the ones on the blockchain, filling in all the transactions to and from known Mt. Gox addresses that had been mysteriously deleted from the exchange's records. He'd soon created two graphs of Mt. Gox's total funds over time, one based on the exchange's own incomplete records and one based on the blockchain's ground truth.

The first graph showed the exchange's balance climbing steadily over the years until it reached 850,000 bitcoins. The second, blockchain-based graph showed a far more distressing trend. Starting in October 2011, the climbing balance had reversed and begun to tumble as mysterious outflows of money—largely deleted from Mt. Gox's records—slowly sapped the exchange of its balance.

Gronager overlaid the two charts. They both showed dramatic ups and downs that reflected the normal variance in Mt. Gox's Bitcoin holdings over time. But despite those irregularities, he could see that the space between the graphs created an ever-widening, jagged wedge of missing money.

Gronager tried subtracting the true, blockchain-based Mt. Gox balances from the false ones to create a graph of the missing transactions alone over time. When he saw the results on his screen, he was hit with a feeling of both epiphany and disbelief, shocked by the sheer clarity of the story that the graph told. Over nearly two years, ending in the summer of 2013, the missing funds had slowly and steadily swelled until they reached a total of 650,000 bitcoins—almost exactly the number known to be missing from Mt. Gox.

Gronager hadn't quite tracked down the missing money. But he'd identified it, isolated it, and shown that the problem had begun *years* before Mt. Gox had publicly revealed that it had gone broke. It was as if the exchange's staff had been counting all the gold bars going into and out of its vault, while thieves had been quietly and persistently pulling out those bars through a hole in the floor, month after month, for nearly the entire life of the business.

• • •

Gronager began writing emails to the bankruptcy trustees and to Karpelès, showing them the graphs and asking if they could explain any of the thousands of mysterious transactions.

Karpelès responded, pointing to a few early cases when Mt. Gox's staff had dipped into its stored bitcoins for expenses like buying computers without noting it in the database—not exactly responsible bookkeeping, but hardly criminal theft. Otherwise, neither Karpelès nor anyone else had answers to offer.

After a flight home to Copenhagen, Gronager was determined to use his Chainalysis application to trace all those phantom transactions. Scrutinizing the funds trickling out of Mt. Gox's vault, he could see that the thefts appeared to be automated. Most of the bitcoins were swiped out of Mt. Gox addresses the very moment they were received, immediately siphoned off to the thieves' wallets, which grew over days or weeks. Then, whenever the hackers periodically checked on these swelling caches of stolen funds, those wallets would be manually emptied into other addresses.

Gronager began to slowly chart where the hacked funds had flowed, forking into three distinct destinations. At first, they had been cashed out through an American exchange called Trade Hill, eventually accounting for more than a quarter of all the money traded on that exchange, until Trade Hill shut down in February 2012. At that point, Gronager saw that something very curious had happened: The missing money had begun to flow *back* into Mt. Gox. It made a kind of sense. For thieves trying to liquidate stolen bitcoins, why not sell them at the world's largest cryptocurrency exchange? Especially when no one knew they'd been stolen from that very exchange in the first place.

In the end, though, the thieves had cashed out the most coins of all through yet another, more mysterious trading platform. It was called BTC-e.

That cryptocurrency exchange, nearly as old as Mt. Gox, had been on the rise since Mt. Gox's bankruptcy, but it remained a near-total cipher. Its ownership and even the location of its management remained unknown, a subject of suspicious chatter within the cryptocurrency economy and a bizarre blank spot on the global map of the Bitcoin industry. Drug dealers and even dark web market administrators who traded in Bitcoin under concealed identities were one thing, but completely faceless owners of an active cryptocurrency exchange visible on the normal, unconcealed web were a far stranger phenomenon.

Even so, with this broad picture of where the stolen funds had ended up, Gronager could finally draw a few conclusions about the Mt. Gox heist. First came a gutting discovery: He calculated the total value of the theft using the exchange rates at the time each bit of the stolen fortune had been cashed out over two years, rather than the date in 2014 when the absence of those stolen funds was finally noticed. The results showed that because the burglars had been trading out their bitcoins as they stole them—instead of holding on to them and watching them accrue value—their profits from the heist had come nowhere near the half a billion dollars that Mt. Gox had seemingly lost. Bitcoin had swelled in value by well over a hundredfold over the previous three years. But unbeknownst to Mt. Gox's staff, the thefts had largely occurred *before* that appreciation. The result was that the thieves had made only around $20 million, pennies on the dollar when compared with Mt. Gox's perceived loss of $530 million.

The vast majority of the Mt. Gox fortune was almost certainly gone for good. The thieves had essentially taken a collection of rare coins and sold them for scrap metal. Even if the culprits could be found and forced to repay their victims, they wouldn't have anywhere close to the money to make Mt. Gox whole.

Just as important to Gronager as that unfortunate calculation, however, was the apparent geography of the thieves' transactions. Gronager broke down the times when the burglars' coins were manually moved out of the wallets that held the stolen Mt. Gox funds, plotting the money movements across a twenty-four-hour cycle. All of them seemed to fall from morning to night in a certain time zone, one that lay a couple of hours east of Greenwich mean time and nowhere near the waking hours of the average person in Japan, where Mark Karpelès lived.

Gronager knew that his time zone test wasn't airtight: Hackers and coders work at all hours. But all night, every night? The timing contributed to his sense that Mark Karpelès must in fact be innocent of the theft, just as he'd suspected.

"Okay," Gronager thought to himself with a certain finality. "Mark didn't do this."

The culprits seemed to be external hackers, then, who had patiently, methodically stalked Mt. Gox, hollowing out and ultimately destroying the world's largest cryptocurrency exchange. And Gronager realized, with a sinking feeling, these hackers likely weren't based in western Europe or the United States, either—countries where extradition treaties meant there was still hope of arresting the thieves and potentially even recouping Mt. Gox's money.

The time zone of the transactions Gronager had plotted on his screen formed a column that included the western, most populated region of a country known as a haven for cybercrime, a nation impenetrable to Western law enforcement, where even blockchain-based follow-the-money investigations reach a dead end. The money, Gronager now believed, had gone to Russia.

BTC-e

When the criminal complaint against Force and Bridges went public, just a few weeks after Tigran Gambaryan's meeting with Michael Gronager in March 2015, it included a note stating that Gambaryan had "conferred with an individual who has a substantial background in blockchain analysis," a tacit credit to Gronager's double check of the IRS and Justice Department's work. Afterward, Gambaryan called Gronager and asked him to serve as an adviser and expert witness in the case if it went to trial. Soon Gambaryan and Gronager were emailing and speaking on Skype constantly, chatting and checking notes. Gronager, with the permission of Mt. Gox's bankruptcy trustees, started sending Gambaryan regular updates on his Mt. Gox investigation.

One increasingly frequent subject of their conversations was BTC-e, this mysterious bitcoin-trading platform that seemed to exist nowhere and be run by no one. Even before Gronager had told Gambaryan about the flow of Mt. Gox's funds into that enigmatic exchange, Gambaryan and Frentzen had begun to focus on this blockchain black hole. Carl Force had cashed out some of his criminal proceeds through BTC-e, and when Gambaryan and Frentzen had looked into the business, they'd seen that it had almost zero know-your-customer or anti-money-laundering protections; in other words, anyone could cash out cryptocurrency through BTC-e with practically no questions asked. "You could say you were Mickey Mouse and lived at Disney World, and they let you convert bitcoins into cash," Frentzen says.

Gambaryan looked into the company's provenance and discovered an utterly confounding mix of clues to its origins. The exchange's website stated that it was hosted in Bulgaria but also noted that the business was subject to the laws of Cyprus. The managing entity behind BTC-e, called Canton Business Corporation, suggested Chinese origins, but it was registered in the Seychelles and listed a Russian telephone number. And the business's various web domains had belonged to shell companies in Singapore, the British Virgin Islands, France, and New Zealand.

Gronager, too, started to scrutinize BTC-e more closely, tracing its money flows in Chainalysis's software. He began to see that all sorts of apparent illicit funds were ending up at this anarchic, crime-friendly exchange. They included dark web market cash-outs, stolen bitcoins, even the proceeds from a relatively new but fast-growing hacker scheme called ransomware: Hackers would infect and lock up victims' PCs, sometimes encrypting their hard drives, and then offer to unlock or share the key to decrypt data only if victims paid a ransom of hundreds or even thousands of dollars in bitcoins. More often than not, those ransomware payments would end up cashed out through BTC-e's mysterious exchange.

As for the dark web markets, still the central players in the criminal side of the cryptocurrency economy, they had bounced back in fits and starts since the takedown of the Silk Road. Just a month after Ross Ulbricht's arrest, a "Silk Road 2" had popped up, a clone of the original site complete with a reborn Dread Pirate Roberts to administer it under the same ultra-libertarian banner. In all, more than two dozen other market sites modeled on the Silk Road had sprouted around the dark web, with names like 1776, Underground Marketplace, Cloud-9, Outlaw Market, Hydra, and Pandora.

Just a year after Silk Road 2 appeared, in November 2014, the FBI and Europol had launched a major takedown known as Operation Onymous, exploiting a rare security vulnerability in Tor—and likely intelligence gleaned from Ross Ulbricht's laptop about Silk Road moderators who had joined Silk Road 2—to arrest several of Silk Road 2's staff and rip half a dozen of the marketplaces off-line. After that culling of the dark web market herd, however, another site had risen to prominence, this one called Evolution. It sold not only drugs but the sort of hacked data and stolen credit card numbers that Ross Ulbricht had deemed too unethical to allow on his site. When Evolution's administrators disappeared in March 2015, absconding with the millions of dollars held in users' escrow accounts, another market called Agora simply absorbed its users and took over the top spot in the dark web's criminal economy.

The Bitcoin-based black market was proving to be surprisingly resilient—and growing. A study by Nicolas Christin's research group at Carnegie Mellon found that in February 2015, before Evolution had gone off-line, Evolution and Agora together were generating as much as $400,000 a *day* in sales, about $100,000 more than the Silk Road had ever earned. And as Gronager and Gambaryan followed the funds of that burgeoning dark web drug trade, they found that an ever-widening current of the markets' dirty money was ending in cash-outs at—again and again—BTC-e.

Just months had passed since the promise of bitcoin tracing had been proven out for the first time in Gambaryan's case against Force and Bridges. Now, already, BTC-e seemed to pose a fundamental threat to blockchain analysis as a law enforcement technique: an exchange at the heart of the crypto-crime world that was seemingly invulnerable to subpoenas for its users' information. What good did it do to follow the money if that tracing led to a den of total anonymity?

. . .

Just as he began to look into BTC-e, Gambaryan had gotten calls from IRS and FBI officials in Washington, D.C. They wanted him to help create a new D.C.-based computer crimes unit at IRS-CI and, at the same time, a virtual currency group within the new National Cyber Investigative Joint Task Force. Based in the nation's capital, that NCIJTF would cut across different agencies, including the Department of Defense, Secret Service, and Homeland Security Investigations.

Senior law enforcement officials around the country were beginning to see what Gambaryan had sensed all along: that cryptocurrency tracing could be an incredibly powerful new investigative tool for law enforcement. Gambaryan, whose crypto-tracing in the Force and Bridges case had been the first of its kind, was now being offered the job he'd dreamed up and sought to create for years, hunting the biggest criminal kingpins of cryptocurrency, full time.

He didn't hesitate: He took the leap and moved his young family to D.C.

When Gambaryan arrived at the new D.C. computer crimes unit field office, however, he found that it was hardly the IRS mother ship he'd imagined. The team's handful of agents were set up in a small, undistinguished, largely empty gray-and-beige office space nearly two miles away from the IRS's stentorian D.C. headquarters next to the National Mall. "They hired a bunch of guys, put us in a room, gave us laptops, and told us to go hunt cybercriminals," Gambaryan says. The group had to take up a collection to buy a coffeemaker.

But over the months that followed, the IRS-CI D.C. computer crimes unit team learned to appreciate their outsider status, adopting the atmosphere of a kind of motley tech start-up. Gambaryan donated one of his years-old, homebuilt desktop PCs to serve as their central data repository. Another agent hung a hammock outside his cubicle and brought in a TV and speakers they'd use to play hip-hop music videos while they worked. Gambaryan hung up a world map on a wall, and the team would put colored pins in it to mark the locations of their successful operations and their targets who were still at large. They permanently "borrowed" a three-foot-long large-format printer from another office down the hall and used it to print massive Chainalysis graphs of cryptocurrency transactions.

In September 2015, Gambaryan was invited to join another interagency team, a nascent virtual currency "strike force" created by a money-laundering- and national-security-focused prosecutor named Zia Faruqui. The strike force met for the first time in the main conference room of the U.S. attorney's office in Washington, D.C.'s Judiciary Square. Seated at the polished-wood, thirty-person conference table, prosecutors began laying out the mission of the virtual currency group—to follow digital money trails as their central investigative technique and prosecute whatever crimes they led them to.

Faruqui remembers Gambaryan chiming in and agreeing to vastly increase the number of cryptocurrency cases they took on. The prosecutor was struck by his enthusiasm; it was unusual to hear that sort of immediate commitment from an agent. Most felt the need to check with superiors before committing to any assignment. He wondered if this young IRS agent was just an ambitious blusterer, flexing for show.

The conversation turned to the subject of building cases against unlicensed money transmitters, and again Gambaryan piped up, suggesting the group investigate illegal exchanges not just in the United States but internationally, if they had U.S. customers. Faruqui was impressed that Gambaryan had read the statute—that even foreign exchanges were subject to U.S. money-laundering laws whenever they carried out transactions with Americans.

Most agents considered investigations of unlicensed money transmitters a "foot foul," Faruqui says, not the sort of major crime that they would be eager to be assigned. But Gambaryan—who by that time was already deep into the BTC-e investigation—seemed not only willing but highly driven to take on these unlicensed exchange cases.

"Who is this guy?" Faruqui remembers asking himself. "Is he a ringer, or is he crazy? It turns out he was both."

WME

For the Northern District of California team that worked the Force and Bridges case—Will Frentzen, Kathryn Haun, and Tigran Gambaryan—BTC-e represented an obvious next target. Now that Gambaryan was based in D.C., he took up the case with a young prosecutor named Alden Pelker in the Justice Department's computer crimes division, who had been tracking BTC-e's use by hackers for months. "When we looked at the platforms that cybercriminals were using to launder their money, it was BTC-e, BTC-e, BTC-e," Pelker says. Together they opened an investigation into this Bitcoin exchange that was quickly growing into a global nexus of crypto-crime.

Gambaryan knew that to investigate BTC-e, he would need to find its servers' real location—the first step in tracking down the people who operated those machines behind the scenes.

Despite the obfuscation of its origins, the computers where the exchange was hosted weren't on the dark web, protected by Tor. They ought to be discoverable with a simple "traceroute" command, an operation that anyone with a computer and an internet connection can run to find a site's IP address—no harder than looking up a commercial service's number in a phone book. Gambaryan checked, and it turned out the only layer of misdirection that had prevented curious observers from learning the location of BTC-e's servers in the first place was a company called Cloudflare, a web infrastructure provider and security service that shielded the exchange's IPs from prying eyes like Gambaryan's.

Cloudflare was an American company, based in San Francisco. So

Gambaryan sent the firm a legal demand to cough up the IPs of BTC-e's servers. He quickly had those addresses in hand, and they revealed something he had never expected. BTC-e's infrastructure was being hosted by a company not in Bulgaria, Cyprus, the Seychelles, or any of the other far-flung locations its owners had pointed to in their attempt to throw off snoops. They were in Northern Virginia. In fact, the IP addresses led to a data center just six miles away from Gambaryan's desk at the NCIJTF in Washington, D.C. For a brief moment, Gambaryan wondered if BTC-e might even secretly be a CIA honeypot, then dismissed that theory as too absurd.

Together with the other agents in the NCIJTF and his old co-workers back in California, Gambaryan began the delicate legal and technical process of working with the Virginia hosting provider firm to gain access to the BTC-e servers and stealthily copy their contents—to "image" them, as computer forensic analysts say.

Soon the agents had a snapshot of the computers' hard drives and logs of their communications. The data the agents pulled from the BTC-e servers showed that three administrators were routinely connecting to the exchange's servers to manage them. Gambaryan could see IP addresses for each of the administrators, too. Those back-end machines were configured to block all direct connections except an "allow list"— the few IP addresses belonging to the administrators' computers. These IPs, however, led only to proxy machines. The canny admins had ensured their real locations would be opaque even to someone who had access to their servers.

The investigators weren't just looking at IP addresses, though. The hosting provider had responded to their subpoena for customer information with names and addresses associated with the account, individuals at a shell company who had rented the servers. That information pointed Gambaryan toward a place that he had long suspected might be the true home of BTC-e's staff. Given all of the misdirection, it was far from a definitive clue. But now, just as Michael Gronager was zeroing in on the suspected time zone of the Mt. Gox thieves, Gambaryan too had his eyes on Russia.

Amid all the conflicting geographic clues pointing to countries around the world, Gambaryan had sensed all along that Russia, the nation where he'd spent much of his own childhood, was the most logical place to run a lawless cryptocurrency exchange like BTC-e. Even the notion that the servers for an exchange run by Russians would be based in the United States made sense to him. The exchange would need high-quality U.S. infrastructure for the sort of rapid trading that BTC-e customers demanded. He also understood from his own background that Russians running a highly profitable, legally questionable business with indiscriminate associations are often just as fearful of their own government as any Western one, and they might want to place their business abroad to protect it.

Soon, the investigation into Mt. Gox's missing loot and Gambaryan's digging into BTC-e began to converge, and not just geographically. Around the time that Gambaryan's D.C. group started snooping on BTC-e's infrastructure, a separate group of agents reached out to him to ask a favor: A New York–based team of FBI and IRS agents had quietly taken on the case of Mt. Gox's missing money, just as Gronager had begun searching for that same fortune. Unbeknownst to Gambaryan—and to Gronager—this team had been consulting with another investigator in the Bitcoin world, a Tokyo-based Swede named Kim Nilsson. He'd traced the 650,000 stolen coins across the blockchain, just like Gronager, and he had similarly seen the largest chunk of them flow into BTC-e. Nilsson had shared those results with Gary Alford, the New York–based IRS agent.

When the New York agents heard that Gambaryan's team in D.C. now had access to BTC-e's back end, they wanted to know if Gambaryan could help them find out more about whoever was cashing out those stolen Mt. Gox bitcoins through BTC-e.

Gambaryan dug into the data his team had copied from the BTC-e server. What he found was a revelation: The IP address for the account trading in stolen Mt. Gox coins on BTC-e matched one of the few IP addresses on the BTC-e server's allow list for the administrators' connections. In other words, the person who had siphoned hundreds of thousands of bitcoins from Mt. Gox into BTC-e wasn't just any BTC-e user. They were a BTC-e administrator. Specifically, an admin with the username WME.

"The gears started turning in my head," Gambaryan remembers. "What better way to launder hundreds of thousands of bitcoins than to launch your own Bitcoin exchange?"

. . .

It was after midnight, Denmark time, when Gronager's phone rang with a call from Gambaryan. Gronager was getting ready for bed in his home in the Kartoffelrækkerne neighborhood of central Copenhagen, along the city's Sortedam Lake, one of the quaint terraced houses known as potato rows, packed together like rows of potato plants in a field. Half-naked, Gronager stumbled into his bathroom to take Gambaryan's call without waking his wife.

Gambaryan, without explanation, began asking Gronager to confirm some data points he'd shared with Gambaryan in a recent email. Since some of the stolen Mt. Gox coins had flowed *back* to Mt. Gox and been sold there—and Gronager had a copy of Mt. Gox's user database—Gronager had been able to run a check similar to the one Gambaryan had just performed on the stealthily copied BTC-e data. After looking over Mt. Gox's account data, he'd sent Gambaryan an email noting that for some of the stolen coins he could see Russian IP addresses for the user who'd been trading them in. These, he suggested, must be the IP addresses of the Mt. Gox thieves—or else whoever in their group was cashing in the stolen Mt. Gox bitcoins.

"Damn," Gronager remembers Gambaryan muttering in response. "Damn, damn, damn. Are you sure?"

Chainalysis's founder, standing shirtless in his bathroom, told Gambaryan that yes, he was confident the Russian IPs he'd shared must belong to someone involved in the Mt. Gox hack.

Gambaryan explained what he'd found: The IP address of the person trading stolen Mt. Gox coins on BTC-e matched the IP address of a BTC-e administrator—one with the username WME. So did one of the IP addresses that Gronager had just confirmed.

It all supported Gambaryan's conclusion: Whoever was cashing out Mt. Gox's 650,000 stolen coins had been *running* BTC-e. The person profiting from the proceeds of the biggest Bitcoin heist in history and the administrator of the shadiest exchange in operation appeared to be one and the same. And that single enterprising criminal seemed to go by the handle WME.

Vinnik

Gronager barely slept that night. By the next morning, he'd finally made sense of the story in his mind: This person they knew as WME must have been part of a group of hackers who had found a security vulnerability in Mt. Gox in its earliest months online (though Gronager never found out what that entry point might have been). The group had used its access to steal a pile of coins from the exchange. One of them, WME, had cashed those coins in on Trade Hill. But as the group had grown more daring, siphoning out more and more money in the years that followed, they'd become worried about getting caught—especially as WME began to use Mt. Gox itself to exchange stolen funds for dollars after Trade Hill went down. Eventually, the sum of stolen coins had grown so large that WME had made a very bold business decision: He would build his own exchange to cash it out.

The hackers' haul had been so massive that they had built an entire company to launder their millions, like mobsters launching their own Wall Street trading floor just to have somewhere to cash out their stolen funds. Having once run an exchange himself, Gronager understood that having a reserve of tens or hundreds of thousands of bitcoins made it far easier to bootstrap a trading platform. BTC-e had grown into much more than WME's personal money-laundering outfit, acting as its own stand-alone, profitable business, as well as a magnet for criminally tainted bitcoins around the world.

Gronager couldn't help but admire one of the most epic illegal operations in the history of cryptocurrency. "It was pretty entrepreneurial," he admits. "And somewhat impressive, I would say."

. . .

As for Gambaryan, once he knew that WME was not only a BTC-e admin but one of the Mt. Gox hackers, it didn't take long to connect those three letters with a real person. A Secret Service agent on Gambaryan's virtual currency-focused team with a particularly good memory recalled that a suspect that went by WME had years earlier been an active "carder," a cybercriminal focused on stealing and selling credit card information. The agent had looked up the handle in the Secret Service's broad database of cybercriminal profiles and found a name: Alexander Vinnik.

The team quickly confirmed that name through another avenue. Whoever used the WME pseudonym had also been an active user on the forum Bitcointalk, Gambaryan found, posting publicly, even as he ran an underground operation. The account had answered questions there as a BTC-e administrator—in Russian, no less. WME's posts had included an email address for further customer support questions at the domain wm-exchanger.com, an abbreviation for WebMoney Exchanger, another business WME had apparently created years earlier.

Back in 2012, WME had posted a long series of messages and screenshots to Bitcointalk, part of a dispute with the staff of another exchange in Australia called CryptoXchange, which had frozen one of the Russian's accounts. At one point in the thread, WME had gone so far as to post a letter from his lawyer to the offending exchange—and forgotten to redact a crucial piece of information. At the top of the page, in bold, were the words "Demand for the release of Alexander Vinnik's funds."

The BTC-e admin's real name had apparently been there all along, hiding in plain sight.

Gambaryan's investigation seemed to be taking the opposite shape of the case against Force and Bridges. In that earlier mystery, he'd gone looking for one Bitcoin thief and found two. Gambaryan and Gronager, in their tandem detective work on Mt. Gox and BTC-e, had been looking for the individuals behind two criminal operations. Instead, they had converged on a single Russian man. And now they had a name.

. . .

The identification of Vinnik, for Gambaryan, was bittersweet. He now believed he knew the name of the administrator behind the most popular money-laundering exchange in the world. But that admin was in Russia, where a name alone is far harder to connect with all the other personal information he'd need to indict Vinnik—not to mention to somehow arrest him.

In a country with friendlier ties to the U.S. government, Gambaryan could build out a profile of his suspect that would include their photo, identifying documents, bank records, and other evidence. But in Russia—which has no mutual legal assistance treaty with the United States—all of that was essentially off limits to American law enforcement. And Gambaryan found that Vinnik, egregious Bitcointalk slipup aside, had been careful about his digital presence. There were no photos of him online, no social media accounts. To Gambaryan, it seemed he never even accessed a website from his own IP address, always relying on proxy servers or VPNs to cover his tracks.

"He was very good," Gambaryan admitted. "Identifying Vinnik was probably the hardest thing I've ever had to do."

For months, Gambaryan and his virtual currency group pored over records from around the world looking for any lead, any shred of personal information they could tie to Vinnik's name. Gambaryan hunted through thousands of IP addresses, representing everywhere WME had left a digital trail for years, looking for one that might offer a useful lead.

Then, finally, in mid-2016, fully six months after they first stumbled across Alexander Vinnik's name, Gambaryan hit pay dirt. He dug up an IP address from which Vinnik had logged in to one of his known accounts—without a VPN. The IP belonged to an international luxury hotel outside Russia (which hotel, in which country, he declined to say). Gambaryan sent a subpoena to the hotel chain's U.S. corporate office and confirmed that Alexander Vinnik had indeed stayed there.

Eventually, the hotel handed over the prize Gambaryan had spent half a year searching for: an image of the passport Vinnik had given the front desk when he'd checked in, complete with his name and date of birth. It showed the photo of a kind-looking, handsome man with short-cropped brown hair and a mole on his left cheek. He looked a bit like a young Mikhail Baryshnikov.

. . .

When Gambaryan had first pointed out to Gronager the thread on Bitcointalk that included Alexander Vinnik's name, Gronager had immediately wanted to publicize their finding. They'd cracked the case—with the help of the bitcoin-tracing software Gronager and his start-up had developed. His months of work on a seemingly impossible quest to find the Mt. Gox millions hadn't been in vain. And he knew that taking credit for this win would lead to enormously valuable publicity for his young company.

But Gambaryan told Gronager they'd need to keep their discovery to themselves. They couldn't give Vinnik or the other BTC-e admins any hint that they'd been identified.

Even with a copy of Vinnik's passport, any immediate indictment they made against him would be in absentia—a hollow victory. Russia wasn't about to hand over one of its citizens to the United States. If they wanted Vinnik to face justice, they needed him to let his guard down, to believe that any investigation into BTC-e and the stolen Mt. Gox money had lapsed. He needed to be lulled into a sense of security, leading him to—eventually, hopefully—travel abroad to another country, one where he could be arrested and sent to the U.S. Gambaryan had no idea when that might happen.

Gronager saw the logic of Gambaryan's argument. He agreed not to share Vinnik's name with anyone—not even with Mt. Gox's trustees, who had originally put him onto the case. Together, Gambaryan's investigative group and Gronager had solved the biggest mystery in cryptocurrency since the identification of the Dread Pirate Roberts. And they couldn't tell anyone.

Consolation Prizes

As Gambaryan was denied closure in one case, he got it in another. In October 2015, not long after he had moved to D.C., Carl Force was sentenced to seventy-eight months in prison. Two months later, Shaun Bridges was sentenced to seventy-one months. Both men had pleaded guilty.

The full story of Force and Bridges had come to light just a few months after Ross Ulbricht's guilty verdict, and his defense team had argued that Force and Bridges's corruption meant Ulbricht deserved a retrial—that the agents' foul play should invalidate the evidence against their client. But Ulbricht's prosecutors countered that the Baltimore agents had no role in the New York–based investigation that had finally captured Ulbricht. Judge Katherine Forrest ruled in closed chambers that revealing the story of the corrupt agents to the jury wouldn't have changed their findings. A panel of judges at Ulbricht's appeal hearing would uphold her decision.

When it came time for Force to be sentenced, he chose not to speak. But Bridges, at his sentencing hearing, gave a short statement. The former Secret Service agent told the court that he'd known from the moment he'd signed his name to the suspicious activity report for Carl Force that the investigation into Force would lead to him. "I mean, the person turning him in worked with him; they're obviously going to look at me," Bridges said, perhaps exaggerating his role in the Force investigation, in which he'd been more of a roadblock than an ally. "But I accept that. I don't diminish one bit of it here." He apologized and added that he now took full responsibility for the actions that had led to his conviction.

The judge in Bridges's case had released him on bail for the long months between his arraignment and his sentencing. That decision went against the vocal warnings of prosecutors, who pointed out that after his conviction Bridges had tried—and failed—to legally change his name to "Calogero Esposito," taking his wife's surname. If that name change wasn't suspicious enough, he had even asked the government to have the change "shielded" so that it wouldn't be visible in the public record. Nonetheless, the former Secret Service agent was released and instructed to self-report to a minimum-security prison in New Hampshire in late January 2016.

A few weeks before that prison entry date, a Secret Service agent happened to check a Bitcoin address in which Shaun Bridges had stored 1,600 bitcoins seized from Bitstamp as suspected criminal proceeds. It was empty.

When Tigran Gambaryan learned of the missing money—worth close to $700,000 at the time—he immediately called Michael Gronager, and they began hunting the wayward coins on the blockchain. They found that the money had moved to a now-familiar destination: BTC-e. Gambaryan confirmed with a dozen Secret Service agents that none of them had access to the emptied Bitcoin wallet. He learned that the agency had, instead, made the mistake of leaving the money at an address for which Shaun Bridges still possessed the key.

Just two days before Bridges was due at the New Hampshire prison, a judge granted Gambaryan a warrant to search Bridges's home.

On a quiet, snowy morning in late January, Gambaryan and about twenty agents surrounded Bridges's two-story house in an upscale neighborhood in Laurel, Maryland. When they pounded on the door and announced themselves, no one answered. The only response was the high-pitched barking of a small dog. The agents debated what to do. If Bridges didn't respond, they might have to ram the door open. But Gambaryan worried that if they did, the door would slam into the tiny dog, who was yapping at them from the other side.

After a while longer with no response other than the dog's barking, they decided they had no choice but to force the door. At that moment, Shaun Bridges finally opened it. The former Secret Service agent stood in the doorway, bald and goateed like Carl Force but thinner, with what Gambaryan describes as a surprised look on his gaunt face.

When the agents searched the house, they found the preparations of someone who appeared very much as if he were about to go on the run: a MacBook with its serial number scratched off, along with two duffel bags, which contained Bridges's passport, records for three different offshore companies he'd created in a collection of tropical island countries, a cell phone, and a thumb drive. Gambaryan had apparently caught Bridges just before he put his escape plan into action.

Bridges was arrested on the spot. Eventually, he confessed to the theft of the 1,600 bitcoins—a theft he had brazenly attempted *after* he had already pleaded guilty to stealing more than 20,000 others. A judge would, soon after, add another two years to his sentence. This time he was not granted bail.

. . .

Michael Gronager would never receive much public recognition for tracking down the missing Mt. Gox millions. His discovery, with Gambaryan, of one of the alleged culprits' names remained a secret. Meanwhile, Kim Nilsson, the Swedish blockchain investigator who had worked with Gary Alford and the New York–based investigative team, had published a blog post that laid out his own findings—without naming WME or Vinnik—not long after Gronager came to the same conclusions. Nilsson was profiled for his detective work in *The Wall Street Journal* and credited with cracking the case in a *Fortune* magazine feature. Gronager's work, meanwhile, remained unknown to virtually everyone other than himself, Gambaryan, and a few others in U.S. law enforcement.

But Gronager says he wasn't bothered by that lack of publicity. That was in part because, by the end of 2015, he'd already won a significant consolation prize: His company was taking off.

Not long after his first meeting with Haun and Gambaryan, word began to spread within U.S. law enforcement that Chainalysis possessed a powerful new tool for tracing cryptocurrency. By May, two agencies agreed to start paying for access to that application. Around the same time, three of the largest cryptocurrency exchanges began to shell out for the software, too.

Late that spring, a third co-founder joined the company, a young U.K.-born South African economist named Jonathan Levin. A year before Gronager started Chainalysis, Levin had attempted to create his own blockchain analysis start-up, Coinometrics, but had never quite got it off the ground. When a friend introduced him to Gronager, they met in Copenhagen and found they had an almost identical ideology around Bitcoin's potential: not a weapon in an anarchist or even libertarian revolution, but a pure technology that was sure to transform finance around the world—if they could use its inherent transparency to weed out the bad actors.

Levin also displayed an incredible sense of hustle and an impressive network of contacts across the cryptocurrency community that made him what Gronager calls "a walking Rolodex." He operated with a certain start-up swagger that the unassuming Gronager had never quite possessed, and traveled so much that he lived out of a backpack with no fixed address—the ideal head of sales for a fully global company.

Levin quickly became one of the two main public faces of Chainalysis, with Jan Møller receding into the company's quieter internal work. Soon Gronager and Levin began renting a shoebox apartment in the SoHo neighborhood of downtown New York. It was infested with little cockroaches—"the real New York experience," Gronager happily remembers. They used that home base to pitch Chainalysis to private sector and government customers from Wall Street to Washington, as well as a growing number of exchanges and law enforcement agencies worldwide. It was Levin who finally came up with a name for the tracing application they were selling, a play on "chain reaction" and a reference to its ability to serve as a powerful catalyst in their customers' investigations: Reactor.

By the end of 2015, Chainalysis had more than fifty Reactor customers and a healthy revenue stream of more than $300,000 a year, enough that in February 2016 a group of venture capital firms led by Point Nine Capital invested $1.6 million in their fast-growing operation. Other companies, including one called Elliptic and another named Cipher-Trace, had entered the blockchain analysis industry, too. But those firms couldn't quite catch up with Chainalysis's adoption—particularly among law enforcement agencies. One prosecutor described Chainalysis to me as the Coca-Cola to those competitors' Pepsi. "Everybody used it," he said simply.

Gronager didn't dwell on the glory he never received for his work on the Mt. Gox mystery. He didn't even care about the 100 bitcoins that he'd left in Mt. Gox, which the hackers stole along with the rest. (By today's exchange rate, those coins would be worth several million dollars.) Chasing the Mt. Gox fortune, Gronager says, was a "formative experience." It drove him not only to prove that Bitcoin was inherently traceable but, as he describes it, to help *make* it traceable—to build what would become the go-to bitcoin-tracing software firm: By the time he knew Alexander Vinnik's name, Chainalysis had become the largest and most valuable blockchain analysis company on the planet, one that would change the way the world thought about cryptocurrency forever.

The company had built a floodlight capable of piercing the veil of the Bitcoin economy, and law enforcement investigators around the globe were about to use it to peer into that economy's shadows like never before—to expose the secret workings of a burgeoning underworld of drug sales, cybercrime, money laundering, and even child exploitation in a way that many of its inhabitants were entirely unprepared for.

Gronager was pleased with his contribution. "We fixed the system," he said. "Bitcoin is transparent."

PART III

ALPHABAY

Alpha02

Robert Miller just wanted to be on the SWAT team.

The young DEA agent—Miller is not his real name*—had been assigned to the agency's Fresno, California, field office right out of the academy. He'd never been to Fresno before, but he had high hopes it would give him a chance at the sort of law enforcement operations he'd always wanted to be a part of: making arrests, carrying out search warrants, "hitting doors," as he put it. He was attracted to the physicality of that work, the adrenaline rush, escaping paper-pushing bureaucracy to "take down bad guys" in the flesh.

When Miller joined the DEA in 2012, he found he wasn't the brawniest trainee in the academy or the best shot on the firing range. But instructors praised him for his instinctive judgment and thoroughness—how, in training raids on the academy's mock-ups of drug dens, he always meticulously cleared his corners and covered his blind spots.

Fresno certainly seemed to offer opportunities for the kind of action Miller was seeking. The sunbaked, dusty, agricultural city in the middle of California had long served as a corridor for cocaine, heroin, weed, and methamphetamine smugglers, as traffickers from the southern border made their way to buyers in the Northwest and the East Coast. Agents spent their days carrying out undercover buy-and-busts, following trucks packed with dope along Highway 99, and tracking, raiding, and arresting cartel operators.

---

* I've also changed some personal details related to Miller to better obscure his identity.

Then, not long after completing training and moving to Fresno, just when he was ready to take up his own small part in America's war on drugs, Miller injured both his foot and his shoulder while rock climbing. Both injuries required surgery. There would be no SWAT team, no "hitting doors" for Miller—not, at least, for the two years at minimum it would take to recover.

So Miller was assigned to surveillance. He'd stake out suspects from his car, or sit in the Fresno office's wiretap room, listening to suspects' phone calls and reading their texts—for weeks or sometimes months on end. The work was often mind-numbingly mundane. "Ninety-nine percent boredom and 1 percent excitement," as he remembers it.

At one point in 2013, Miller's partner on a surveillance assignment had suggested they try to work on a new sort of case. What about this booming dark web drug market she'd heard about called the Silk Road? But when Miller asked his DEA superiors about the site, he was told that a team in New York and a task force in Baltimore were on top of it. Not long after, he was on a surveillance assignment in his car in a mall parking lot when his phone buzzed with an alert that the notorious market had been busted.

It was only after two more years of stakeouts and phone-call eavesdropping that, one day in early 2016, Miller's boss came into the wiretap room, where the young agent was spending yet another hour of his life listening in on yet another narcotics suspect. He asked if Miller wanted to join a different team. A local assistant U.S. attorney by the name of Grant Rabenn had assembled a dark-web-focused group, and he was asking for volunteers from all the federal agencies clustered around Courthouse Park in Fresno's downtown square: the IRS, Homeland Security Investigations, and the DEA. Someone in the office had remembered Miller's inquiry into the Silk Road.

The assignment, Miller knew, was pretty much the opposite of the SWAT team. But at least it would be something new. "Okay," he said. "I'll do it."

. . .

When Miller joined Fresno's dark web strike force, it quickly became apparent to him that it had not been assembled to take down the next

Dread Pirate Roberts. Grant Rabenn, the young prosecutor at the helm, had more modest goals: They would be going after individual money launderers and drug dealers on the dark web, not its kingpins and masterminds. "We are not the Southern District of New York. We are in a dusty town in the Central Valley of California," as Rabenn put it. "Let's hit singles before we try to go for a home run."

That humble starting point was fine with Miller, who had little idea at the time of how the dark web drug trade even worked. When Rabenn asked Miller to start making undercover heroin buys, he initially couldn't figure out how to buy bitcoins, not to mention drugs themselves. He drove two and a half hours to San Jose to find a physical Bitcoin ATM where he could convert dollars to bitcoins rather than simply use an online exchange. Even then, Miller discovered that after transaction fees he hadn't bought nearly as much cryptocurrency as he'd intended and could purchase only half a gram of heroin, instead of the two grams he'd planned on for his first undercover operation.

But slowly, as Miller poked around the dark web and perused the various markets, he got a feel for the post–Silk Road online drug economy. And he soon came to see that this underworld was dominated by a single entity: AlphaBay.

AlphaBay had first appeared in late 2014, just one of the broad scrum of markets vying for a share of the growing dark web criminal trade. But the site's administrator, who went by the handle Alpha02, seemed cannier than those behind many of the competing markets. Alpha02 was a well-known if not exceptionally talented "carder," a cybercriminal hacker focused on credit card theft and fraud. He'd become a significant player on Tor Carding Forum, a cybercrime-focused dark web site where hackers traded in stolen data. He'd even sold his own sixteen-page "University of Carding Guide," designed to teach beginners the tricks of the trade, like knowing which credit cards were most profitable to exploit, or how to take over victims' accounts on e-commerce sites, or how to "social-engineer" customer service representatives at banks, calling from spoofed telephone numbers to deceive them into approving fraudulent transactions.

Alpha02 bragged in his guide about his own carding wins, like buying a $10,000, high-end gaming rig with one of his victim's accounts. These were hardly the sorts of multimillion-dollar heists that more elite and professional cybercriminals were pulling off at the time, but perhaps just enough to establish his bona fides for AlphaBay's earliest users.

Indeed, for its first months online, in late 2014 and early 2015, Alpha-Bay was devoted almost exclusively to cybercriminal wares such as stolen account log-ins and credit card data—not narcotics. But as Alpha02 bootstrapped the site from its carder origins, its portfolio of vendors quickly expanded to offer the dark web's more lucrative contraband: ecstasy, marijuana, meth, cocaine, and heroin.

Soon it became clear that Alpha02 had a grander vision than the average carder market admin. He aimed to unite the distinct spheres of the dark web devoted to cybercrime and drugs.

To the merchants operating on the dark web, AlphaBay's cyber-criminal origins meant they would be held to none of the ideological restrictions of the Silk Road, which, at least in theory, had limited sellers to offering only "victimless" products. Aside from a ban on child abuse materials and murder for hire, the only rule Alpha02 imposed on AlphaBay's vendors was that they not sell data or accounts stolen from Russia or other former Soviet states and not infect those countries' computers with malware. This strict prohibition, common among cyber-criminals from that part of the world, was typically designed to avoid trouble from Russian law enforcement—a kind of "don't shit where you sleep" principle. For Miller and any other federal agents and prosecutors sniffing around the site, it also suggested that AlphaBay and its mysterious founder were likely based in Russia—an impression cemented by Alpha02's signature in messages on the site's user forums: "Будьте в безопасности, братья," Russian for "Be safe, brothers."

In an interview in April 2015 with the dark-web-focused news site and directory DeepDotWeb, Alpha02 reassured his users that he and his site were beyond the reach of any Silk Road–style seizure. "I am absolutely certain my opsec is secure," he wrote, using the shorthand for "operational security," and added, "I live in an offshore country where I am safe."

From the start, Alpha02 declared that AlphaBay's "goal is to become the largest eBay-style underworld marketplace." He used almost none of the flowery libertarian rhetoric of the Dread Pirate Roberts and instead seemed to have a steely focus on the bottom line. In his DeepDotWeb interview, Alpha02 wrote in the style of a corporate press release: "We have made sure to have created a stable & fast marketplace web application which has been built with security in mind right from the start," adding, "We would like to assure all of our users (both vendors & buyers) that their security, privacy and anonymity rank first place in our priorities list."

What Alpha02 lacked in political inspiration, he seemed to make up for in technological aspiration and coding competency. Alpha02 boasted about features ranging from auction-style bidding to search tools that helped fraudsters comb through stolen data to carefully choose their victims, to a multi-signature transaction scheme designed to reassure users that it would be far harder for law enforcement or rogue staff to steal users' funds held in escrow than on older sites.

"We want to have every imaginable possible feature to be the #1 market," he wrote to DeepDotWeb. On each page of AlphaBay, he'd signed his work: "proudly designed by Alpha02."

When Judge Katherine Forrest had imposed a double life sentence on Ross Ulbricht in May 2015, she had intended to scare off future dark web drug buyers, dealers, and administrators. By the time of AlphaBay's rise, that unprecedented punishment seemed to have exactly the opposite effect. A study in *The British Journal of Criminology* found that sales on what was then the top dark web site, Agora, more than doubled in the days following the news of Ulbricht's sentencing, to more than $350,000 a day. The study's author, trying to interpret that unexpected increase, reasoned that by imposing such a shocking, draconian prison term, Forrest had only generated new awareness of the dark web's drug trade. Rather than deter users, Forrest seemed to have created a massive advertisement for the world's burgeoning cryptocurrency black markets.

As for Alpha02, he was hardly fazed by the news. Following Ulbricht's sentencing, in an interview with Joseph Cox, a reporter from *Vice*'s tech news site *Motherboard*, Alpha02 momentarily affected a revolutionary posture, picking up the Dread Pirate Roberts's torch. "Courts can stop a man, but they can't stop an ideology," he wrote. "Darknet markets will always be around, until the War on Drugs stops."

But in response to other questions, AlphaBay's boss seemed to let that thin veil of ideology slip. He put forth a seemingly more authentic motive, better aligned with those the pragmatic profiteer had laid out from the start. "We have to carry on with business," he wrote. "We all need money to eat."

. . .

By the fall of 2015, AlphaBay was the biggest market on the dark web. Agora's administrators had taken their site off-line the previous August, citing concerns about a vulnerability in Tor that its administrator feared might be used to locate its servers. As AlphaBay eagerly absorbed Agora's tens of thousands of buyers and vendors, the inheritor of the dark web's throne appeared to have no such security flaw. In fact, for the growing crowd of federal agents surveilling the site, like Miller and his more technical colleagues at law enforcement agencies around the world, AlphaBay seemed to have made no coding or opsec slipups that could give them the slightest clue as to where they might find its servers, not to mention its founder.

Shortly before AlphaBay took over the dark web's top spot, Alpha02 had changed his username on the site to merely "admin" and announced that he would no longer accept any private messages sent to him by anyone other than AlphaBay's staff. Instead, he left much of the site's communications to his second-in-command and head of security, a figure who went by the pseudonym DeSnake.

This metamorphosis was a kind of reverse of the Dread Pirate Roberts years earlier, who had allowed his online personality to flower only after the Silk Road had taken off. Once Alpha02 had obtained the coveted crown as the kingpin of the dark web, he seemed to have none of DPR's interest in notoriety or politics. The Alpha02 moniker had served its purpose, lending the site its initial credibility. Now he intended, like discreet criminal bosses the world over, to slip into the shadows, raking in his fortune as quietly and anonymously as possible.

That fortune was, by the time of Alpha02's name change, growing at an unprecedented rate: By October 2015, AlphaBay had more than 200,000 users and more than 21,000 product listings for drugs, compared with just 12,000 listings on the Silk Road at its peak. Sometime around the middle of 2016, AlphaBay surpassed Agora's peak sales rate of $350,000 a day, according to Nicolas Christin's research team at Carnegie Mellon. AlphaBay had become, in other words, not only the biggest black market on the dark web but the biggest cryptocurrency black market of all time. And it was still growing wildly.

For Grant Rabenn, the Fresno-based prosecutor, it was clear that Alpha02 was now the most wanted man on the dark web, a persona whose notoriety among digital crime investigators he compared to Osama bin Laden. As the site's numbers swelled, AlphaBay and Alpha02 began to be invoked at every cybercrime-focused law enforcement conference, every interagency meeting, every training event, Rabenn says. And as the target on Alpha02's back loomed larger, so too did the unspoken fear that perhaps, this time, the agencies had met their match—that this dark web mastermind might actually stay a step ahead of them indefinitely.

"Is this person just a pure genius who has figured out all of the possible mistakes? Has this person cracked the code?" Rabenn remembers asking himself. "Has this individual found the perfect country with the right IT infrastructure to run a marketplace, and he's able to bribe the officials there so we'll never touch him?

"As every day passed, there was, more and more, a sense that this might be the special one," Rabenn says. "You begin to wonder: Is this the Michael Jordan of the dark web?"

The Tip

Grant Rabenn and his small Fresno team had no ambitions of taking down AlphaBay. "It's not expected for people like us," he says simply, "to go after a site like that." But that didn't mean he and his strike force didn't have plenty of lesser dark web denizens to chase. And although Rabenn had little idea of how to decipher the secrets of the blockchain, he had sensed from the beginning that he might be able to pluck the lower-hanging fruit of the crypto-crime world, the same way he'd made so many other cases in his short but eventful career as a prosecutor: by following the money.

Before becoming an assistant U.S. attorney, Rabenn had spent years on the other side of the money-laundering ecosystem, working for a boutique law firm in Washington, D.C., devoted to white-collar criminal defense. A young, olive-skinned lawyer with dark hair and a Hollywood smile, he had sought an escape from his mind-numbing first job out of law school, doing regulatory reviews at a white-shoe law firm—only to instead end up representing Russian oligarchs and corporate executives accused of bribing foreign governments. "Very interesting, wealthy people trying to hide their assets and avoid scrutiny," as he described them, or alternatively, "James Bond characters who are jet-setting around the world with suitcases full of cash."

Rabenn was captivated by the glimpses he'd gotten of this hidden world of billions and even trillions of dollars in invisible transactions—so fascinated, in fact, that he rarely felt any compunction about the high-level criminals he might be enabling. But Rabenn also found that he admired and envied the federal prosecutors on the other side of the table, the way they made their own cases and worked in the public interest. So he began applying for Justice Department jobs, finally finding one in Fresno—a city he says he'd vaguely heard of growing up in Southern California but could never have placed on a map.

As soon as he arrived at Fresno's DOJ office in 2011, he found it was exactly what he'd always wanted: a "wild west," with almost no hierarchy or bureaucracy, where Rabenn was simply told to focus on money-laundering cases and otherwise given free rein. For the next few years, he and local agents in Fresno investigated and prosecuted a vast array of crimes that all created covert money trails: fraud and extortion, child exploitation, corrupt cops, and, of course, the drug trafficking operations that used Fresno as their artery, pumping narcotics out to the rest of the country. "We were just running and gunning," Rabenn says of those years of prolific prosecutions, with a typically boyish enthusiasm. "It was a really fantastic experience."

Rabenn's money-laundering cases very often began with one of the steady stream of suspicious activity reports he received from banks, which they were required to file under the Bank Secrecy Act. By mid-2013, Rabenn found that more and more of those reports had been triggered by financial transfers out of cryptocurrency exchanges—what the banks suspected were cash-outs of dirty digital money. So the young prosecutor immersed himself in dozens of hours of YouTube videos to understand this still-new currency called Bitcoin—its mechanics and how it seemed to be monetizing an anonymous underworld of online commerce.

Rabenn quickly realized that the dark web presented an opportunity to work cases on a scale that would otherwise be impossible in Fresno: As long as a dark web drug dealer could be coaxed into sending a package to the Eastern District of California, the crime had officially occurred in his jurisdiction. "I wasn't necessarily happy with just prosecuting drug mules driving meth up the 99 freeway," he says. If he could arrange an undercover buy online and identify the seller, he could arrest dealers all over the country. "All I have to do is order dope from them, and then we can go get them. And that's what we did."

．　．　．

In 2014, Rabenn began forming his dark-web-focused group of agents, collecting local investigators from Fresno's Homeland Security Investigations and IRS-CI offices to join it. Soon he had assembled a small team of "odd ducks," as he describes them—agents on the more cerebral side, content to work cases largely on a computer screen instead of kicking down doors like their Central Valley colleagues.

Rabenn still focused on following the money, but he stuck to his bottom-up approach to making cases: He and his agents would take aim not at bosses—as Gambaryan's team was simultaneously doing with BTC-e—but at more prosaic forms of crypto-laundering. On a site called LocalBitcoins, individuals were offering to meet in person and buy bitcoins for cash, advertising services that would come to be known as over-the-counter or peer-to-peer exchangers.

Rabenn figured that these individual exchangers must be acting as human ATMs for the dark web drug trade, given that they had practically none of the know-your-customer restrictions that traditional banks are held to. As a trial run, Rabenn and a Fresno-based IRS agent arranged a deal with one such Bitcoin trader, recruiting an undercover agent to meet the exchanger at a Buffalo Wild Wings restaurant in Bakersfield, California. The undercover customer explained that he was a steroids dealer looking to cash out hundreds of thousands of dollars' worth of bitcoins—much of which he proceeded to trade, on the spot, for a brief-case full of cash. After that first face-to-face meeting, the IRS agent set up further undercover deals with the man, swapping cryptocurrency that he described as drug money for cash that the trader shipped through the mail. Rabenn and the IRS used that evidence to get a search warrant for the exchanger's home. They hit pay dirt when they found a spreadsheet there that he'd kept of all his customers, including many of their home addresses.

Rabenn's Fresno team carried out this form of money-laundering sting again and again, playing both sides of the game. In one operation, undercover agents took on the role of the exchangers themselves, meeting with a Colorado man to trade six-figure dollar sums for the bitcoins he'd amassed selling hundreds of pounds of marijuana and then charging him with drug conspiracy. On another operation they tracked down and searched a particularly prolific LocalBitcoin exchanger—who was also a licensed pilot—at an airport in Sacramento; the man routinely flew his own Cessna aircraft around the country, personally transporting bags of cash in his plane to exchange for bitcoins.

The Fresno detectives began to mine these exchangers' Rolodexes to find leads on bigger dark web targets. They started with a Merced, California, man who had cashed out millions of dollars through peer-to-peer exchangers. A Homeland Security agent got a warrant to plant a GPS tracking device on the suspect's truck and followed him to a nearby post office, where he shipped three packages that the agent intercepted and found to be loaded with marijuana. When agents searched the man's house and cracked the encryption on his laptop—the password was "asshole209," a reference to his Modesto, California, area code—they found he had also been selling cocaine, going back to the years of the Silk Road. He had in fact been the third-biggest U.S.-based dealer on the site. Another Los Angeles man they ID'd from the exchangers' lists had trafficked marijuana, cocaine, and LSD and later turned out to be part of a massive marijuana operation that had sold $7 million worth of pot on the dark web, blending the illegal revenue into the proceeds he made in his legal marijuana business.

Grant Rabenn and his team were generating steady wins with their targeting of peer-to-peer exchangers. But by the time he had recruited the DEA's Robert Miller out of the wiretap room, Rabenn had started to wonder whether they really needed to go to all that effort to achieve their busts. By then they'd done plenty of undercover buys; Rabenn had begun to suspect that many of the dealers they targeted were sloppy enough in their operational security that they could simply purchase their wares and look for clues either in their packaging or in the vendors' online profiles.

Miller, starting his new assignment, assembled the usernames of the top heroin and fentanyl dealers on AlphaBay and began to buy dope from them, one by one. As the packages arrived, triple sealed in silver Mylar and plastic, Miller and the team scrutinized both the shipments and their sellers' opsec. They found that one vendor had made an elementary mistake: He'd linked his PGP key—the unique file that allowed him to exchange encrypted messages with customers—with his email address on the PGP key server that stores a catalog of users' identities.

Miller and Rabenn quickly tied that email to the dealer's social media accounts and real name. They learned that he was based in New York. Miller then found fingerprints on a package of heroin sent from one of his accounts, which matched those of another New York man. Finally, the DEA agent worked with postal inspectors to obtain photos taken by a post-office self-service kiosk. They showed the second New Yorker putting a dope shipment in the mail. Miller and a team of agents flew across the country, searched the two men's homes, and arrested them both.

The same simple PGP trick allowed Miller to find the real name of another dark web opiates dealer—which turned out to be part of his dark web handle, only written backward—and then caught him shipping dope, again using evidence from a post-office kiosk camera. When Miller and a group of agents raided the man's home, this time in San Francisco, Miller says they found piles of fentanyl and heroin powder sitting on tables and in open plastic containers.

Rabenn's team was now on a roll, building significant cases—and even a reputation. When Miller had ordered a package of opiates from their San Francisco suspect, addressed to Fresno, he was amused when the suspect warned him that a particularly aggressive group of feds operating out of the Central Valley seemed to be targeting players on the dark web and that he had better watch his back.

But Miller and Rabenn didn't kid themselves: Fresno's strike force was still taking down minor players, not masterminds. Alpha02 remained, it seemed, untouchable, his marketplace still growing. Busting a few of the site's dealers wasn't any more likely to topple that black market than the DEA's efforts to defeat Mexican cartels by chasing yet another meth mule up Highway 99.

. . .

By December 2016, Miller was ready, again, to try something new. He'd achieved a couple of decent dark web busts, but he didn't love the paperwork or the weeks upon weeks spent in front of a screen. By then, his shoulder and foot had recovered. Perhaps it wasn't too late to get onto the SWAT team after all.

Then, one afternoon, Miller returned to the office after picking up lunch, his In-N-Out Burger bag still in hand, when he found he'd received an email from an intriguing stranger.

The email explained that the sender had been googling dark web arrests, looking for a law enforcement contact. They'd tried the FBI tip line, but no one had responded. So they'd tried Homeland Security and had no luck there either. Finally, they'd found Miller's contact information in one of the Fresno team's criminal indictments of an AlphaBay drug dealer.

So the stranger had decided to try getting in touch with Miller. And now they were ready to share a very good tip about the identity of Alpha02.

CHAPTER 26

Cazes

More than a year before that fateful tip, around the beginning of 2015, a Canadian tech entrepreneur from the small city of Trois-Rivières in Quebec—I'll call him Paul Desjardins—had been planning a trip to Thailand. A friend recommended that during his stay he meet up with a contact from their hometown who now lived in Bangkok. The man's name was Alexandre Cazes.

When Desjardins visited Cazes in his Bangkok home, an unremarkable, midsized house in a gated community in the Thai capital, he found that Cazes seemed to be doing well for himself. He had invested early in Bitcoin, the baby-faced Canadian in his early twenties told Desjardins, and it had paid off.

Cazes's biggest problem, financially, seemed to be that he now had more cash than he could deal with. He alluded to having sold bitcoins to Russian mafia contacts in Bangkok. A foreigner depositing the resulting voluminous bundles of Thai baht at a bank would raise red flags with local regulators, he worried. So instead he had piles of bills accumulating around his home, even hidden in recesses in the walls.

"There was money everywhere," Desjardins remembers. "You open a drawer, and you find money."

Despite Cazes's liquidity issues and his somewhat alarming mention of the Russian mob, Desjardins couldn't see any evidence that his strange new acquaintance was involved in anything overtly criminal. He didn't use any drugs; he seemed to barely drink beer. Cazes was friendly and intelligent, if socially aloof and emotionally "very cold," like someone going through the motions of human interaction rather than doing so naturally. "It was all logic," Desjardins says, "ones and zeros." He did note that his new friend, while otherwise generous and good-natured, had ideas about women and sex that struck him as very conservative, bordering on misogynistic.

During that first visit, the two men discussed Desjardins's idea for a new e-commerce website. Cazes appeared interested, and Desjardins suggested they work on it together.

Back in Quebec later that year, around Christmas, Cazes met with Desjardins again, this time to hear a full business pitch. After no more than fifteen minutes' discussion of the details, Cazes was in. He impressed Desjardins by spending $150,000 without hesitation on a web domain for their business, not even bothering to haggle with the seller.

In another pleasant surprise, Cazes also paid a six-figure legal bill Desjardins had racked up in a dispute with another business. Cazes turned out to be a coding savant, too; Desjardins had planned to hire a team of coders, but Cazes quickly proved capable of doing most of the initial programming work for their fledgling site single-handed.

As they worked to get their business off the ground, Desjardins could see that Cazes's wealth was much bigger than he had first estimated. He learned that his partner was in the process of buying a villa in Cyprus and making some sort of real estate investment in Antigua, too. When Desjardins next visited Cazes in Bangkok, his friend and business partner arrived at the airport to pick him up in a dark gray Lamborghini Aventador.

Desjardins pointed out that there was nowhere in the super-car to fit his large suitcase. Cazes told Desjardins to get in anyway and gamely struggled with the luggage until it fit onto Desjardins's lap.

Desjardins remembers seeing that the suitcase had scratched parts of the Lamborghini's interior, but Cazes didn't seem to care. It struck Desjardins, in fact, that Cazes didn't seem to have much emotional connection to the car at all; he didn't even know how to use its radio. Desjardins thought that Cazes appeared to own it out of a sense that he should, that it was the socially correct way to display his wealth.

As they left the airport, Cazes asked Desjardins if he'd ever been in a Lamborghini before. He responded that he had not.

Within seconds, Desjardins was flattened against the Aventador's passenger seat as his eccentric friend rocketed the car down the Bangkok highway at more than 150 miles per hour.

. . .

In late November 2016, just before Thanksgiving, Rabenn was in his office, working to wrap up his caseload and prepare for the holiday, when he got a call from Miller. "Hey, Grant," Miller said. "I think I've got something big that we should talk about."

They met at the Starbucks a block from Fresno's courthouse. Miller explained what his tipster had told him: In AlphaBay's earliest days online, long before it had gained its hundreds of thousands of users or come under the microscope of law enforcement, the market's creator had made a critical, almost laughable security mistake. Everyone who registered on the site's forums at the time had received a welcome email, sent via the site's Tor-protected server. But due to a misconfiguration in the server's setup, the message's metadata plainly revealed the email address of the person who sent it—Pimp_alex_91@hotmail.com—along with the IP address of the server, which placed it in the Netherlands.

That shocking mistake had been quickly fixed, but only after the tipster, who made a habit of scrutinizing dark web sites, had registered and received the welcome email. The source had kept it archived for two years as AlphaBay grew into the biggest dark web market in history.

And now they had given it to Miller. It seemed that even the man Rabenn had once thought of as "the Michael Jordan of the dark web" was capable of elementary opsec errors—with permanent consequences.

Rabenn received Miller's revelation coolly, he remembers: He'd heard from overexcited agents before, whose incredible leads led only to dead ends or hoaxes. Surely, he thought, if his little team in Fresno had these clues, someone else, somewhere in the U.S. government, must have them too and would be miles ahead of them. But he had found Miller to be a careful and thorough agent, and the prospect of a lead on the identity of Alpha02 was too significant to ignore. So they decided to drop everything and follow it.

There was, in fact, more to the source's tip, all of which they could corroborate with a few Google searches: The Pimp_alex_91@hotmail.com address also appeared on a French-language social media site, Skyrock .com. On that site, someone named "Alex" had posted photos of himself from 2008 and 2009, dressed in baggy shirts covered in images of dollar bills and jewels, wearing crisp new baseball caps, with a large silver pendant hanging from his neck. In one picture, he'd written his hip-hop handle, "RAG MIND," at the top of the image in the style of a debut rap album. The words on his shirt read "HUSTLE KING."

A dating profile the man had posted to a "singles" portion of the site identified his hometown, Trois-Rivières in the French-Canadian province of Quebec, and his age at the time, seventeen. The "91" in his email address, in other words, was his birth year. If this was indeed AlphaBay's founder, he would have been twenty-three at the time of its creation.

Nothing about this young French-Canadian hip-hop wannabe matched their idea of the kingpin known as Alpha02. Had all of the allusions to Russia and Russian-language snippets been a ruse? Based on the IP address that had been included in the tipster email, the site's forums, at least, seemed to be hosted in western Europe.

To Miller and Rabenn, the conclusion that this "Alex" character was Alpha02 seemed almost impossible at first. But the deeper they looked, the more plausible it became: The young Quebecker had used his Pimp_alex_91 email address years earlier on a French-language technology forum called Comment Ça Marche—French for "how it works." He had signed his messages with his full name: "Alexandre Cazes."

Searching for that name, the investigators came upon a more recent profile on LinkedIn for a decidedly more adult Cazes, sans hip-hop outfit, advertising himself as a web programmer and the founder of a Quebec-based hosting and web design company called EBX Technologies. His photo on the site showed an unremarkable-looking businessman wearing a gray suit and white shirt with no tie. He had a round face with a cleft chin, slightly thinning hair in the front, and an innocent openness to his expression.

Cazes listed his location as British Columbia, Canada, but they could see from his social media connections that he seemed to actually be based in Thailand. It wasn't Fresno's backyard, but not quite the "offshore country" Alpha02 had claimed he was hiding in, either. Digging further on social media revealed Facebook accounts for Cazes's fiancée, a pretty Thai woman named Sunisa Thapsuwan. A telling photo on a relative's profile showed Cazes in a suit and sunglasses, standing next to a dark gray Lamborghini Aventador—hardly the typical ride of a small web-hosting service founder.

Still, only once Rabenn and Miller began to dig deeper, using archival tools to look for web clues beyond those left in the open, did the DEA agent and prosecutor truly start to believe the links they'd been gifted. On Comment Ça Marche and another programming forum called Dream in Code, they found older profiles for Cazes. Years earlier, it seemed, he had written posts there under a username that left little room for doubt: Alpha02.

Alpha02 had tried to erase his tracks, deleting messages from the forums and changing his now-notorious username. But the evidence had been preserved by the Internet Archive, a nonprofit project that crawls and copies web pages for posterity. Just as with Ross Ulbricht, Alexandre Cazes's operational security slipups had been permanently etched into the internet's long memory.

. . .

Within days, Rabenn and Miller believed their Alpha02 lead was real. They also knew the case was too big for them to take on alone.

They decided to bring their findings to the FBI field office in Sacramento, a much larger outpost just a few hours' drive north, with significantly more computer crime expertise and resources than their small Fresno office. It turned out the FBI agents in Sacramento had an open case into AlphaBay—that, in fact, they had been tracking the site from its inception. Nonetheless, Miller's tip was new information to them.

Rabenn brought on the office's assistant U.S. attorney Paul Hemesath as an investigative partner. He'd been friendly for years with Hemesath, an older and more deliberate prosecutor with the air of a college professor, balancing out Rabenn's aggressive "run and gun" approach with cooler-headed analysis. Hemesath in turn asked for help from the Computer Crime and Intellectual Property Section at Justice Department headquarters, the Washington, D.C., office where a small army of cybercrime-focused agents and computer forensics analysts were based.

As they assembled their broad team, Miller and Rabenn began the delicate process of "deconfliction," figuring out if other agencies and task forces around the country had their own open cases on Cazes. They knew they needed to make sure they weren't stepping on another investigation's toes. But they also didn't want to simply cede the case to another group of agents and hand over the lead of a lifetime.

Soon, they found themselves butting heads with a usual suspect: Baltimore. When Rabenn called the same office that had produced Carl Force and Shaun Bridges's Silk Road team, he was told they were hot on the trail of Alpha02 themselves. Baltimore, just as in the Silk Road case, was focused on infiltrating AlphaBay's staff with undercover agents, in the hopes of working their way up to the market's kingpin.

Rabenn could sense this was a losing strategy. AlphaBay's dozen or so moderators and administrators, like the Silk Road's, didn't know their boss's identity, or even one another's. Each was simply a pseudonym hiding behind a Tor connection. There was no way to "roll up" a conspiracy from the bottom when the boss at the top was as careful and anonymous as Alpha02 seemed to be. And besides, Rabenn told Baltimore, they had a tip that went right to that apex figure. Rabenn worried that Baltimore's infiltration of the market would only spook Alpha02, causing the staff to pull an "exit scam" like so many markets before it: running away with users' money and then destroying evidence, making a case against them far harder to prosecute.

Baltimore refused to back down. Rabenn, who knew Baltimore's reputation after the Force and Bridges indictments, had no intention of teaming up with them. So, in a replay of the Silk Road case, the two groups decided to meet face-to-face to sort out their differences. In early 2017, Miller flew to Virginia to argue their case in a meeting that Rabenn—who called in by phone—describes as "everyone sitting in a room and yelling at each other."

In the end, they decided that the two teams would investigate Alpha-Bay in parallel. For Rabenn's California group, that meant their investigation was now a race—not simply against a black-market kingpin who could flee with his millions in profits at any time, but also against a team whose tactics the young Fresno prosecutor feared were bound, sooner or later, to trigger that exit.

In the meantime, Rabenn continued to poll his fellow prosecutors across the country, and even foreign law enforcement agencies, to check if they, too, were on his lead suspect's trail. Again and again, he would hear that another team in another city was investigating AlphaBay but that they had made no real headway. None appeared to recognize the name Alexandre Cazes.

Against all odds, Rabenn began to realize, his little team from Fresno was now at the vanguard of the dark web's most significant global manhunt.

CHAPTER 27

Thailand

If Alexandre Cazes had moved halfway around the world to Bangkok in an attempt to run AlphaBay beyond the reach of Western law enforcement, he had chosen, by some measures, exactly the wrong foreign destination.

For more than half a century, the U.S. government has had an enormous presence in Thailand. Even before the DEA was founded in 1973, a U.S. agency called the Bureau of Narcotics and Dangerous Drugs had stationed a field office in Bangkok. American agents had long been sent there to disrupt the flow of so-called China White heroin from the Golden Triangle opium-growing region that covers parts of Thailand, Laos, and Myanmar. In the late 1950s that triangle produced fully half the world's heroin supply and fed an epidemic of addicted U.S. soldiers in Vietnam in the 1960s and 1970s—a problem that made quashing the Thai drug trade one of the DEA's earliest and highest priorities. Fifty years later, Bangkok remains one of the largest and most active DEA offices in the world, the regional headquarters for the entire East Asia operations of a U.S. law enforcement agency that has more overseas agents than any other.

For Jen Sanchez, it was also a plum assignment: beautiful weather, low cost of living, incredible food, and not particularly dangerous—at least not relative to other DEA hot spots.

Sanchez, a twenty-six-year-veteran DEA agent in her mid-fifties with white hair cut to her shoulders and a zero-bullshit, profanity-laden approach to conversation, felt she'd earned her coveted Bangkok job. She'd spent years as a money-laundering-focused agent in Mexico City, followed by a stint in Texas, where her work had led to the arrest of three Mexican governors for taking bribes from the Zetas drug cartel and massive embezzlement from their own state governments. In that case, dubbed Operation Politico Junction, she'd tracked the crooked governors' dirty funds into the businesses they'd bought to launder it, along with mansions, luxury cars, and even private aircraft. In total, Sanchez had signed affidavits for seizures worth more than $90 million. As she modestly put it, "I paid for myself."

By December 2016, Sanchez had been in Thailand for nine months, mostly helping to track the financing for violent Islamic movements in the south of the country. Then, one day at the Bangkok DEA office—situated in the U.S. embassy, a white stone building surrounded by tropical trees, with a canal surrounding its foundation and a grass lawn where six-foot-long monitor lizards emerged from the foliage in the evening—her boss told her they had a visitor: a DEA official who was set to give them a presentation on virtual currency.

Sanchez didn't know anything about virtual currency. Nor, with just a few years left until retirement, did she particularly care to learn about it. But she figured it was her job to sit in on anything that had to do with money, so she listened politely throughout the presentation.

Only at the end of that meeting did the visiting agent truly get her attention: He mentioned, almost in passing, that the DEA had recently found a lead on the administrator of the biggest dark web market in the world and that he seemed to be right there in Thailand.

Sanchez had heard of the Silk Road. She asked if this site was as big as that legendary black market. The agent responded that it was at least three or four times the Silk Road's size, and growing. "Holy shit," Sanchez thought to herself. The biggest dark web kingpin in history was in her backyard? The scale of the money laundering alone would be enormous.

"He's going to have *stuff*," she remembers thinking. And she wanted to be the one to track it down and take it.

Another group of agents in Bangkok was assigned to handle the AlphaBay case. Sanchez's own supervisor, to her constant frustration, seemed more interested in busting small-time dealers on the tourist beaches of Pattaya than in big-game, long-term investigations. But Sanchez was not about to be left out of what she suspected might be one of the largest asset seizures—virtual or otherwise—in the history of the

DEA in Thailand. As soon as the presentation was over and the visiting agent left, Sanchez walked into her boss's office, pointed a finger at him, and told him she wanted the AlphaBay case.

. . .

When Sanchez got her wish, her new supervisor on the assignment was a forty-seven-year-old Puerto Rico–born DEA agent named Wilfredo Guzman. Guzman had started his career hunting drug-laden speed-boats by night in helicopters off the coast of Puerto Rico, and he'd risen through the agency's ranks following a series of massive Caribbean and South American cases. Working years earlier under the legendary agent Javier Peña—whose investigation and takedown of Pablo Escobar in the 1970s had made Peña one of the protagonists of the Netflix series *Narcos*—Guzman's team had in 2010 helped the Dominican Republic and Puerto Rican governments track down and capture the most wanted drug kingpin in the region, José Figueroa Agosto.

Now, as a supervisor in the Bangkok office, he prioritized, above all else, maintaining a hand-in-glove relationship with the Thai police's DEA equivalent, known as the Narcotics Suppression Bureau. Doing so required near-constant late-night business dinners of painfully spicy Thai food, drunken banquets, and karaoke outings with Thai counter-parts, belting out John Denver lyrics onstage with high-ranking Bangkok cops.

The Royal Thai Police have a far from sterling record when it comes to drug trafficking and corruption. Shakedowns of petty drug dealers, for some elements of the agency, are understood to be a perk of the job. One RTP official named Thitisan Utthanaphon had earned the nickname Joe Ferrari for his collection of sports cars of mysterious provenance. He would later be caught in a leaked video suffocating a suspected meth dealer to death, alongside six fellow cops.

So when the DEA agent Robert Miller in Fresno had asked Guzman in the agency's Bangkok office for help in hunting Cazes, Guzman had brought the case to his most trusted contact at the NSB, Colonel Pisal Erb-Arb, who led the agency's Bangkok Intelligence Center. Pisal was a spry, fatherly officer in his mid-fifties who frequently used his unassum-ing look of a balding middle-aged dad to personally take on undercover assignments. He had assembled a small team that held a rare reputation within the DEA: They were known for squeaky-clean, by-the-book investigations, as well as for Pisal's rare practice of elevating female agents.

Almost immediately, Guzman, Pisal, and the NSB team got to work tracking down their new target. Starting with just Cazes's name and a telephone number, they began to map out his properties: one home in a quiet gated community that he visited intermittently—what they'd come to call his "bachelor pad" or "safe house"—and another in his wife's name in another gated neighborhood on the other side of town, where he seemed to work and sleep. He had bought and was remodeling a third home, a $3 million mansion, farther out in Bangkok.

Soon the investigators were shadowing Cazes's every move around the city. The Thais were particularly fascinated to discover his Lamborghini, a super-car that cost nearly $1 million, as well as a Porsche Panamera and a BMW motorcycle, all of which he drove at speeds well above a hundred miles an hour whenever Bangkok traffic allowed.

Following Cazes proved to be a moderate challenge: He frequently zoomed away from the agents tailing his sports cars on stretches of unbroken highway, or lost them while snaking between cars and tuk-tuks on his motorcycle. Pisal used a bit of personal tradecraft to plant a GPS tracker on Cazes's Porsche, posing as a drunk and collapsing next to the car in a parking garage, then planting the device in its undercarriage. The police tried attaching a similar tracking beacon to the Lamborghini, but found that the car's chassis rode so low on the street that their gadget wouldn't fit. They resorted to tracking Cazes's iPhone instead, triangulating its position from cellular towers.

As Pisal's team began to assemble a detailed picture of Cazes's daily life, they were struck by how aboveboard it all seemed. He was a "home-body," as one agent put it, spending entire days without stepping outside. When he did leave his home during the day, he would go to the bank or to his Thai language classes downtown or take his wife out to restaurants or the mall. He lived, as Pisal put it using an English phrase commonly adopted by Thais, a "chill-chill" life of leisure.

Cazes did, it soon became apparent to Guzman and the Thai police, have one very significant secret in his non-digital life: He was a woman-izer. He frequently ventured out in the evenings to pick up dates—from 7-Eleven, from the mall, from his language class—and take them to his bachelor pad, or else to "love motels." These encounters were business-like and brief. By the end of the night, Cazes would be back at home with his wife.

So-called sexpats, foreigners using their wealth to live out their polyamorous fantasies, were common in Thailand. And as scandalous as Cazes's affairs might have been, there was no law against philandering.

Still, the Thais needed little convincing that Cazes must be some form of crime boss. At one point the surveillance team trailed his Lamborghini to a restaurant called Sirocco, situated on the roof of Bangkok's Lebua hotel; at sixty-three floors up, it claimed to offer the highest "alfresco" dining in the world, with two Michelin stars and $2,400 bottles of wine on the menu.

When Cazes and a group of his friends left the restaurant, the cops entered and spoke to Sirocco's management, demanding the receipts from the entire day to hide their intentions. Including wine and lavish tips, they found that Cazes had spent no less than 1.3 million baht—nearly $40,000—in a single meal for his entourage, an amount that flabbergasted even the agents accustomed to tracking high-rolling drug kingpins.

Drug lords who never touched narcotics themselves or directly carried out crimes were nothing new to the NSB agents. They were used to the notion that the cleaner a suspect's hands, the more senior the position they likely held in a drug trafficking syndicate. But those high-ranking bosses at least *met* with associates connected to hands-on crime, or those a step or two removed from them.

Cazes's criminality, by contrast, was channeled entirely through the opaque aperture of the dark web. In the physical world, his hands were cleaner than those of any kingpin they'd ever encountered.

. . .

Jen Sanchez was no more experienced in dark web investigations than the Thais; she had never used Tor, never visited the Silk Road. But as she began to get a sense of the full extent of the massive commerce in hard drugs AlphaBay now facilitated on a daily basis, she became incensed. The American opioid crisis was, by that time, in full swing; forty-two thousand Americans had died of opiate overdoses in 2016, more than in any year on record. That surge in fatalities was due in part to an influx of fentanyl, an opium derivative as much as a hundred times stronger than morphine. And here this twenty-five-year-old French Canadian was running a massive open-air heroin and fentanyl bazaar in public view? She was haunted by the thought that every day they left AlphaBay online, anyone, even children, could order fentanyl from the site, receive it in the mail, and die of an overdose in a matter of hours.

In a phone call with Miller in Fresno, she swore they would have AlphaBay off-line and Cazes behind bars in less than six months. "I'm going to take his shit, and he is going to go to jail, and we're going to get him in Florence supermax," she remembers telling Miller, referencing the prison where Ross Ulbricht was then serving his life sentence. "I want this kid gone."

But when it came to digital drug busts, Sanchez had far more enthusiasm than know-how. In the first of many conference calls among all the different agencies now hunting Cazes as a single team, including Rabenn, Miller, Hemesath, and the Sacramento FBI office, an FBI agent laid out AlphaBay's basic mechanics, its use of cryptocurrency for payments, and its escrow system. Sanchez interrupted to ask the agent what payment processor the site used. There was a short pause. Sanchez repeated her question. She wanted to know what processor held the bitcoins so that she could subpoena it and then seize AlphaBay's funds, as she'd done with criminal payments countless times before.

There was a longer silence still, and Sanchez started to get angry. Why were these agents refusing to tell her such a basic fact of the case? Finally, the lead FBI agent in Sacramento cut in to diplomatically explain to Sanchez the basics of Bitcoin and the blockchain: There was no payment processor, no bank, no middleman. Realizing that this sort of Bitcoin 101 would be necessary for some members of the team, "we were all kind of horrified," Rabenn said.

For an old-school money-laundering agent like Sanchez, cryptocurrency still represented a serious impediment to forensic accounting, just as its criminal users intended. But by early 2017, there was already a new, growing class of investigators who saw Bitcoin very differently. And it was those blockchain tracers who would offer the next breakthrough in the race to take down Alpha02.

28

Tunafish

As Alpha02 had risen to become the most wanted man on the dark web, so too had his marketplace become the most pressing puzzle for the world's top cryptocurrency tracing firm, Chainalysis. By late 2015, the company's third cofounder, Jonathan Levin, had heard a frequent refrain from their growing roster of law enforcement clients. They wanted to know if Chainalysis's core tool, Reactor, could help them identify the full breadth of AlphaBay's wallet—the massive constellation of that black market's addresses hidden within the blockchain.

The Silk Road, for all the Dread Pirate Roberts's promises of tumbling users' bitcoins into a state of supposed cleanliness, had been relatively straightforward to spot amid what were, at the time, tens of millions of transactions: When a user sent their coins into their Silk Road account's wallet, it was typically pooled with other users' money and ended up stored at one of a small number of centralized addresses—the trait that had allowed Sarah Meiklejohn to so easily spot my marijuana purchases on the Silk Road back in 2013.

That made it tough to trace the route of a buyer's coins to any particular Silk Road drug dealer, Levin says, but easy to see that the money had touched the Silk Road itself. Just send a few test transactions to any Silk Road account, and the market's wallet system would soon bundle up your coins with others, leading to a cluster of other Silk Road addresses— like a briefcase full of cash with a homing device inside, brought back to a criminal's hideout.

But as Levin sent test transactions into AlphaBay accounts, he found that this market functioned differently. It seemed to carefully avoid pooling users' money, keeping it instead in many small, disconnected addresses. By April 2016, AlphaBay had advertised to users that, like the Silk Road, it functioned as a Bitcoin tumbler: Put money into an AlphaBay account and it purportedly severed any link that could be used to follow it from where it entered the market to where it left. "No level of blockchain analysis can prove your coins come from AlphaBay because we use our own obfuscation technology," read one 2016 post from AlphaBay's staff to users on the site. "You now have ironclad plausible deniability with your Bitcoins."

Those claims, Levin says, turned out to be partly true. Most of the time when he put coins into AlphaBay and took them out again, they remained traceable. But unlike the Silk Road, AlphaBay's deniability claim was more than marketing hype. Because it never gathered coins into large, easily identifiable purses, AlphaBay's buyers and sellers were far tougher to distinguish from other, noncriminal users on the blockchain.

That meant, for Chainalysis, the task of mapping AlphaBay's wallet among what by 2016 were *hundreds* of millions of Bitcoin transactions soon became the most difficult problem the company had ever taken on. AlphaBay "was the number one priority of anyone looking at dark web crypto investigations," Levin says. It was also, more than any market they'd previously encountered, a target that was actively working to flout their ability to identify it.

Chainalysis, by this point, had around thirty employees, though the co-founders, Levin, Gronager, and Møller—along with the Czech programmer Aleš Janda, the creator of WalletExplorer, which Chainalysis had acquired—remained the most experienced blockchain analysts at the company. The small team began to grapple with their challenge.

They began by carrying out the same sort of blockchain observation experiments Sarah Meiklejohn had performed in her UCSD office years earlier, only now on an industrial scale. For month after month, they performed hundreds of test transactions with AlphaBay wallets—still never actually buying anything from the market, only moving money into and out of accounts—and watched the patterns those transactions formed on the blockchain, in the hopes of finding clues they could use to spot patterns elsewhere in the vast expanse of Bitcoin's accounting ledger.

At this stage of the game, the two clustering techniques that Meiklejohn had pioneered in her early experiments were no longer enough on their own. Instead, the Chainalysis founders were now hunting for distinct tells in the way AlphaBay moved its users' money—properties that weren't inherent in Bitcoin's protocol, but instead defined by the highly specific choices of Alpha02 and whoever else was writing the code of AlphaBay's wallet. Every time that software was rewritten, the Chainalysis team would have to shift their lens again, hunting anew for idiosyncrasies that could be used to recognize the trails it left behind.

Levin refused to divulge most of the clues that Chainalysis unearthed; some he described as "secret sauce" (a term that would come up in interviews with Chainalysis analysts with greater and greater frequency). But Levin offered as an example the trade-off that every wallet has to make between the speed of a transaction's "confirmation" and the fees it pays.

In order to persuade the Bitcoin network to record a transaction, a wallet has to offer a fee. The greater a fee the wallet is willing to pay, the better incentivized other nodes are to quickly rebroadcast the transaction so that all the Bitcoin nodes around the world eventually come to agree that the transaction occurred. Most wallets allow users to set their own fees along a sliding scale of speed versus cost. Dark web markets, however, typically use their own set configuration.

Chainalysis began to see the unique way that, for AlphaBay, the fee settings shifted depending on the size of a transaction. This set of fingerprints didn't offer a complete solution, isolating all AlphaBay addresses at once. But it represented a tell—one of many, Levin says—that would allow them to delineate the market's tangled web of payments. And just as with Meiklejohn's clustering tricks, every discovery of a new trick like these fee fingerprints produced a new set of addresses that would help them refine again the profile of the other hidden addresses they still sought.

By the end of 2016, Chainalysis had labeled more than 2.5 million addresses as part of AlphaBay's wallet. But even that years-long project of excavating the entire, massive shape of AlphaBay's finances was only a starting point. For Chainalysis's users at law enforcement agencies, the task ahead would be following the money from somewhere in that vast pile of numbers out to the bank account of a real human being.

. . .

Tigran Gambaryan, after half a decade of monitoring Bitcoin's rise as a cybercriminal tool and the currency of the dark web, was now far from alone among federal agents in his blockchain fixation. By late 2016, a pair of FBI analysts, both likewise based in Washington, D.C., had gained a reputation as perhaps the very best team of cryptocurrency tracers in the U.S. government. The two women had quietly followed cryptocurrency flows, tracking online fraudsters and black-market vendors for years. But they only ever produced leads that they quietly handed off to other investigators, clues that appeared in no criminal affidavits or courtroom evidence.

They both deeply value their privacy, so I'll refer to them here by the first names Ali and Erin. It was Ali who, just days before Robert Miller would receive his Alpha02 tip, decided that the pair of analysts should try something no one had ever pulled off before: tracking down a dark web administrator through blockchain analysis alone.

Ali and Erin worked for different investigative groups in different offices; Ali typically focused on dark web cases and Erin on more traditional cybercriminal hackers. But they shared a focus on digital money laundering, a fascination with cryptocurrency, and a years-long friendship. They had come to form a two-person team of their own, a unit that was inseparable, practically mind melding into two lobes of a single Bitcoin-obsessed brain.

On that winter day, Ali had left the FBI satellite office where she worked in a grim beltway office park in Chantilly, Virginia, and driven for half an hour through D.C. traffic to Erin's desk at FBI headquarters. Ali, the more ebullient and ambitious of the two analysts, had an idea she wanted to share with Erin, her more heads-down, details-oriented partner, and now Ali wanted the two to push aside all their other work to pursue it. Before Erin had time to protest, Ali had hijacked her workday, squeezed a chair into Erin's tiny cubicle, and impatiently grabbed her mouse to start clicking through Bitcoin addresses on her computer screen.

Ali had come to a realization: Every time a dark web market administrator pulled an exit scam, absconding with all the money his users held in their dark web market wallets, the dark web's forums were flooded with users lamenting their stolen funds and others offering reminders that no one should store any amount of cryptocurrency on a market beyond what they plan to spend immediately.

But there was one person, Ali figured, who would never have to worry about an exit scam when considering where to keep his crypto savings: the dark web administrator himself. "Who would have the most faith to leave their money on the market?" Ali asked Erin. "Of course it would be the guy in charge."

What if they simply searched for the black-market addresses that had held the largest sums of bitcoins for the longest time, even while exit scams on other markets spooked every other high roller into pulling out their funds? The biggest, most stationary piles of money might just belong to the boss.

Erin admitted it was a good idea. But after identifying a few addresses to look at, she shooed Ali out of her office to get on with her other work. After all, no one had asked them to track down Alpha02; they had intelligence reports to write and more realistic, achievable targets to hunt.

The next day, however, Ali began calling Erin every few minutes to give her breathless updates: She had started with the address of the biggest sum of bitcoins that had sat unmoved for the longest time among all the wallet addresses tied to the AlphaBay cluster. And, observing where the money had eventually transferred out of AlphaBay, she'd been able to track its movements in Chainalysis's Reactor software—the FBI, like most U.S. law enforcement agencies, was by then a Chainalysis customer—among the branching tendrils forking off from the market.

"It's still going!" she'd tell Erin excitedly on the phone as she followed it from one address to the next.

Soon Erin, infected by Ali's enthusiasm, was digging through other unmoved piles of potential administrator commissions. Talking constantly on the phone from their offices across the D.C.-Virginia border, they began to devote hours to their Alpha02 hunt, scanning through hundreds of AlphaBay addresses in Reactor.

Whoever owned these piles of criminal money had, at least in some cases, taken pains to hide their footprints on the blockchain. The funds would sometimes flow into clusters of addresses created by services known as mixers, advertised on dark web sites with names like Helix and Bitcoin Fog. These bitcoin-laundering services offered to take in coins, pool them with other users' funds, and then return all the coins in the pool to their senders at new addresses. In theory this would cut the forensic link for any tracer, like a bank robber who slips into a movie theater, takes off his ski mask, and walks out with the crowd, evading the police on his tail.

Ali and Erin did sometimes hit dead ends in their work to trace Alpha02's profits. But in other cases, they were able to defeat his efforts at obfuscation. Neither of the two FBI analysts would reveal how they overcame Alpha02's use of mixers, but crypto-tracers like those at Chainalysis offered hints.

A mixer, Jonathan Levin explained, is only as good as its "anonymity set"—the crowd of users all mixing their coins to render them untraceable. Despite whatever claims mixers made to their customers, examining their work on the blockchain revealed that many didn't actually offer an anonymity set large enough to truly flummox an investigator. The more money someone tried to launder, the harder it became to avoid those coins remaining recognizable when they reappeared on the mixer's other end.

Any decent mixer splits large sums of coins into smaller, less conspicuous payments when returning the money to its owner. But at some point, the transaction fees for every payment put a limit on any effort to break big sums of money up into small, less remarkable chunks, Levin says.

Mixers, of course, weren't the only tools that attempted to defeat blockchain analysis. Some wallet software offered a feature called Coin-Join, which could combine transactions from different users to muddle who had sent money to whom. But Michael Gronager hinted—without further explanation—that Chainalysis could often defeat that technique too, particularly when a spender was trying to hide a conspicuously large sum.

In truth, Chainalysis didn't need to offer its users *proof* of the path money took on the blockchain, so much as probability. Grant Rabenn candidly explained that the bar for sending a subpoena to a cryptocurrency exchange for a user's identifying information was low enough that they could simply try multiple educated guesses.

All of that meant that, in spite of criminals' best efforts, investigators were often left with suspicious outputs from both mixers and CoinJoin-enabled wallets, ones that they could follow with *enough* likelihood—if not certainty—of staying on their target's trail. Even the crowded movie theater trick, it turns out, breaks down when the robber is carrying a large enough sack of loot and the cops are watching every exit.

. . .

As Ali and Erin followed what they increasingly believed to be Alpha02's personal transactions, they gave nicknames to the most significant Bitcoin addresses they were scrutinizing, turning the strings of meaningless characters into pronounceable words. An address that started 1Lcyn4t would become, in their private language, "Lye sin fort." One that began with the characters 3MboAt would be pronounced "Em boat." The two analysts spent so much time examining and discussing these names that the addresses began to take on "personalities" in their minds. ("It's not exactly healthy," Erin said.)

Of all of their nicknamed addresses, one loomed largest in the two analysts' conversations. They refused to reveal even its nickname, for fear that someone might reverse engineer the actual address and learn their tricks. For the purposes of this book, let's call it "Tunafish."

Tunafish lay at the end of a long string of hops Ali and Erin had followed out from one of the initial addresses they'd hypothesized might be Alpha02's. It held special significance, however: It connected directly to an exchange. For the first time, they realized with excitement, they had managed to trace what they suspected might be a collection of the AlphaBay admin's commissions all the way to a transaction in which Alpha02 had traded them for traditional currency. They knew it was at those cash-out points, the blockchain's connections to the brick-and-mortar world of finance, that they might be able to match the transactions to a real person.

It was here, just as they were on the verge of ferreting out a name behind Alpha02's money that Ali heard a rumor of a criminal suspect's identity that was spreading among law enforcement agents across the country. As a longtime dark web analyst, she had kept in close contact for years with the cybercrime-focused FBI agent in Sacramento who had first opened a file on AlphaBay. So when the Sacramento office joined forces with Grant Rabenn's Fresno team, Ali was among the first people the agent called. He told her that they had finally matched a real person to Alpha02's online persona. He gave her the name.

The Sacramento agent knew Ali was already busy tracing AlphaBay's blockchain tentacles. He asked her to join their growing investigative team. Ali returned to Erin's office at FBI headquarters, cornered her in the hallway, and insisted she join, too.

"This is going to be a massive case," Ali told her. "We need to do this together." Erin agreed.

Now they were hunting Alpha02 no longer as an obsessive hobby but as part of an official investigation. Ali and Erin explained their Tunafish discovery to a D.C.-based assistant U.S. attorney who had also joined the team: a seasoned cybercrime prosecutor named Louisa Marion. She, Rabenn, and Hemesath immediately filed a subpoena for the identifying records on the exchange where the Tunafish address had been cashed out.

That legal request took weeks to bear fruit. Finally, one evening in the early weeks of January 2017, Ali was in the middle of a law school night class when she got a call from the Sacramento-based FBI agent with the news: The subpoena results had come back.

The agent told her the name on the exchange account tied to the Tunafish address. It was Alexandre Cazes.

CHAPTER 29

Rawmeo

As they followed up on the initial lead that Robert Miller had received—the Pimp_alex_91 email address that had first pointed the investigators to Alexandre Cazes—the assistant U.S. attorneys from Fresno and Sacramento, Rabenn and Hemesath, had periodically asked each other whether they truly had the right guy. Could their too-good-to-be-true tip have been some sort of elaborate misdirection? Could someone have purposefully leaked the address—and even chosen the handle Alpha02—as a way to frame this Cazes, to use him as a patsy? "The nightmare scenario would be that the source was setting us up," Rabenn remembers thinking.

The AlphaBay welcome email that the tipster had shared with Miller offered more than just an email address; it offered the Netherlands IP address, too. That was another golden lead, but the investigators hadn't dared to do much with it yet: They feared that if they approached the Dutch hosting provider the IP address pointed to, the firm might tip off Alpha02 that they were snooping around his site's infrastructure, blowing their cover.

When the subpoena results from Ali and Erin's blockchain tracing came back with the same name, however, it instantly vaulted the investigators to a new level of confidence: They were on the right track.

Over the next weeks and months, Ali and Erin continued to trace more high-value addresses out of the AlphaBay cluster into one cryptocurrency exchange after another. They came to recognize what seemed to be Cazes's identifying tells, even in his bitcoin-laundering habits; in some cases, his attempts to obscure his ownership of the bitcoins became, themselves, a kind of fingerprint.

In total, the two analysts would trace Cazes's commissions to fully a dozen cryptocurrency exchanges, which the prosecutors then subpoenaed, one by one, finding accounts registered in both Cazes's and his wife's names. And as those results came in, they found a years-long pattern: Cazes would open an account with an exchange and attempt to use it to cash out a chunk of AlphaBay's profits. At some point—often within months of his cash-out transactions—the exchange would grow suspicious about the origin of these massive cryptocurrency trades and ask for more know-your-customer information from him.

Cazes would send a note explaining that he was merely an early investor in Bitcoin (the same vague story told by every crypto criminal from Carl Force to Ross Ulbricht). In some cases, the AlphaBay founder claimed to have bought thousands of coins from Mt. Gox in 2011 or 2012, knowing that it would be difficult to check the records of a defunct exchange. In others, Cazes claimed to have bought them from a "private seller" at the exchange rate of a dollar each. "Since then, I've been pretty much juggling the coins like stocks, buying and selling, but never cashing out," he wrote in one emailed explanation to an exchange.

By 2017, however, legitimate Bitcoin businesses had learned to be wary of these unverifiable stories. In most cases, they'd close or freeze Cazes's account, and he'd have to move on to another exchange. Ali and Erin, meanwhile, could see the true source of Cazes's wealth, traced out in strand after strand of the blockchain's connections.

For years to come, the investigators involved in the AlphaBay case would debate whether, in another scenario—one in which they had never gotten the Pimp_alex_91 tip—their cryptocurrency tracing alone would have cracked the case. Would the appearance of Cazes's name on those exchange accounts have been enough to put them onto his trail, or would they have treated it as just another vague lead that they were too busy to chase down?

Coming as it did, however, in the immediate wake of the tip about Alpha02 that Miller had received, the two FBI analysts' blockchain work nailed to the wall a theory that would have otherwise hung by only a few threads. Every exchange subpoena and its results drew another line between Cazes and AlphaBay's fortune.

"When we saw millions of dollars in crypto flowing to him from what appeared to be AlphaBay-associated wallets, I was fairly confident that we had the right person," Rabenn says. "When you hit that point, you start gearing up to indict."

. . .

By March 2017, the always-aggressive Rabenn was ready to charge Alexandre Cazes with running AlphaBay. But his more cautious fellow prosecutor Hemesath wanted more evidence. They were still busy filing subpoenas for not only Cazes's cryptocurrency exchange accounts but all of his online activity, from email to banking, which had begun to coalesce into a portrait of Cazes's entire online existence. It was only in April that they found a new element of that digital life, one that revealed Cazes's daily thoughts to them with a level of detail they had never thought possible.

Their investigation had led them to an online forum called Roosh V. The site, the team quickly learned, was a kind of hypermasculine, "alpha male" pickup artist community, as well as a hive of shocking misogyny, alt-right racism, and anti-LGBTQ bigotry. Founded by the blogger Daryush "Roosh" Valizadeh in 2008, it had tens of thousands of registered users, men who coached one another on maximizing their sexual conquests and living an "alpha" lifestyle.

The Fresno team had found a curious individual on that forum. He had joined Roosh V in late 2014 and went by the name "Rawmeo." The pseudonym appeared to be an allusion to his love of "rawdogging," or unprotected sex. Rawmeo had written well over a thousand posts and achieved "True Player" status on the forum. He described himself as living large in Thailand, possessing a fortune in Bitcoin, and owning a web-hosting and design firm—all attributes that matched Alexandre Cazes's public persona. When the prosecutor team subpoenaed Cazes's PayPal account, they confirmed it: Cazes was using his account to pay a fee for a premium subscription to Roosh V. Rawmeo was another of his many personalities.

In some respects, Rawmeo represented the opposite facet of Cazes from Alpha02. As a dark web kingpin, Alpha02 was all business: He had restricted his communications with AlphaBay's community to the bare minimum, issuing only the occasional colorless pronouncement about the site's functions. Rawmeo, by contrast, was a full-color, tell-all persona, an outlet for Cazes to enjoy the rewards of his larger-than-life success, to stretch out his ego, and to soak up adulation, much as the Dread Pirate Roberts had been for Ross Ulbricht. But whereas DPR had built his following around a radical ethos of libertarianism and personal freedom, Rawmeo seemed to adhere to a much less idealistic philosophy. As he put it: "The person who gives the least amount of fucks will always have the upper hand."

Cazes, it turned out, was a prolific poster to a particular Roosh V section known as the "I-Just-Had-Sex" thread, where he described how he'd frequently pick up Thai women—impressing them with his Lamborghini or Porsche—and attempt to sleep with them, with as few strings attached as possible. He described the women as "his harem," or else "plates," a reference to the common Roosh V analogy of a juggler who keeps as many plates as possible spinning, never giving too much attention to any of them to become distracted and let one fall.

Every Rawmeo post ended with his lengthy signature, which summed up his lifestyle and extolled the paradoxical virtues of promiscuity for men and virginity for women: "Living in Thailand, enjoying life, making money, not interested in Western woman, not giving a fuck about millennial problems, addicted to rawdogging. #NoHymenNoDiamond #PoppedCherryDontMarry #RealMenDontDateSingleMoms."

Cazes, like many pickup artistry adherents, believed in a strict system of "sexual market value," or SMV, that could be calculated to determine a man's sexual fortunes. "The four pillars of SMV are Fame, Looks, Money, Game," he wrote. "I'd say fame is #1."

He described how he would explain to the Thai women he seduced that he was of a higher social class than them and they were lucky to have his attention, even briefly. "Once she started showing 'strong personality' I had to let her go," he wrote of one woman. In another post, he counseled his fellow alphas to seek out single mothers for easy sex, but never a longer-term relationship. "Not interested in being a cuckold before even having started the relationship, but for the bang, it can be good," he wrote. "Just let out a 'fatherly' vibe and you're in."

Cazes, like many Roosh V members, was obsessed with the threat of false rape allegations. He boasted of his solution, one that, for someone obsessed with privacy, was a shocking admission. "I secretly record EVERY new sex intercourse with a girl with a hidden camera in my room," he wrote. "This is stored on an encrypted hard drive, ready to be pulled in case the shit hits the fan. If nothing bad happens, nobody will ever know that the video exists. I respect my girls' privacy."

In other posts, Rawmeo explained that he was married and in fact loved his wife, who was pregnant with their first child. He described her as possessing "everything a wife needs to have: virgin, well preserved body, university degree, complete family, no LGBT in social circle, cooks for me, doesn't complain" (throwing in the sort of casual homophobia that was common on the forum). He said he kept tight control of her financially, storing most of his money in cryptocurrency, cashing out only what he needed, and never revealing his full net worth.

In some respects, Cazes was as privacy-minded as Rawmeo as he was as AlphaBay's boss. He had fully compartmentalized his life, sealing off his philandering from his family life almost as completely as he'd sealed off his Alpha02 persona from his real-world identity. "I am what we call a *professional cheater,*" he wrote. He kept his wife ignorant of the second home he used for sex. He used fake IDs to prevent his "plates" from learning his real name. He even used separate phone numbers for his different personas' communications and bragged that he spoofed the IMEI identifiers that a phone carrier can use to link two numbers on the same device, even when the SIM card has been swapped.

"I have a completely different identity with my plates," he wrote, "and there's no way that my two lives can be linked together."

. . .

Among the global group of agents now assigned to the AlphaBay case, no one spent more time with Rawmeo than Jen Sanchez of the Bangkok DEA office. She read and reread his every Roosh V message with morbid fascination, amazed by the lurid details of his sexual escapades, marveling at the hypocrisy of his commentary. "I strongly favor ethics rather than money," wrote the secret kingpin of a massive marketplace for hard drugs and cybercriminal wares, explaining his decision not to do web design work for "social justice warrior" customers or rent his real estate properties to LGBTQ couples for weddings. "It is important to follow our principles even if it implies a loss."

As a money-laundering-focused agent, Sanchez's central task in the AlphaBay case wasn't to catalog Cazes's affairs but to trace his financial assets, in Thailand and around the world. She did so with professional thoroughness, mapping out his four homes in Bangkok—the bachelor pad, his primary residence, another for his in-laws, and his mansion under renovation—as well as his $6 million five-bedroom seaside villa in Phuket, his two sports cars and motorcycle, and even the Mini Cooper he'd bought for his wife. Despite years tracking corrupt politicians and organized criminals, she was amazed by Cazes's casual extravagance. In one email, a complaint he'd sent to his favorite rooftop restaurant, Sirocco, about disappointing service, he mentioned in passing that he'd spent roughly $120,000 at the restaurant in just the previous two months.

At another point in their daily surveillance, Sanchez's supervisor Wilfredo Guzman and the Thai police watched Cazes enter a Mail Boxes Etc. store to ship a package of documents. The police intercepted it after he left and found inside an application for economic citizenship in Cyprus, one of several countries where he sought to cache his wealth and perhaps find a safe haven, should the Thai authorities get onto his trail. The documents provided a detailed accounting of Cazes's finances, helping Sanchez track down bank and cryptocurrency exchange accounts in not only Thailand but Liechtenstein and Switzerland, as well as millions of dollars in real estate investments in Cyprus. Later, she'd find yet another property in the Caribbean island nation of Antigua and Barbuda.

But as she carried out that financial tracing, Sanchez found herself becoming more and more obsessed with Cazes's Roosh V persona and the view into his personal life it offered. She discovered, just as tellingly, that his posts as Rawmeo revealed exactly *when* Cazes was online. A small gray figurine on Roosh V users' profiles, next to their usernames, would turn green if they were active on the site. When she saw that figure light up next to Rawmeo's name, she knew she was watching Cazes in real time, practically looking over his shoulder, into a part of his life he still believed to be secret.

In some cases, Sanchez's online surveillance and the team of agents physically watching Cazes could now match up his real-world behavior with his online confessional. Guzman and the Thai police, following Cazes and tracking his cell phone location, would see Cazes pick up a young woman from 7-Eleven, take her to his bachelor pad, and disappear inside. The next day, almost without fail, Sanchez would see Cazes describe in detail on Roosh V the sex he'd had with the woman. It was as if they now had eyes not only on Cazes's movements but into the private recesses of his mind.

Into *one* recess of his mind at least. Cazes was careful never to give any hint on Roosh V of his other secret life as AlphaBay's creator. But his writing on the forum nonetheless displayed, Sanchez came to believe, a deep psychological portrait. He wrote in one post, for instance, of his childhood and how his parents' separation had affected him. "My father was pretty alpha, but he was absent," Cazes wrote. "He tried hiring the best lawyers to fight for custody, but because of equality, i was able to see him 4 days per month. He got dumped by my mother when I was around 19 months old, because she found someone more exciting—who dumped her 1 year after."

Cazes complained that because he never had a chance to live with his father as a child, he'd been denied masculine experiences until the age of eighteen. He listed these essential male activities with bullet points. "Using a chainsaw, driving a motorcycle, go-kart racing, approaching girls, changing a tire. All this stuff had to be learned from scratch," he lamented.

To Sanchez, this was Alpha02's origin story. She read it, perhaps a bit reductively, as the autobiography of a man trying to overcompensate, blaming his mother for what he perceived as his lack of masculinity, seeking in his adult life to become the ultimate "alpha" male.

Another autobiographical document the investigators dug up seemed to capture Cazes's lifelong feeling of being an outsider, smarter than most everyone around him but struggling to find his place in society. Cazes had filed an official form with the government of Grenada, another country where he was seeking economic citizenship, in which he described his work history. It offered in abbreviated, blunt terms his life story, from skipping the second grade at his elementary school in Trois-Rivières— "due to being too 'advanced' in regards to the rest of the class"—to dropping out of college, to his attempts to find a normal job.

He wrote that he had worked, for instance, at McDonald's part time for a few months during his first year of college but was fired "for not fitting in the gang." He was fired from another Quebecois chain restaurant the next year for, he noted, "excessively eating on the job." Cazes found another job at an insurance company for a few months, but left "because the pay was too low and the work hours too long." He wrote that he was fired from yet another job at a Canadian telecom firm for, again, "not fitting in the gang." And yet another summer job between college semesters lasted only a month because "one of the shareholders hated me for having got the job without a diploma," he wrote, "and I got fired when they found out that I was seeing his wife."

. . .

Sorting through the detritus of Cazes's private life could seem almost voyeuristic at times, Sanchez admits. But it wasn't merely a distraction. Occasionally, amid all his prurient and sordid posts, the investigators would find a gem of precious information for their case.

One such morsel appeared in a thread on Roosh V in which members of the forum were debating Windows versus Mac operating systems. Cazes, a talented programmer and IT administrator who would never miss an opportunity to one-up his fellow alphas, chimed in to describe his personal computer setup: He ran Linux, the "Cadillac" of operating systems, he said. What's more, he described how he used LUKS encryption, or Linux Unified Key Setup, a free encryption tool specific to Linux that would securely scramble his laptop's entire hard disk whenever he so much as closed the lid of his machine. Without his passphrase, not even the world's most powerful supercomputers would be able to crack that encryption within many human lifetimes.

For the team of investigators now close on Cazes's heels, this had enormous implications: As the Silk Road investigation had taught them, there were three central components to a truly successful dark web bust. To have dead-to-rights evidence of their target's guilt, they would need to seize AlphaBay's servers, arrest its administrator, and access the admin's laptop.

Now, when they came for that laptop's secrets, they knew exactly what to expect. Just as the FBI had snatched Ross Ulbricht's laptop from across the table where he was working in a public space, they understood they'd need to seize Cazes's computer while he was using it, if they wanted to capture it in an unencrypted state.

This presented a daunting challenge: Based on their physical surveillance of Cazes, he never seemed to log in to AlphaBay from anywhere other than his home. He had learned, it seemed, the lesson of the Glen Park Public Library.

The team was six months into the AlphaBay investigation, and they had Alpha02 in their sights, practically within their grasp. But if they couldn't also lay hands on his laptop in a live, open state, his most incriminating secrets would remain eternally locked inside it.

Hansa

By May 2017, a core team of AlphaBay investigators—including Rabenn, Hemesath, Miller, and the prosecutor Louisa Marion from the DOJ's computer crimes unit—convened at the U.S. attorney's office in Sacramento to review the mountain of evidence they'd accumulated. The question of the day: Were they ready to indict Alexandre Cazes?

For about an hour of the meeting, as the agents and prosecutors talked over piles of bank documents, crypto exchange records, and social media clues, Paul Hemesath remained bent over his laptop, silently typing. Some around the conference table wondered whether the Sacramento prosecutor, who had a reputation for professorial eccentricity, was rudely doing other work or answering emails in the midst of their meeting.

Then Hemesath suddenly broke in to show what he'd assembled: He connected his laptop to a large monitor on the wall and displayed a graphic to the room. It showed a flowchart, a tangle of nodes and lines that he'd illustrated. Each node represented a piece of evidence, with the different lines between representing blockchain connections from Chainalysis's Reactor software, traditional payments they'd tracked, usernames and email addresses they'd linked to their target. On the left was the name Alexandre Cazes—the real-world person. On the right was Alpha02. Some lines meandered through multiple nodes, but every line began with Cazes, branched out into the mess of his online life, and then converged on his dark web persona.

It was no smoking gun. For that, they'd still need to catch Cazes with his hands on the keyboard. But looking at the chart, summing up the totality of Cazes's opsec failures and the indelible tracks he'd left across the blockchain, the group agreed. He was no patsy; these were no coincidences. They had found Alpha02, and they were ready to charge him.

. . .

Around the same time that spring, more than five thousand miles to the east, in a long, four-story black office building flanked by forest and highway in the leafy central Netherlands town of Driebergen, a secret had begun to spread among the Dutch National Police: The Americans were close to achieving a takedown of AlphaBay.

When the U.S. team had been tipped off to AlphaBay's Netherlands IP address, the FBI had discreetly alerted the Dutch that the bureau might soon need their cooperation to surveil and eventually seize a major black-market server hosted in their country.

The news that the United States was seeking to bust the world's largest dark web market soon reached one group of Dutch agents for whom this represented an intriguing coincidence. They were already deep in pursuit of a site that was quickly growing into the world's *second*-largest dark web market. And they began to wonder if there might be an opportunity to make this confluence of events work in their favor.

Since the fall of 2016, a newly formed team of dark-web-focused investigators based at the Dutch National Police's Driebergen office had been hunting a dark web drug market called Hansa. While far smaller than AlphaBay, Hansa had thousands of its own vendors and tens of thousands of listings for every narcotic imaginable. The Dutch investigation into Hansa had started with a tip from a security firm called Bitdefender, sent to the European police cooperation agency Europol. The company had found what appeared to be a Hansa server, also in a Dutch data center. Though the main server actively running Hansa's market was protected by Tor and couldn't yet be found, this one appeared to be an older machine that the administrators had left vulnerable (Bitdefender has never revealed how it spotted the server's unprotected IP address).

When the Dutch set up a wiretap on that computer, they found that the administrators had connected to it from yet another Dutch server, along with a couple of others in Germany, adding up to four servers in total. They quickly made a plan with the help of the German federal police to seize all four machines. The Dutch investigators intended to strike what they called a *korte klap,* or "short blow": By grabbing those computers, they hoped to quickly take down the site with the minimal amount of investigative resources and, if they were lucky, to obtain enough data to identify and arrest the administrators.

When the Dutch police got their hands on the German servers and saw what they contained, however, they realized their "short blow" might have been a missed opportunity. On those machines, the Dutch found an utter bonanza of Hansa's sensitive data. It included the source code of the market, a collection of usernames and passwords, the database of all the market's transactions, and messages between users, mostly encrypted—even the two administrators' PGP private keys, allowing them to both decrypt messages the admins received and verify their identities on messages they sent.

The seized Hansa database listed only the pseudonyms of the site's users, and each of those users' connection to the site had been anonymized by Tor. It was hardly a simple Rolodex of customers' identities. But the data also included another prize: a massive chat log between Hansa's two administrators, one who went by the names HL and RonSwanson. This was a treasure trove of seventeen thousand messages. In some of those conversations, they'd even referenced each other's full legal names. One had revealed his home address. Some quick social media searches shed more light on their lives: One was a thirty-year-old based in the German city of Siegen, the other a thirty-one-year-old in Cologne.

On a fall day in 2016, not long after the servers were seized, two Dutch investigators pored over that bounty of data at a desk on the second floor of the Driebergen police building. One investigator, Nils Andersen-Röed, was an agent on the Dutch National Police's newly formed dark web team; the other—who asked to go unnamed—was a technical adviser to the Dutch prosecutor. Both sat entranced by the highly sensitive information unspooling on the screen before them. They wondered aloud how they could capitalize on this rare windfall.

Andersen-Röed, thinking of the two administrators' PGP keys, made a comment that he intended as a joke: With those two keys, he pointed out, they could go onto dark web forums and impersonate the two German admins, writing messages and "signing" them as the founders of Hansa market. They could essentially *become* the administrators.

As the two men batted around that impersonation idea, their conversation turned more serious. They'd both seen dark web markets rise and fall over the past half decade, ad nauseam: When law enforcement busted one—or when its administrators ran off with their users' money—a new one would simply emerge to replace it, an endless game of whack-a-mole.

"We should be able to do something more with this than just take the marketplace down and go on to the next one," one man said to the other. "We're in a unique situation; we should do something different."

Soon, the notion of becoming Hansa's bosses was no longer a joke. What if, instead of merely arresting the admins and seizing their site, they secretly commandeered the market? With one of the most active sites on the dark web under their control, there was no telling what powers they might gain to identify Hansa's users, including its most high-volume drug dealers.

If and when they did ultimately reveal their sting operation, the two Dutchmen daydreamed aloud, the psychological blow to the community would be insidious: No one would ever again be able to fully trust that a dark web administrator wasn't actually an undercover agent working on behalf of the feds.

. . .

Sharing their idea with the rest of their team at the Dutch National Police, and then the German federal police who had helped seize the servers, the two Dutch investigators learned of another lucky break: The Germans were already on the trail of the two suspected Hansa admins—not for the massive drug market they had created, but for a book piracy site they were running on the side.

Rather than presenting a conflict, the Dutch police realized they could play this to their advantage: When the Germans arrested the men for their book piracy site, the Dutch would have the perfect opportunity to stealthily slip into their places, running Hansa with minimal publicity or disruption. "We could use that arrest," says Gert Ras, the head of the Dutch National High Tech Crime Unit that was soon brought in to take charge of the operation. "We had to get rid of the real administrators to become the administrators ourselves."

Just as this bold plan began to come together, however, it faced a fundamental problem. Their initial "short blow" seizure of Hansa's Dutch and German servers had shown their hand. By the time the investigators had gotten to the market's core server, hosted in the Netherlands, the spooked admins had relocated it to an unknown data center, shuffling it back into Tor's vast deck of anonymized machines around the globe. "That was a setback," Ras said with grim understatement.

At that point, the Dutch cops might have simply cut their losses, given the Germans the go-ahead to arrest Hansa's administrators—after all, they knew their names and locations—and then charged them with running a massive drug market, for which they had ample evidence. Instead, remarkably, they decided to double down on their stealthy takeover plan. That meant they had to find not only the admins but the servers that had just disappeared from their radar, too.

They spent the next months patiently hunting those machines, looking for any clue that could help them reestablish the trail. It was only in April 2017, more than six months after their "short blow," that they got another lead. This time, it came from the blockchain.

Among the two administrators' thousands of messages to each other, logged on the seized German servers, were a handful in which they'd mentioned Bitcoin payments. When the Dutch police fed those addresses into Chainalysis's Reactor software, they could see that the transactions led to an account on BitPay, a payment processor designed to let users spend cryptocurrency on traditional goods and services. In this case, unlike for most dark web payments, there *was* a middleman to go after: The Dutch subpoenaed BitPay's Netherlands office and discovered that the admins had funneled bitcoins into the service in order to rent servers at a Lithuanian hosting provider.

So a team of Dutch investigators flew to the Lithuanian capital of Vilnius and explained their first-of-its-kind takeover plan to the local police. "They were literally flabbergasted," says Petra Haandrikman, a chief inspector for the Dutch police who had become team leader for their Hansa operation. "You want to do *what*?" she remembers them responding. But they agreed to cooperate. The Dutch detectives now had Hansa's infrastructure back in their sights.

It was around that time, just as their Hansa-hijacking scheme became a real possibility again, that the Dutch learned of the U.S. investigation into AlphaBay, the Americans homing in on an even bigger target. They discussed what this might mean for their own operation, which was now the better part of a year in the making.

Their takeover idea was already the most ambitious undercover operation to ever target the dark web drug world. But maybe, they thought, they could push their luck just a little further.

. . .

Early on a May morning, a delegation from the U.S. AlphaBay investigation team arrived at the airport in The Hague—a city on the Netherlands' North Sea coast, forty miles west of Driebergen. Jet-lagged and hungry after their red-eye flight, they stopped for breakfast at a Dutch-style pancake restaurant in an underground cellar.

Paul Hemesath, who could never sleep on airplanes, had used the time to assemble a list of potential names for their AlphaBay takedown operation. He recited his list to the group, which included Operation Blockbuster, Operation Block Party, Operation Chain of Fools—all references to their blockchain tracing evidence—Operation Siamese Dream, Operation Not-So-Darknet, and Operation Rawdogger. ("In retrospect," Hemesath admits, "some of these were just kind of unfortunate.") The sleep-deprived group rejected all of Hemesath's submissions and began brainstorming other ideas. Finally, they settled on a pun that combined an element of the name AlphaBay with the notion of the net they were tightening around it, along with an allusion to piercing the dark web's veil: Operation Bayonet.

A few hours later, the group arrived at Europol headquarters, a fortresslike building of blue-gray brick, complete with a moat in front of its entrance. They were set to present the progress they'd made on their newly christened investigation to an international group of law enforcement agencies. The team sat down in a vast conference room, with tables for each delegation arranged with placards and microphones like a kind of UN General Assembly of dark web snoops.

The meeting was a routine event, mostly designed to prevent the agencies from getting in each other's way. The Americans went first, presenting the latest developments on AlphaBay: They believed they had both AlphaBay's server and its administrator, Alexandre Cazes, within reach. They planned to indict Cazes under seal in a matter of days and were working with the Thai police to arrest him soon thereafter.

After a short coffee break, it was the Dutch delegation's turn to speak. The technical adviser to the Dutch prosecutor's office made a proposal, one he had received approval for just minutes earlier, after hurriedly telling prosecutors about the Americans' presentation. The Dutch police were ready, he explained, to arrest the administrators of Hansa with the help of the German federal police, take control of the market, and run it in secret.

They now could see just how close the Americans were to taking down AlphaBay. What if, the Dutch technical adviser suggested, they combined their operations?

All the Americans would need to do, he explained, was to wait for the Dutch takeover of Hansa before green-lighting their takedown of AlphaBay. Then, after they'd arrested Alpha02 and seized his servers, they would simply delay any official announcement of their victory. If all went according to plan, a massive throng of the dark web's users would flee from the seized market to the next-best option—a market under Dutch police control.

Then, only after the Dutch had a chance to spy on the internal workings of the dark web economy like never before—from the privileged position of its newly crowned kingpins—they would publicly announce their Hansa and AlphaBay operations simultaneously. Together, their sting operation would be what the Dutch technical adviser described as a "one-two" punch.

At the American table, eyes widened. Ali, the FBI analyst, remembers her exhilaration at the epic ambition of the plan. The prosecutor Louisa Marion's mind excitedly raced through the risks and rewards. Was this even legal? Was it ethical?

Paul Hemesath, still deeply jet-lagged, remembers being both impressed and wary of the complexity the Dutch were adding into their AlphaBay operation. There had been prior investigations in which law enforcement had secretly taken control of a dark web site. In 2014, for instance, the Australian Federal Police had run a site trafficking in child sexual abuse materials called the Love Zone for six months. Cases like the Love Zone were operational successes, but controversial ones. Journalists and legal scholars would later point out that in order to more deeply infiltrate the underground community they were targeting, law enforcement had essentially engaged in the same crime they were investigating.

Now the Dutch were suggesting doing something similar, but for the second-biggest online narcotics market in the world. There was no precedent for it.

"In terms of dark web drug market impersonation," Hemesath says, "this was the first monkey being shot into space."

Aside from the legal or ethical implications, he wondered if it wasn't a little "pie in the sky," as he put it. Coordinating among the agents across the United States was difficult enough. Now they were going to coordinate among the Dutch, the Germans, half a dozen U.S. agencies, and the Thais, too?

Still, the serendipity of these two investigations unfolding in tandem was uncanny. When would they have another opportunity to try something like this again?

"To time this and to count on it happening, who knows?" Hemesath thought. "But let's give it a shot."

Takeover

A few weeks later, in early June, a team of Thai police arrived at the Courtyard Marriott in Sacramento. Jen Sanchez's boss Wilfredo Guzman had assigned her to bring the delegation on a flight from Bangkok to California to coordinate with the U.S. team—to iron out any intercontinental wrinkles on the Bangkok end of what had come to be known as Operation Bayonet. She was quietly annoyed to be made a "babysitter," as she put it, for the Thai group, which had swelled in the days preceding the trip from just three specialists to eight officers, some of whom had never been on an airplane before, not to mention halfway around the world.

The Thai police met the American agents, analysts, and prosecutors at the U.S. attorney's office, with more than two dozen people arrayed around the room. The two countries traded off PowerPoint briefings. Ali and Erin, in town from D.C., walked the Thais through "Bitcoin 101" and their tracing of Cazes's crypto cash flows. The Thais shared everything they'd learned in following Cazes's physical movements for months. The police then explained the particulars of the Thai legal system—what U.S. agents would and wouldn't be allowed to do with Cazes after, if all went well, they laid hands on him.

Between meetings, Sanchez took the Thai group on field trips: to a golfing range, to a shopping mall—where the officers practically bought out the entire contents of a Coach outlet—and on an outing to San Francisco in rented vans. The Thais, accustomed to the tropics, nearly froze on Fisherman's Wharf; they were so exhausted that they slept through the drive over the Golden Gate Bridge in both directions. On another day, the FBI gave the Thais a tour of the bureau's Sacramento field office's explosives lab, impressing them with their bomb-defusing robots. Hemesath later brought out his HTC Vive VR headset, and the two countries' agents took turns walking a plank over a digital abyss and swinging virtual swords at zombies.

When they weren't busy with tourism and team-building exercises, the agents were grappling with the practical details of raiding a dark web kingpin. At one point, the case's lead FBI agent presented the looming problem of Cazes's laptop encryption. Sanchez and the Thais explained that based on their surveillance, Cazes almost never opened his machine outside his own home. The agents agreed: They'd have to catch him in his house, logged in to AlphaBay, and yet somehow off guard, so that he couldn't shut the laptop's lid before his arrest.

Almost as important as the computer was Cazes's iPhone. The FBI told the Thais they'd need to grab it unlocked, or it too would be irretrievably encrypted. That phone, after all, might hold keys to Cazes's cryptocurrency wallets or other crucial data. The question of how to thread the needle of capturing these two devices and their information hung in the air, unanswered.

Then Sanchez spoke: She asked the FBI agent if it would be helpful to know more about how Cazes spent his days, hour by hour. After all, she explained, he had laid it all out on Roosh V. The FBI agent invited her to go ahead.

So Sanchez walked the group through Cazes's daily schedule as he had, himself, described it in exacting detail: Wake up at dawn and check his email and social media, including the Roosh V forum. Work out at home until the late morning. Have sex with his wife. Then go to his laptop and take care of business until the evening, with only a short break in the afternoon for a light lunch. At seven, he'd quit work for the day to go out for dinner and cruise for girls in his Lamborghini. Almost without fail he'd be back home and asleep by eleven.

Then Sanchez offered another observation from her Roosh V trawling: She could see on the forum exactly when Cazes was online. The little green light next to Rawmeo's name wasn't merely a reminder that they were seeing into Cazes's thoughts in real time. It might also serve as an indicator of when his laptop was open—and when Alpha02 was vulnerable.

. . .

In the late morning of June 20, 2017, in Driebergen, half a dozen Dutch police were huddled around a conference room where they'd been anxiously waiting since early that day. Finally, one of the investigators' phones rang with a call from German federal police. The Germans had just arrested the two Hansa administrators in their homes. Both men were in custody. The first phase of Operation Bayonet's one-two punch could now begin.

For weeks, the Dutch National High Tech Crime Unit had been preparing for this moment. They'd used the source code for Hansa that they'd pulled from the German servers to reconstruct their own, off-line, practice version of the market, to familiarize themselves with how it was built and administered. They'd even gone so far as to create their own play-money version of Bitcoin, with its very own blockchain—what cryptocurrency developers call a "testnet"—to privately experiment with how the site handled its monetary transactions.

Now, with the real admins arrested, they had to take over and run the actual, live version of Hansa, with millions of dollars moving between tens of thousands of users. And they had to do it seamlessly, without knocking the site off-line or, worse, giving its users or staff any clue that the two administrators were, in fact, a team of undercover Dutch police impostors.

At the Germans' signal, the Dutch team immediately called a pair of agents they'd sent to a data center in Lithuania, where the server actively running Hansa was hosted. Those agents physically pulled out a hard drive from the rack that held the machine so they could access a backup copy of its data. The teams in Driebergen and Lithuania then began feverishly duplicating every digital component of the market, piece by piece, on their own computers and then on a server in a Netherlands data center, reconstructing an exact copy of the site that was now under their control.

For the next two days, the Dutch investigators sat at their keyboards from morning until well after midnight, fueled by pizza and Red Bull. At one point early on, someone spilled a soda onto the conference table, nearly soaking a laptop that stored the entire collection of the Hansa data; only a desperate lunge by one of the investigators managed to save it. At another point, a typo in a single command caused the site to go down for several panicky minutes before it could be restored.

Finally, around 3:00 a.m. on the third night after the arrests, a Dutch investigator, Marinus Boekelo, was troubleshooting a final problem in their reconstructed site, one that was causing error messages to cascade across the screen whenever someone used the search bar at the top of the page. "Fuck, fuck, fuck!" Boekelo muttered, bent over his laptop, his hands on either side of his face as he attempted one fix after another.

Then, after a moment, he leaned back with a look of relief. The error messages were gone. The last serious bug had been ironed out.

After nearly seventy-two hours, they had the site running smoothly and now fully under their own command. The skeleton crew still working in the conference room exploded in jubilation. Aside from the two or three minutes of downtime caused by a single brief hiccup, the migration of the site into a Dutch data center had been nearly invisible to its users.

The most conspicuous sign of the takeover, the Dutch police worried, was that for almost three days there had been complete radio silence from the two Hansa administrators. The takeover team needed to immediately reestablish communication with the site's staff of four moderators, all of whom looked to the two admins for orders and to resolve any disputes between buyers and dealers that they couldn't handle themselves. The police could see that the admins communicated with Hansa's staff using an encrypted messaging system called Tox Chat—the server they'd seized contained some limited records of their past communications—but they didn't have the password to log in to their chat accounts.

So they tried a simple solution: They asked the real admins for help. The two German men quickly agreed to cooperate in hopes of a lighter sentence. They handed over their Tox Chat passwords to the German police, who passed them on to the Dutch. The team in Driebergen then resumed day-to-day chatter between the bustling black market's bosses and staff. With the cooperation of the real admins and their Tox Chat logs, they were able to pick up the business of the site without a hitch. Their only initial error was paying one moderator the incorrect amount for his Bitcoin salary, pegged to the wrong non-digital currency. The undercover police fixed their mistake, paid the staffer the difference, and all was forgiven.

The Dutch team had come up with a cover story for the admins' three days off-line: They would tell anyone who asked that they were heads down coding an upgrade to the market. But in fact, no one asked. The hierarchy of the marketplace's org chart and the secrecy of dark web operations, where no one on staff knew their co-workers beyond a username and a shared chat history, meant the cops-in-admin-clothing were spared all curious questions about their absence.

Nor did there seem to be any inside jokes or watercooler gossip to catch up on, they were relieved to discover. "It actually turned out that they did not discuss anything personal with each other," one investigator remembers. "It was pure business."

The cover story about an upgrade wasn't exactly a lie, anyway. In reconstructing the site, the Dutch police had actually ironed out some of its bugs and rewritten parts of its code to be more efficient. And because they now had a team of half a dozen rotating agents acting as the administrators, instead of two overworked men, they found that the site's customers considered the day-to-day operations of the market to be significantly improved.

One of the younger Dutch agents had been an IT help-desk admin years earlier. He found his new job helping to run Hansa to be remarkably similar. He got to work efficiently resolving disputes over the site's drug deals, assisted by a collection of pre-written answers the administrators had helpfully prepared in an online control panel. The undercover agent even came to the rescue of one grateful, sight-impaired drug dealer, helping him figure out how to get his screen reader software properly integrated with his Tor Browser.

Ethical quandaries aside, the team couldn't help but take a certain pride in the professionalism of their work. "The quality really went up," said the head of the Dutch National High Tech Crime Unit, Gert Ras. "Everyone was very satisfied with the level of service they got."

. . .

For their first day acting as Hansa's bosses, the team had cautiously watched the site's internal clockwork, almost in disbelief that they'd gotten away with their takeover undetected. But when it was clear they could control Hansa seemingly indefinitely, they settled in, working in shifts to run the site from the small conference room in Driebergen they'd turned into a kind of twenty-four-hour war room.

On one wall, they set up a sixty-five-inch screen where someone started a stopwatch, measuring exactly how long they'd been in control of the market. Then slowly, silently, they began to spring the trap they'd assembled.

Hansa, like any good dark web drug market, had been designed to learn as little as possible about its users beyond what was necessary to facilitate reliable drug transactions. The passwords for users' accounts were stored only as cryptographic "hashes," indecipherable strings of characters that let the site avoid having to protect a collection of those sensitive log-in credentials. Hansa also offered to let users automatically encrypt all their messages using PGP—including, most important, the mailing addresses that buyers would share with sellers when they made an order. All of that meant that, in theory, the site itself would never have full access to its users' accounts or know their most personal secrets, such as the locations of their homes.

Now the police began to invisibly sabotage those safeguards. They started recording all of Hansa's usernames and passwords when buyers and sellers logged in. They also began secretly archiving the full text of every message users sent on the site before the text was encrypted. Soon they were collecting hundreds, then thousands of buyers' addresses from orders, turning the business of the entire market into a glass aquarium under their real-time surveillance.

According to Dutch law, the police had to record and attempt to intercept every drug order made on the market while they controlled it. So the half dozen undercover agents working in their small conference room were soon joined by dozens of others, working on the same floor, who were tasked with manually cataloging every single purchase. They forwarded the data for sales destined for the Netherlands to Dutch police, who could seize the packages of heroin, cocaine, and meth shipped through domestic mail. Non-Dutch orders would be sent to Europol, which was charged with distributing the ever-growing pile of drug deal data to their respective nations' law enforcement agencies.

Already, the Dutch police had accomplished something that law enforcement had never attempted before: hunting, capturing, and vivisecting a dark web drug market in real time, unbeknownst to the site's users. But Operation Bayonet was only getting started. The Dutch—and their collaborators from Sacramento to Bangkok—still had other, bigger game in their crosshairs.

CHAPTER 32

"Advanced Analysis"

On June 22, 2017, two days after the Hansa takeover and less than two weeks before the date of the planned AlphaBay takedown, Tigran Gambaryan and the Chainalysis co-founders Michael Gronager and Jonathan Levin happened to be in the Netherlands, too. They had flown to The Hague, halfway across the small country from the Driebergen office where the Dutch were pulling Hansa's puppet strings, for a Europol conference focused on virtual currency investigations.

By this time, all the interlocking pieces of Operation Bayonet were falling into place. The Dutch Hansa takeover was under way. A team of Americans targeting AlphaBay planned to set up surveillance of that market's Dutch servers early on July 5, taking a snapshot of its contents while Cazes was logged in to it. They would pull it off-line only after the Thais arrested Cazes in Bangkok; touching it any sooner might spook him and cause him to destroy evidence or flee. U.S. prosecutors would then interrogate Cazes and swiftly extradite him. Even the Royal Canadian Mounted Police, the RCMP, had been roped in to simultaneously search Cazes's mother's home in Quebec.

As this international whirlwind of detective work picked up speed, Gambaryan remained on its periphery. He'd learned about the AlphaBay case early on from a friendly IRS criminal investigator in Fresno, the hometown he still returned to when visiting his parents. He'd followed the investigation's progress. But he'd never been assigned to the case.

Still, he couldn't help but take an occasional, curious poke at the biggest dark web market in history. For months, Gambaryan had followed AlphaBay's tracks through the blockchain, obsessively pestering Levin—

who had largely taken over Chainalysis's day-to-day relationship with the IRS from Gronager—with new ideas about how to circumscribe the edges of the AlphaBay wallet or trace its most incriminating money trails. He was, as Levin put it, "completely relentless."

That spring, Gambaryan and Levin had together come up with an idea—a new, experimental method to examine AlphaBay's use of cryptocurrency. Prosecutors in the AlphaBay case have referred to it using only the hideously vague term "advanced analysis." But Gambaryan and Levin hoped they could use it to unearth a major finding: the IP address of the server that hosted AlphaBay's Bitcoin wallet.

By all conventional wisdom, that data point shouldn't have been possible to learn through blockchain surveillance. The blockchain, after all, is a ledger of transactions between Bitcoin addresses. It doesn't record IP addresses. Since Chainalysis's early, controversial attempt to set up nodes to monitor for those IP identifiers years earlier, Bitcoin's protocol had been updated to make intercepting IP addresses from transaction messages far more difficult.

By the spring of 2017, of course, the AlphaBay investigators believed they already knew an AlphaBay IP address; the one in the Netherlands that had been leaked in the welcome email passed on by Miller's tipster. But Gambaryan figured it couldn't hurt to independently verify this critical piece of evidence. For his part, Levin had been doing his own hands-on research into AlphaBay for years, and he was eager to try out a new investigative technique that, if it worked, Chainalysis could potentially sell to other customers.

So, on that June morning in The Hague, Levin sat at a desk in an apartment in the coastal city's quiet western periphery, a few blocks from the beach, next to a fishing harbor that fed into the wind-churned North Sea. Levin and Gronager had rented the Airbnb and were sharing it—more out of habit than financial necessity, given their funding and swelling cash flow—with one staying in the bedroom and the other on the couch.

Levin and Gronager were both up early, before the conference began. So Levin used this spare moment to check the results of his and Gambaryan's "advanced analysis" experiment. Neither Levin nor Gambaryan has revealed a word of how their method works. (In fact, in our conversations, they never treated any piece of cryptocurrency-tracing tradecraft with more secrecy.)

Nonetheless, there the answer appeared, without fanfare, on Levin's screen: an AlphaBay IP address. Or rather, a handful of IP addresses that were likely to belong to the site's wallet server, with one especially likely candidate. A quick search revealed that the most salient IP wasn't, in fact, in the Netherlands. It was in a data center in Lithuania.

Levin remembers his reaction in the moment as less of an epiphany than a brief flash of recognition. "Huh," he thought to himself. AlphaBay seemed to be hosted in a data center in the Baltics. He made a mental note to tell Gambaryan about the Lithuanian IP the next time he saw him.

He felt no particular sense of urgency about the finding. As a contractor with no security clearance, he didn't have privileged access to the secrets of the AlphaBay investigation. He had no clue that the coordinated global takedown of AlphaBay was planned for just over ten days later and that it was targeting a server in the wrong country.

Levin's next meeting with Gambaryan happened to arrive that evening. After a day spent at the Europol conference, he sat down beside Gambaryan at dinner. A dozen agents, analysts, prosecutors, and contractors had gathered at a long table at Flavor's, a ribs-and-steak restaurant a few blocks from Europol headquarters, its walls covered in paintings of a medieval feast. They had just ordered drinks when Levin thought to mention to Gambaryan that their experimental idea had apparently worked. He showed Gambaryan the three IP addresses on his phone, pointing out the Lithuanian one that seemed most likely.

The IRS agent went silent. He pulled out his own phone and took a picture of the IP addresses on Levin's screen. Then he stood up, blank-faced, and quickly walked out of the restaurant without explanation.

Levin watched him go, dumbfounded. Gambaryan hadn't even paid for his beer.

· · ·

Gambaryan ran the eight blocks through the streets of the residential neighborhood, past The Hague's art museum, to the Marriott next to Europol headquarters, where he and most of the other international agents at the conference were staying. He went directly to the building's top floor, overlooking the darkened forest of Park Sorghvliet, ringed by international government buildings. At a table in an empty conference room, he opened his laptop, confirmed that the IP address Levin had found was indeed in a Lithuanian data center, and then began calling prosecutors—Grant Rabenn and Paul Hemesath from California, as well as Alden Pelker, the D.C.-based cybercrime attorney on the case, and Erin, the FBI bitcoin-tracing analyst who was there in The Hague attending the Europol conference—to tell them that he and Chainalysis had found what appeared to be the true location of AlphaBay's central server, and it wasn't in the Netherlands but instead a thousand miles to the east.

Soon Erin joined Gambaryan in the hotel conference room, with Hemesath and Rabenn on speakerphone from California, where it was still early in the day. Levin arrived not long after, then Gronager, who'd been attending a different business dinner. For the rest of the night, until the early hours of the morning, the group worked frantically to sort out the logistics of seizing AlphaBay's infrastructure not from the Netherlands, as they'd intended, but from Lithuania, with their July 5 deadline just days away. At one point, a Dutch hotel worker came into the lounge to try to tell the group the room was closed. Gambaryan, who technically wasn't even a part of the AlphaBay operation, flashed his badge at the man instinctively—a badge that had no actual authority outside the United States—and the startled Dutchman retreated, leaving them to their work.

Ultimately, Gambaryan and Chainalysis's "advanced analysis" spared Operation Bayonet, at nearly the last minute, from what could have been an embarrassing error. The investigators would later learn that the Netherlands IP address they'd been focused on for months pointed to a data center that held only an older server for the site, rather than the holy grail they were looking for. Just like Hansa, AlphaBay had apparently moved at some point from a Dutch hosting provider to Lithuania. Without the Lithuanian IP address, passed from Levin's phone to Gambaryan's in a steak restaurant, the investigators would have been raiding the equivalent of an abandoned hideout, leaving AlphaBay's actual criminal headquarters untouched.

The mechanics of that Hail Mary "advanced analysis" technique remain a blank spot in the story of Operation Bayonet—a black box with mysterious internal workings, one that investigators refuse to open. That's because, as Gambaryan and other officials would later explain, they would continue to use this technique for years to come, identifying the IP addresses of dark web services' Bitcoin wallets again and again. Law enforcement agencies wanted to make sure it kept working as long as possible—that dark web administrators, Bitcoin developers, or whoever might have the ability to fix the vulnerabilities they exploited didn't wise up to their trick.

"We're using this to go after the real bad guys out there, and it's something that I wouldn't want to burn," Gambaryan later confided, using the law enforcement and intelligence term "burn" to mean expose—and thus render useless—a secret technique. "I know if it does get out, it could potentially compromise what we do."

For anyone who followed the early days of Chainalysis, though, it would be hard not to take one particular educated guess at how the company's "advanced analysis" worked. After all, just months after the company's founding, the start-up had caused a brief, very public blowup in the Bitcoin community with a technique capable of identifying Bitcoin users' IP addresses—exactly as their secret technique would years later.

Gronager and Møller had created a collection of their own Bitcoin node servers, capitalizing on the way Bitcoin users broadcast their IP addresses in transaction messages, with the purpose of creating a global map of Bitcoin users' geolocations. Could that technique somehow also have been updated and adapted to target—and locate—the Bitcoin wallets of very specific users? Even when the transactions were sent from a computer running on Tor's anonymity network?

For Operation Bayonet, all that mattered was that Gambaryan and Levin had course corrected a massive, coordinated, international investigation at a critical moment, deploying a new, secret weapon with hardly a day to spare. But secret weapons don't tend to stay secret forever.

CHAPTER 33

The Athenee

In the last days of June, the Americans descended upon Bangkok like a tropical law enforcement convention. They included nearly twenty agents, analysts, computer forensics experts, and prosecutors from the FBI, DEA, DOJ, IRS, Canada's RCMP, and even two DHS agents from the parallel Baltimore AlphaBay investigation. Mirroring the path of the Silk Road saga, the Sacramento team had ended up light-years ahead of the Baltimore agents who were hunting Alpha02 by infiltrating the site. But in a peacemaking gesture, over Grant Rabenn's objections, the Sacramento-based coalition had ultimately invited the competing Baltimore group to bury the hatchet and join their takedown.

More than a dozen members of the group checked in at the Athenee, a five-star luxury hotel a few blocks from the U.S. embassy, which advertised that it was built on grounds once owned by a nineteenth-century Siamese princess, featuring eight restaurants and a rooftop complete with a garden and swimming pool. It was, Rabenn noted, certainly the nicest hotel he'd ever managed to book on the government's per diem.

With just days until their planned bust, Rabenn, Hemesath, and the D.C. prosecutor Marion remained swamped with the bureaucracy of coordinating law enforcement agencies in five countries—the United States, Thailand, Canada, the Netherlands, and now Lithuania, where they had a fresh plan to seize the central AlphaBay server. The team also met repeatedly with the Thais at the headquarters of their Narcotics Suppression Bureau across town, gathering in a conference room on the building's eighth floor to talk through the details of Cazes's arrest.

The central problem remained unsolved: how to distract Cazes and lure him out of his house with his phone unlocked and his laptop open and unencrypted. Set fire to a dumpster outside the house? Too dangerous, they decided. Have a female undercover agent begin screaming and crying outside his house? Cazes might simply ignore her, or else close the laptop before checking out the noise.

What if they dressed an undercover agent as a postal worker who knocks on the door and asks Cazes to come sign for a package? That, they concluded, might work.

Amid all this frantic eleventh-hour planning, a core group still managed to cap off each day at the Athenee's lounge for its all-you-can-eat sushi happy hours. It was during one of those evening gatherings that something surprising appeared in the group chat the Thai police had set up on a messaging app called Line, popular in Thailand. The Thais used the group chat to post constant updates to one another and to the DEA on their physical surveillance of Cazes. That day, Colonel Pisal and his team had been following their target on an early evening outing, tracking him in his Porsche Panamera as he approached central Bangkok. Jen Sanchez, who lived near both the Athenee and her workplace at the U.S. embassy building down the street, had just returned home when she saw a photo, taken by one of the Thai officers, pop up. It showed a white Porsche, parked at a swanky-looking hotel entrance.

"What the fuck?" she thought, with a sudden rush of adrenaline: Wasn't that the Athenee, where much of the U.S. team was staying?

At that same moment, in the Athenee lounge, Rabenn remembers seeing the same Porsche out of the corner of his peripheral vision and instantly remembering that a white Panamera was one of Cazes's stable of pricey vehicles. He pointed it out to Hemesath, as well as the DEA's Miller and an FBI agent, all of them sitting together at a table in the lobby. They half jokingly suggested the FBI agent go check it out.

The agent gamely strolled across the lounge as a figure walked through the front door of the Athenee that threw Rabenn's mind into a spasm of shock.

It was him. Alexandre Cazes. And he was walking directly toward Rabenn, Miller, and Hemesath's table.

Rabenn froze. "It was like seeing a ghost," he remembers. He glanced over at Hemesath, who seemed equally paralyzed, in disbelief.

The image in Rabenn's mind during that first in-person encounter with Cazes, after nine months of obsessively tracking Alpha02, remains burned into his memory. Cazes was dressed, Rabenn remembers, in a slim, expensive-looking blue suit, his white shirt unbuttoned underneath in the style of someone too rich to wear a tie. Yet Rabenn also observed that Cazes moved with a certain nerdy awkwardness, that he seemed soft and pale under his costume—that he looked "more like a pudgy programmer pretending to be a rock star than an actual rock star," Rabenn said.

The FBI agent, thinking quickly, avoided eye contact with Cazes and walked directly past him to the door. In the short seconds it took for Cazes to cross the room, seemingly in slow motion, thoughts raced through Rabenn's mind: How did Cazes know who they were? Or that they were on his trail? Or which hotel they were staying at in Bangkok? Had there been a leak? Had they been meeting too conspicuously, blowing their opsec? Had this criminal mastermind ultimately outsmarted them?

In mere moments, Rabenn expected Cazes to sit down next to them at their table, smug expression on his face, and say, as he imagined it, "Fuck you guys, I know you're here, and you're not going to get anything."

Rabenn realized he had no idea how he would respond. They could arrest Cazes on the spot, but they'd lose all hope of getting access to his laptop, or any smoking-gun evidence of his control of AlphaBay. Just as they were on the cusp of victory, it seemed, their plan had failed.

"Oh, shit," Rabenn silently concluded, in a state of blank panic. "This thing's over."

Then, when Cazes was about five feet away from their table, he turned and sat down at the table next to them, across from a pair of Israeli businessmen wearing suits and yarmulkes.

The Americans looked at each other in confusion. After a moment, the FBI agent returned and sat down casually. He and Miller began to silently signal to the rest of the table that everyone else should leave.

Rabenn, recovering his composure, allowed the thought to cross his mind for the first time that, perhaps, all was not lost—that this was simply the most stunning coincidence of his life.

Doing their best to act natural, the prosecutors cleared out and walked up the curved staircase to the mezzanine floor of the hotel, while the FBI agent and Miller hung back to eavesdrop on Cazes's conversation at the neighboring table. On the floor above, Rabenn and Hemesath shared a moment of wide-eyed relief. Text messages from the FBI and DEA agents still at the table began to roll in, reporting on Cazes's meeting: He was talking with the Israelis about one of his real estate investment deals in the Caribbean.

The two prosecutors could hardly believe it. The man they had come to Bangkok to arrest had, entirely by chance, arrived at a meeting at the exact hotel where they were staying and sat down at the table next to them. He still had no idea they were on his trail.

As their panic subsided, they now saw that a group of Thai undercover police, including Colonel Pisal himself in plain clothes, had stationed themselves around another table across the hotel lounge from Cazes and were discreetly watching him, even stealthily taking photos of each other that captured Cazes in the background. The AlphaBay founder gave no sign of having spotted them.

As Rabenn and Hemesath silently rejoiced, the FBI agent joined them on the mezzanine floor and pulled out his phone. He started googling, trying to calculate the odds of what had just happened. How many hotels were there in Bangkok, anyway? He quickly showed them the answer: more than ten thousand.

Takedown

On a typical day, the Private House Buddhamonthon development on the western edge of Bangkok offers a quiet respite from the traffic jams and diesel fumes of the city's central neighborhoods. The cul-de-sac where Alexandre Cazes lived in that semi-suburban enclave was dotted with yellow trumpetbush blossoms, its idyll accompanied only by the sounds of palm fronds and banana trees rustling in the breeze and the chatter of tropical birds. But on the morning of July 5, that street would have seemed unusually busy to anyone paying attention.

At one end, a gardener worked trimming the foliage, and an electrician was busy with a nearby wiring box. Inside the house at the street's dead end, a model home and sales office for Private House's real estate developer firm, a man and woman were getting a tour of the property and inquiring about moving into the neighborhood. Their driver sat waiting in a car outside. Another car with two women in it was slowly pulling in to the cul-de-sac, looking lost after taking an apparent wrong turn.

In fact, every one of the characters in this bustling scene was an undercover agent. Pisal's NSB team had assembled an entire theatrical production's worth of actors around their unwitting target, busily performing their roles and waiting for a signal for Operation Bayonet's takedown to finally begin.

The only non-Thai player in this pantomime was the DEA's Guzman. He stood inside the real estate spec house at the end of the cul-de-sac wearing a Red Hot Chili Peppers T-shirt and jeans, posing as a wealthy foreign buyer with a Thai wife. Guzman's primary job that morning was to distract the polite real estate agent, straining the limits of his Thai vocabulary to bombard her with questions about the layout of the spec house, the number of bedrooms, the size of the garage, and every other domestic detail that he could think of. All of this was designed only to allow the agent playing his wife to venture to an upstairs window and get eyes on Cazes's house and driveway next door, in anticipation of the action set to unfold there.

Another group of NSB officers, along with the DEA's Miller and a group of FBI agents and analysts, were still at Pisal's own home, where the entire team had gathered that morning; the colonel happened to live a few miles away from Cazes's residence. Pisal himself and a group of uniformed officers had now parked several blocks from Cazes's house. Nearly an hour's drive to the northeast, on the eighth floor of NSB headquarters, yet another group, including Rabenn, Hemesath, Marion, and Sanchez, were assembled in a conference room, with portraits of the Thai royal family on one wall and a collection of screens mounted on another.

The war-room monitors showed video feeds of the cul-de-sac, pulled from a nearby security camera and the dashcam of the car where Guzman's "driver" was waiting. At the center of the long table was a conference phone connected to both the Thai team on the ground and another team of agents in Lithuania, tasked with imaging the AlphaBay server—taking a snapshot of its contents and then, after Cazes's arrest, pulling it off-line.

Rabenn remembers the atmosphere of that war room as dead silence and sweaty, anxious tension, far more than eagerness or anticipation. For his own part, he knew that the possibility of achieving an actual Ross Ulbricht–style arrest and seizing Cazes's laptop in a live, logged-in state—not to mention his phone—was a long shot at best. Even after all their international meetings and coordination calls over the past months, and in spite of his usual hard-driving enthusiasm, Rabenn found himself quietly expecting their plan to fail.

Across the table, Sanchez was logged in to Roosh V. She checked Rawmeo's profile and confirmed to the group that he was online and active: Cazes was at his keyboard. It was time.

Then, almost immediately, they hit a snag. "Oh God," a voice said over the conference phone. "We shut it down."

It was the team in Lithuania. Somehow, the agents there had accidentally crashed the AlphaBay server before they could finish imaging it. In a matter of moments, Cazes would be tipped off that AlphaBay was down, possibly due to foul play. All he would need to do was close his laptop and the game would be over.

Now there was no choice: The team in the conference room frantically told the agents on the ground that they needed to arrest Cazes and do it *now*.

Pisal gave a cue via police radio to the two female agents in the gray Toyota Camry at the mouth of the cul-de-sac. Just the day before, the NSB colonel and his team had scrapped the postal delivery plan. The local post office had warned them that Cazes never signed for packages himself, that his wife often came to the door instead. So they'd had to think up a last-minute alternative. Their Plan B now centered on that inconspicuous Toyota.

The driver of the car, a slight, forty-six-year-old agent with a short, boyish haircut who went by the nickname Nueng, felt her heart pounding in her chest. She knew that the entire global operation to capture Cazes now hinged on what she did in the next few moments.

Nueng slowly rolled the car to the end of the cul-de-sac, trying to give the impression of a nervous driver. She signaled through the windshield to a security guard outside the model home—one of the few people present who was *not* an undercover agent—that she was going to turn around, and she heard him shout at her to instead back directly out, that the street was too narrow for a three-point turn.

Nueng quickly muttered a nearly silent traditional Buddhist prayer, an adapted, high-speed plea to the holy trinity of the Buddha, his teachings, and all the monks and nuns in his service. "Dear Buddha, please bless me with success," she whispered. "Dear Dhamma, please bless me with success. Dear Sangha, please bless me with success."

Then she put the car in reverse, turned the wheel to the left, and ever so gently—almost in slow motion—slammed the Toyota's fender into Cazes's front gate.

A loud *clang* rang out across the cul-de-sac, followed by a grinding of metal on concrete as the gate was bent and then dragged off its rails.

The security guard at the end of the cul-de-sac began shouting in exasperation at Nueng. Hadn't he *just* told her to back straight out?

Nueng and the other agent in her car stepped out of the vehicle, and

Nueng stood on the street, scratching her head in a display of hapless-ness, apologizing and explaining to the security guard that she was still learning to drive. At that moment, a vertical shutter opened partially on a second-floor window on the front of the house—a detail, visible on the surveillance video feed, that sent a wave of excitement through the war room at NSB headquarters.

They had gotten the layout of the home on an earlier trip to the spec house, and they knew that this was the master bedroom. Had Cazes stepped away from his computer?

A moment later, Cazes's wife, Sunisa Thapsuwan, came out from the house's front door and poked her head around the bent gate. The petite Thai woman, wearing a long nightshirt over her pregnant belly, kindly reassured Nueng that it was fine, that she and her friend could leave. But Nueng, doggedly playing her part, shouted—as loudly as possible, trying to project so that Cazes could hear inside the house—that she needed to pay for the damage.

"I want to pay for it!" she pleaded. "I don't want to pay for it in the next life!" Her hands shook as she channeled her adrenaline into the anxiety of a poor person who owes something to a rich person.

Thapsuwan looked up to the open window, and Nueng heard Cazes say something to his wife that she couldn't pick up. "Maybe your hus-band could come down here to assess the damage?" Nueng suggested helpfully.

A moment later, Cazes emerged. He was shirtless and barefoot, look-ing pale and soft, wearing nothing but a pair of baggy gym shorts; he had bragged on Roosh V that he liked to go "commando" when working out in the morning, and apparently hadn't changed since beginning work that day. He had his iPhone in one hand.

Nueng allowed herself a moment of silent internal celebration. "I got you," she thought.

She remembers that Cazes, for a dark web administrator whose site had just dropped off-line and who was now dealing with a minor traffic accident at his front driveway, looked relatively calm and unperturbed. His emails would later reveal that seconds earlier he'd been repeatedly messaging his Lithuanian hosting provider about his server's unex-plained outage. But he seemed to suspect nothing about the scene at the gate; Pisal had chosen the two women for their role in part because he'd guessed that Cazes's misogyny would prevent him from imagining they could possibly be undercover agents. As Cazes walked toward them, Nueng and her partner got back in the car and drove it onto the spec house's driveway, ostensibly to get it out of the way.

Cazes turned to the gate to see if he could pull it back onto its rails, tucking his phone into the elastic band of his shorts. At this point, the driver of Guzman's car, a middle-aged agent nicknamed Pong, walked over. He stood next to Cazes as if to help appraise the situation.

Then, as Cazes yanked on the gate, Pong reached over and plucked the iPhone out of Cazes's waistband, seemingly to prevent it from falling. As Cazes looked over to him, perhaps to thank him, Pong took Cazes by the arm and motioned for him to step aside for a moment. Cazes, seeming confused, walked with him out into the street.

Events suddenly accelerated. Another agent, a younger, compact man with an athletic build who went by M, had emerged from Pong and Guzman's car, where he had been hiding in the backseat. As he walked past them, Pong handed M the phone behind Cazes's back. At the exact moment of that handoff, Cazes looked down the street, away from his home. He saw another police officer—the electrician, now wearing a police vest—sprinting straight toward him.

Cazes spun around, instantly in fight-or-flight mode, trying desperately to run for his front door. Pong and M grabbed Cazes and struggled with him for a fraction of a second. The iPhone clattered to the ground and another officer picked it up. Soon another cop had grabbed Cazes, and then another. Together with Pong they were pinning his arms behind his back and holding him in a headlock as M wrenched free from the melee and ran through the gate.

The moment for M's make-or-break assignment had arrived. He raced into the house, past Cazes's wife, who by now stood frozen in the living room, and up the stairs, taking them two at a time. From studying the layout of the spec house, M had determined that Cazes's home office must be across the upstairs hall from the master bedroom. He burst through the door there and found a pair of young foreigners asleep in a guest bedroom—unexpected guests of Cazes's visiting from Quebec.

M shouted a quick "Sorry! Sorry!" then whirled around and ran across the hall into the master bedroom. On the far end of the room, there it was, on a cheap white desk: Cazes's laptop, a black Asus PC with an external monitor, revealing red-highlighted A, S, D, and W gaming keys.

It was open.

To the right of the desk stood a more curious piece of technology, a massive, sleek, waist-high black cube with a glass front, filled with interconnected computer components and neat coils of blue tubing. M didn't stop to consider what this other science-fictional machine might be. His mission was the laptop. He practically leaped across the room, reached out, and placed a finger on its touch pad. Then he sat down in Cazes's desk chair, keeping one hand on the computer's mouse, finally catching his breath.

A moment later, M's voice crackled over the police radio. "Officers, Officers," he said in Thai. "The computer is unlocked."

In the NSB office war room, someone announced over the phone that they had the laptop, open and alive.

The room's tension broke into an eruption of cheers. Jen Sanchez leaped up, standing in front of the video screens pumping her fist in the air. Rabenn and Hemesath gleefully hugged each other. Four years after the arrest of Ross Ulbricht, it seemed they had pulled off a Glen Park Public Library of their own.

. . .

But there was still the question of the phone. As Pong and two other Thai cops had wrestled Cazes to his knees and handcuffed him, Guzman had run out of the spec house, leaving the bewildered real estate agent behind. As was customary in Thailand, he'd taken off his shoes to go into the model home, and Guzman hadn't had time to put them back on, so he stood in the street in his socks.

A Thai police officer handed Guzman Cazes's iPhone, and he looked down at it in dismay. It was locked.

As the Thai police held Cazes on the ground, he screamed his wife's name. She and her father, who lived with the rest of Cazes's in-laws across the street, came outside and stood over him helplessly as he was handcuffed.

At that moment, Pisal arrived on the scene, wearing a gray polo shirt and a kind of naval cap; the hat wasn't part of his uniform, but he believed it brought him luck. He had already been told by police radio that the phone was locked.

Pisal bent over Cazes, who seemed to calm down as the officers pulled him to his feet. The police colonel introduced himself, put a paternal hand on Cazes's shoulder, and gave him a knowing look. He asked the shirtless, still-panicked young man to please follow him for a moment so that they could speak privately.

Cazes's expression eased slightly. This didn't seem to be the behavior of police arresting someone for running the world's biggest online drug market. Cazes walked with Pisal and the cops holding him across the street, under the shade of a mango tree.

When they were out of earshot of Cazes's wife, Pisal explained in a discreet tone that they knew about Cazes's sexual encounter with a woman two evenings prior. Now that woman was alleging sexual assault. They needed to work this out.

Cazes could see that this must be some sort of shakedown: He, a wealthy foreigner, had flaunted his Lamborghini and now was paying the price. He looked concerned but rational again, his moment of panic over. This was a situation he might be able to handle.

Pisal explained that the woman's husband wanted to speak on the phone. Perhaps if Cazes offered the man something, he wouldn't press charges.

The cops led Cazes into the same Toyota Camry that had pulled in to the cul-de-sac. Pisal sat down next to Cazes and handed him the locked phone Guzman had given him, telling him the number to call.

Cazes unlocked the phone and dialed. The voice on the other end of the line, another undercover agent, played the role of the cuckolded husband. Cazes, nervously speaking in Thai, offered him 100,000 baht to drop the charges, around $3,000. The man demanded ten times that amount. Cazes quickly agreed. When they had finished negotiating, the husband instructed Cazes to hand the phone to the police, and Cazes did as he was told.

Pisal stepped out of the car, the unlocked phone in his hand, and gave it to an FBI agent who had just arrived on the scene.

. . .

Guzman was the first to finally tell Cazes the truth. After the AlphaBay founder had been allowed to go back into his home and get dressed, Guzman sat next to him on the couch of his living room, where Cazes now rested, his hands cuffed in front of him, wearing a worried expression. Guzman, the first foreigner Cazes had seen since the raid of his home began, explained that he was an agent with the DEA and that the United States had issued a warrant for his arrest.

Around the same time, the DEA's Robert Miller arrived, along with a team of FBI agents and analysts assigned to forensically examine Cazes's devices. Ali, the cryptocurrency tracer who had confirmed Cazes's identity as Alpha02 so many months earlier, walked through the gate and past his luxury cars, her first time seeing real, corporeal results of the digital wealth she'd so obsessively tracked.

"That's the Aventador," she thought to herself. "That's the Panamera."

In the master bedroom—which they now knew doubled as Cazes's home office—the FBI's team of computer specialists began exploring his laptop. They found that he was logged in to AlphaBay as its administrator. On the computer's desktop, they found a text file where, just like Ross Ulbricht, he had tracked his net worth. Cazes had counted more than $12.5 million in assets, including houses and cars; $3.3 million in cash; and more than $7.5 million in cryptocurrency, totaling to a fortune of more than $23.3 million.

When Ali was given her turn on the machine, she immediately began examining its cryptocurrency wallets and the addresses associated with them. As she did, she excitedly picked up her phone and called Erin, who was sitting an hour away in the NSB war room with Rabenn, Hemesath, Marion, and Sanchez.

"Tunafish!" she shouted without preamble (or rather, Ali and Erin's actual secret nickname for that address).

"I'm going to need more context," Erin responded drily.

"It's here," Ali said. "I've got the key for it."

She could see before her the one, very specific pot of gold that had first confirmed the identity of Alpha02. It had appeared exactly where the blockchain's rainbow had pointed, arcing halfway around the world, into Alexandre Cazes's Bangkok home.

CHAPTER 35

Captivity

For several days after his arrest, Cazes lived in a kind of comfortable purgatory.

The Thais kept him on the same eighth floor of their Bangkok NSB headquarters building where they had, over the previous months, engineered his surveillance and takedown. Cazes spent his nights sleeping on a couch there, constantly under the watchful eye of the police. During the day he was shuttled back and forth between conference room tables—where he was subjected to paperwork and questions that he almost entirely refused to answer until he could speak to a lawyer—and a black leather massage chair. He was fed whatever he requested: mostly local takeout or, on some occasions, French food from the fast-food bistro chain Paul.

Cazes's relatively gentle treatment—at least compared with what he'd receive in a typical Thai jail—was designed to persuade him to consent to two key forms of cooperation. Rabenn, Hemesath, and Marion hoped to convince him to sign an extradition agreement, allowing them to deport him from Bangkok to Fresno without a lengthy legal battle. And more ambitiously, the Americans hoped he might agree to work with them as an informant.

Flipping the kingpin of the world's biggest dark web market to "Team U.S.A.," as Jen Sanchez put it, would be an incredible coup. There was no telling, the prosecutors imagined, what sort of gold mine of information Cazes might be able to share with them about his AlphaBay co-conspirators, or others in the online underground where he'd been such a key player. What sorts of traps for those co-conspirators could they set with his help?

Among the DEA agents, Jen Sanchez was given the job of speaking to Cazes and coaxing him into agreeing to extradition. After his arrest, Sanchez had experienced a complication in her feelings toward the dark web kingpin, whose opioid sales and misogynistic alter ego had once triggered her revulsion. In her prior postings in Mexico and Texas, she'd taken pride in her ability to convert suspects into informants, a skill that required persuasion and personability. She now took a similar stance toward Cazes: Even after her hard-charging comments to Miller about sending Alpha02 to supermax prison earlier that year, she felt a sense of maternalism toward the young French Canadian they'd captured, with warmth and even empathy mixed in with her contempt.

Sanchez didn't have the authority to negotiate with Cazes for his cooperation or to make promises to him about his future. But she says she tried to show him kindness, to help him keep his spirits up. He asked her about his wife and his unborn child. She reassured him they were safe; his wife had been arrested, too, but quickly released.

"I'm gonna take care of you," she repeatedly told Cazes. He seemed unconvinced.

. . .

In their war room on the same floor of the NSB office, just a few walls away from the defendant in their investigation, the Americans continued their work scouring Cazes's computers for evidence. His iPhone, after all their concerns about hidden Bitcoin keys and the trickery Pisal had employed to unlock it, turned out to have only personal information and nothing related to AlphaBay. The Lithuanian server, too, was initially useless to them; after crashing, it had rebooted in an encrypted state. They were denied its secrets, and would only manage to decrypt the machine months later.

As for the massive cube-shaped computer next to Cazes's desk, it turned out to be a $60,000 PC that Cazes had assembled for the apparent sole purpose of playing video games and that he'd nicknamed the Blue Pearl. The investigators later found a thread on the computer hardware forum Overclock.net in which Cazes described "using only the world's strongest gear" to build an epic gaming rig, complete with its own internal, blue-tinted water-cooling system. Aside from the money that had paid for it, the machine seemed to have nothing to do with AlphaBay.

The laptop, on the other hand, was a gold mine of evidence—quite literally. Aside from being logged in to AlphaBay and containing that incriminating net worth file, the computer had keys for all of Cazes's various wallets, containing not only Bitcoin but also other, newer cryptocurrencies: Ethereum, Monero, Zcash. Rabenn remembers watching the two FBI analysts, Ali and Erin, in the war room as they siphoned that money into wallets under FBI control, announcing every time they had transferred another multimillion-dollar stash. "It was the coolest thing I have ever seen," Rabenn says.

On the evening after the arrest, Rabenn and Hemesath met with Cazes for the first time. He sat in a conference room of the NSB office—accompanied, for the moment, only by a Thai police chaperone and two Thai lawyers, whom Cazes had hired to temporarily oversee his defense. For Rabenn, who had hunted Cazes for the better part of a year across the digital world, sharing a room with his target still felt surreal. But Cazes didn't recognize either of the prosecutors; he had sat down next to them in the Athenee just a few days earlier by sheer coincidence, without the slightest hint that these two men would soon hold his future in their hands.

Rabenn began by warning Cazes not to waste their time or lie to them, his standard opening to criminal defendants. But the two American attorneys had agreed that Hemesath, the more experienced orator, would take the lead. In his usual analytic tone, Hemesath launched into a short speech about the crimes they knew Cazes had committed, the indictment against him, and the potential consequences if he were convicted. He laid out the evidence they possessed, which now included not only archived social media clues and blockchain evidence but Cazes's own unencrypted laptop and phone. He explained that if Cazes didn't cooperate with them, he might very well spend the rest of his life in prison.

That sentence, however, could still be reduced if he made the right decisions. If he cooperated, Hemesath concluded, Cazes might still be able to meet his child as a free man someday.

After a moment's hesitation, Cazes answered this extended soliloquy with a single question: Were they going to charge him with the kingpin statute?

His voice, which neither prosecutor had heard before, was a sort of middle pitch, inflected with a noticeable French accent. But they were struck more by his expression: a slight smile.

Both prosecutors were caught off guard. Was he asking about the kingpin charge out of fear of the severe sentence that it promised? In fact, they hadn't charged him under that statute, which might have left them less room to maneuver if he eventually cooperated. But it was Cazes's glib tone that gave them pause. They wondered if he was in fact comparing himself to Ross Ulbricht, who had been convicted under that same charge. Did he see the "kingpin" label as a status symbol, one that would cement his place in the dark web pantheon?

Rabenn was unnerved. It wasn't that Cazes had the manner of some sort of cold sociopath, he says. But nor did he seem to be taking the conversation seriously. He remembers thinking that their defendant, facing a potential life sentence or even the death penalty if he was tried in Thailand, was treating this encounter like some sort of game.

He tried to drive home the gravity of the situation. "This is not a joke," Rabenn remembers telling Cazes. "We can't help you unless you help us." He reiterated that the rest of Cazes's life hung in the balance. Cazes seemed to hear that admonishment and became slightly more somber.

The two prosecutors finally asked Cazes if he would be willing to waive his extradition rights so that he could be tried—and likely incarcerated—in the United States rather than Thailand. Cazes said he would consider it. But he insisted that he still wanted to speak to a more permanent lawyer who could take on his case before any real negotiation. Their meeting was over.

. . .

A couple of days later, Cazes did speak for the first time to his lawyer of choice, a young American defense attorney named Roger Bonakdar. Bonakdar was in his office, just a block from Rabenn's in downtown Fresno, when he got the call about Cazes from the federal defenders office for the city. Learning of the magnitude of the case—easily the biggest of its kind to ever occur in the state of California, to say nothing of Fresno—he immediately agreed to speak to Cazes.

Bonakdar's impression of the young man on the other end of the phone contrasted sharply with Rabenn and Hemesath's. He says he found Cazes to be "pleasant and articulate," but also deeply stressed and concerned for his safety. Cazes was particularly scared, Bonakdar remembers, that any negotiation with the prosecution could endanger him and his family—that he could be seen as an informant and that any arrests that followed his own might lead to reprisals against him. "He was sensitive to the perception that he was cooperating," Bonakdar says. "Which he wasn't."

They agreed that Cazes had few, if any, real legal protections in Thai custody and that Bonakdar needed to get him out of the NSB headquarters as quickly as possible and into the Canadian embassy. "I was in a scramble to find a way to secure him," Bonakdar says. He told Cazes he would fly to Bangkok as soon as possible to meet with him.

By this time, however, Cazes had spent the better part of a week on the eighth floor of the NSB office. The prosecutors had made no real progress toward getting him to cooperate. So they agreed to let the Thais move him into the jail on the first floor of the building. He was locked behind steel bars in a dingy white cell with a thin blue mattress and a rudimentary toilet that sat behind a three-foot-high wall with a swinging wooden door.

A few days after Cazes's arrest, with the crux of their work complete, Rabenn had flown back to the United States, and Hemesath had taken a brief trip to Phuket to check out the villa that Cazes owned there, which the Thai government planned to seize.

But Sanchez remained in Bangkok. After Cazes was moved to the NSB lockup, he would be brought out—handcuffed, slightly disheveled, with a week of stubble—for occasional chats with her. Together they would deal with yet more paperwork, or else she would hand him a phone to speak with his attorneys or his wife, who also came to visit Cazes daily and spoke privately to him through the bars of his cell.

Eventually, Cazes signed the waiver that would allow him to be extradited to the United States without a lengthy legal battle. After a couple of days in lockup, he shifted into a more conversational, if somewhat defiant, relationship with Sanchez. The DEA agent suspected he was bored, lonely, and ready to talk to anyone.

On one occasion, Sanchez says he brought up with her, apropos of nothing, the question of AlphaBay's morality. What was so wrong, Sanchez remembers him musing in hypothetical terms, with a website that sold marijuana? Sanchez answered by asking him about AlphaBay's sales of fentanyl. In her retelling of the discussion at least, Cazes lowered his head and offered no defense.

During another late-night visit, this one on July 11, six days after his arrest, Sanchez remembers Cazes informing her, in a kind of deadpan, that he planned to escape—that a helicopter gunship was coming to break him out.

"Cut your shit, Alex," Sanchez responded with a wry smile. "Don't play those games with me."

She reminded him that he was going to be an incredibly valuable informant for the American government—a "superstar," as she put it. Sanchez said she would try to get him a computer and that he would do "amazing things" once they had him set up in the United States. She repeated that she would take care of him.

At 2:00 a.m., she wished him a good night and went home.

.   .   .

The next morning, after just a few hours of sleep, Sanchez left her apartment and headed back to the NSB headquarters, where Cazes was due at 8:00 that morning to be taken to Bangkok's main justice center for a hearing. Worried that parking might slow her down, she jumped in a cab. But the car was soon caught in Bangkok's notorious traffic, and the driver made a wrong turn that Sanchez says added another maddening half an hour to the journey.

When she arrived at the police station, she was running a few minutes late, so she headed straight into the ground-floor lockup. As soon as she walked through the door, she heard someone screaming in Thai, again and again, "He's not talking! Alex isn't talking!"

She broke into a run. Her mind immediately flashed back to Cazes's comment the night before that he planned to escape. "Oh my God, that mother—," Sanchez thought as she ran through the station, furious. "He got somebody to spring him."

As she arrived at Cazes's cell, it seemed to be empty. Then she saw that

Thai officers were peering over the cell's internal three-foot wall at something. She walked in and looked down: Cazes's body, hidden behind that wall, was sprawled across the length of the cell's bathroom area.

His corpse was facedown and bluish, she remembers. The flesh of his arms and legs looked darkened, almost bruised. A navy-blue towel was tied around his neck, with one end now draped over his shoulders.

She was momentarily overcome with shock, sadness, disappointment, and anger—albeit a different pitch of anger than she'd felt just a moment before, when she feared he'd escaped. She found herself wishing that he had. It would have been a better outcome, she felt, than the scene she saw before her.

"You motherfucker," she thought. "I told you I was going to take care of you."

Postmortem

The day before Cazes's death, Paul Hemesath had returned to Bangkok from Phuket and was staying at a new hotel close to NSB headquarters. As he walked toward the station the next morning, past the lush gardens of the Royal Thai Police Sports Club, he was in a spectacular mood, still feeling the afterglow of one of the biggest victories of his career. "Here I am in Bangkok, the sun is shining," he remembers thinking. "Things are going great. This is incredible."

Then, as he approached the station, an FBI agent drove alongside him in a car and told Hemesath from the window that Cazes had been found unresponsive in his cell. Hemesath, perhaps in a state of denial, thought to himself that Cazes must be taking a nap. But as he walked into the lockup, Sanchez and Thai police intercepted him and stated it more plainly: Their defendant was dead.

Hemesath's mind went blank. He began to rewind through the nine months he'd spent chasing Cazes, then fast-forward through his plans for the next year that he had arranged around the case, which had just been torn apart without warning.

At that moment, Cazes's wife and her parents walked into the jail, carrying food for Cazes in plastic bags. Hemesath watched one of the Thai police officers explain to them what had happened. He remembers Thapsuwan standing in the hallway, eight months pregnant, stony-faced, silently absorbing the news. Her mother immediately began to wail in sorrow.

Moments later, Rabenn got a FaceTime call from Hemesath. He answered from his car in downtown Fresno, where he was picking up his child from day care across the street from the city's courthouse. He found Hemesath's face on his screen with tears in his eyes. "He's dead, Grant," Hemesath said. "He's dead."

. . .

Fifteen time zones away, Rabenn sat in his car, overwhelmed by a sudden, crushing wave of disappointment. He compares the feeling to that of some sort of treasure hunter who had traveled across the world in search of a precious relic, obtained it, and was about to bring it home, only to have someone casually smash it on the ground into a thousand pieces. He felt a sense of premature finality: The most impactful case of his career was over.

Rabenn admits he felt little sympathy for Cazes, after the initial shock passed. To prepare for a potential trial, he and Hemesath had identified a handful of individual deaths that had resulted directly from AlphaBay's sales. In one case in Luxembourg, a police officer had murdered his sister and her husband with potassium cyanide purchased on the site. In the U.S., an eighteen-year-old woman in Portland, Oregon, and two boys—just thirteen years old—in Utah had all died from taking synthetic opioids bought on AlphaBay. "When I think about the dead kids that are directly attributed to the site that he was making millions of dollars off of, it's hard to feel bad about him killing himself," Rabenn says.

In the years since, trying to make sense of Cazes's death and his brief interactions with AlphaBay's boss, Rabenn says he's come up with plenty of his own explanations for why Cazes would commit suicide. He was a gamer, Rabenn points out, and he played his life like a video game: He sought power, money, and sexual conquests like points on a leaderboard. Rabenn felt he could see it in Cazes's expression during their first meeting—the sense of detachment from consequences, the disregard for his future.

"It's like when you're playing a first-person game," Rabenn says. "When something goes wrong, you hit the reset button."

Rabenn saw in Cazes's apparent decision to end his own life a kind of reflection, too, of the hip-hop ideals of his teenage years and the "alpha" mentality of his twenties: a desire for status, for respect, and for a certain kind of fame above all else—high-risk, high-reward values that were incompatible with quietly serving decades in prison or becoming a federal informant.

"He was the kid who wanted to be the shot caller," Rabenn says. "He achieved that. He touched the sun. And died."

. . .

Roger Bonakdar saw things differently.

When Cazes's Fresno-based defense attorney got the call from Rabenn, informing him of Cazes's death, he went through the same paroxysm of shock. His flight had been booked for Thailand. He'd been checking on his vaccine records. "We were planning our next steps, and then"—Bonakdar snaps his fingers as he recounts the moment—"he was gone."

But unlike Rabenn, Hemesath, or Sanchez, Bonakdar immediately doubted the story that his client had killed himself, and he told Rabenn as much. Bonakdar had never experienced a client committing suicide, but he'd heard defendants consider it in moments of despair. "I know someone who's on the edge when I speak to them," Bonakdar says. "I just never got the sense from Cazes that he felt all was lost, that there was no recovering from this, that he was a dead man."

Over the months that followed, Bonakdar says he asked U.S. prosecutors and the Thai government for video footage of Cazes's cell at the time of his death. He received neither.

I did, years later, request and receive several clips of video inside Cazes's cell from Thai police. One clip shows Cazes looking up and down the jail hallway through the cell's bars, then doing something with his towel just off-screen before disappearing behind the cell's bathroom door. The next clip, which starts more than half an hour later, shows guards rushing in, followed by Jen Sanchez, and looking over the bathroom wall, apparently at Cazes's corpse.

The Thai police explained to me that they hadn't saved the video between those before-and-after moments because they simply showed the empty part of Cazes's cell with no movement and no one entering. But Bonakdar contends that gap in the footage only makes the circumstances of Cazes's death more suspicious.

Bonakdar argues that the physical explanation of Cazes's suicide alone is "biomechanically dubious." He can't imagine how Cazes could have hanged himself from a makeshift, waist-high gallows. "How do you place enough force to crush your carotid artery when your body's not suspended?" he asks. "From three feet off the ground?"

Sanchez, for her part, described to me in detail how she believes Cazes asphyxiated: He tied one end of the towel around his throat and closed another section of the towel in the hinge of his three-foot-tall bathroom wall, essentially fashioning a noose that suspended his neck from the top of that half wall. Then he simply sat down and used his body weight to pull the towel tight around his neck, cutting off his breathing and blood flow. "He willfully checked out," she says. A Thai police coroner's report lists Cazes's cause of death as simply "suffocation," and notes no signs of a struggle, pointing out that there was no one else's DNA found under his fingernails.

Looking into the medical research on hanging deaths reveals that self-asphyxiation can in fact easily occur without someone suspending their full body.* Sanchez and Rabenn both told me, based on his apparent means of suicide, that they believe Cazes had searched for methods of killing himself online. Sanchez also believes Cazes's wife, Thapsuwan, knew he was planning his death. Sanchez heard from Thai police that Thapsuwan had told staff at Cazes's Phuket villa that he would rather die than be extradited to the United States.†

But Bonakdar dismisses that secondhand account and remains unconvinced. He maintains, at the very least, that his client's suicide is far from proven, though he admits he doesn't know who would have killed

---

* A 2016 paper by the Virginia Commonwealth University ear, nose, and throat doctor Michael Armstrong pointed to evidence that just a few pounds of weight, applied to the neck, can cut off circulation and lead to unconsciousness in seconds. As early as 1897, a study by a French forensic pathologist on cadavers found that neck veins can be compressed with less than five pounds of force. And an especially grisly study of fourteen filmed hangings—most of which were cases of accidental deaths from autoerotic asphyxiation—showed that in at least ten cases the person had their feet or knees on the ground and yet lost consciousness in as little as eight seconds and died within minutes.

† Thapsuwan would later herself be convicted of money laundering by the Thai government for her association with Cazes's crimes and served two years in prison before receiving a royal pardon. She declined to be interviewed.

Cazes—or had him killed. A co-conspirator afraid that Cazes might inform on him? Thai police officers on the take, seeking to cover up their corruption? He doesn't expect he'll ever know the truth.

Danielle Héroux, Cazes's mother, who still lives in Quebec, also rejects the story of her son's suicide. She laid the blame for his death at the feet of the American government. "Alex didn't kill himself," Héroux wrote in a text message in French. "Why did the FBI take no action to protect 'their trophy' while awaiting his extradition to the USA? Surely they wanted Alex not to speak, and his assassination was ordered."

Héroux declined to be interviewed and didn't elaborate or share any evidence of her claim. But she did defend her son. "Alex is not at all the person portrayed in the media," she wrote. "I raised him alone and he is an extraordinary being."

Cazes's mother shared a photo of the two of them together, a selfie she'd taken with Cazes in the back of a car. He's smiling, a bit halfheartedly, the same innocent openness to his expression that he'd had in the LinkedIn profile photo that first put prosecutors onto his trail.

She added one more message: "He was my entire life."

37

The Trap

In the days after the AlphaBay takedown but before Alexandre Cazes's death, Paul Hemesath spent a few enjoyable hours by the rooftop pool of the Athenee, scrolling on his iPad through the responses to the sudden, unexplained disappearance of the world's largest-ever dark web market.

Rumors had begun to swirl instantly that the site's administrators had pulled off an exit scam, taking with them millions of dollars' worth of the market's cryptocurrency. But others argued that the site might just be down for technical reasons or to carry out routine maintenance. Few suspected the truth. "People have always screamed exit scam in the past, and they've always been wrong," wrote one user on Reddit. "I really hope this turns out the same." Another added, "until we know otherwise, keep the faith."

Almost immediately, faithful or not, AlphaBay's vendors and buyers went looking for a new market where they could continue business as usual. The natural choice was the second-biggest, well-run, and already fast-growing AlphaBay competitor: Hansa. "wow alphabay exit scam. crazyness!" one user wrote on Twitter. "moving to hansa."

Back in the Netherlands, the Dutch police were waiting for them. For two weeks, they had been overseeing Hansa's vast marketplace, surveilling its users, and collecting their messages, delivery addresses, and passwords. Their Driebergen conference room, where the small team of undercover investigators had continued to work in shifts around the clock, had taken on the atmosphere of a college dorm. Chips, cookies, chocolates, and energy drinks covered the table, a warm, stale funk pervading the air.

At one point the head of investigations for the Dutch National Police paid them a visit to see their landmark operation in action. He was visibly offended by the smell and left after ten minutes. Someone brought in an air freshener. ("It didn't really work," a team member says.)

Hansa's marketplace, meanwhile, was thriving. In the days before the AlphaBay takedown, it was adding nearly a thousand new registered users a day, all falling into the trap the Dutch had patiently set. When AlphaBay went off-line, that number spiked to more than four thousand users a day. Then more than five thousand the next day. Then, two days after that, six thousand.

Soon, as the market absorbed AlphaBay's wayward users, the Dutch team was logging a thousand daily transactions. The paperwork of tracking and sending those order records to Europol—not to mention attempting to intercept every order shipped to the Netherlands—became so massive that the police were briefly overwhelmed. They reluctantly decided to shut down new registrations for a full week. "Due to the influx of Alphabay refugees we are dealing with technical issues," read a message they posted to the site. Those refugees, however, remained so eager to join that some Hansa users began selling their accounts on web forums, like scalpers selling tickets to a concert.

Then, in the middle of that week, on July 13, one prong of Operation Bayonet suddenly slipped into the light. *The Wall Street Journal* broke the news that AlphaBay had been taken down by a joint law enforcement operation involving the U.S., Thai, and Canadian governments and that the site's administrator, Alexandre Cazes, had been found dead in a Thai jail cell.

There was no mention in the article of Hansa or the Dutch police. And when the Dutch reached out to the FBI, they were surprised and relieved to find that the Americans were willing to keep mum—to follow the Dutch team's lead and delay any announcement of the entirety of Operation Bayonet. The still-operational, undercover half of their one-two punch would remain hidden for as long as the Dutch chose to pursue it.

So a week after pausing new registrations on Hansa, the Driebergen team turned them on again. New user sign-ups soon spiked to more than seven thousand a day.

. . .

The Dutch knew that their operation couldn't go on indefinitely. They could see the moment approaching when they would have to take off their masks, reveal their surveillance coup, and tear down the market they'd so carefully rebuilt and maintained. They were, after all, facilitating drug sales, and not all of them were being intercepted in the mail.

The closer they got to the end of the sting, meanwhile, the less they had to lose if they were discovered—and thus the more risks they were willing to take.

Throughout the operation, the Dutch team would hold what they called "evil plan" meetings, brainstorming ever more devious schemes to track and identify the unwitting users of the market they controlled. They created a list of those tactics, ordering the menu of surveillance actions from least likely to most likely to blow their cover. As they reached their endgame, they began to put their most brazen ideas into practice.

Hansa had long ago implemented a standard feature for dark web markets, designed to protect their vendors: When sellers uploaded images for their product listings, the site automatically stripped those images of their metadata—information nested within the file such as what sort of camera had taken the photo and the GPS location of where the image was created. The Dutch had silently sabotaged that feature early on, recording images' metadata before it was stripped, so as to catalog uploaders' locations. But they had managed to pinpoint only a few vendors that way: They found that most rarely updated their listings or posted new photos.

So, a few weeks into their takeover, the police wiped every image from the site. They claimed that a server had failed due to a technical glitch, and they announced that vendors would have to re-upload all the images for their listings. Those fresh uploads allowed the Dutch cops to scrape the metadata from a vast new batch of images. They quickly obtained the locations of fifty more of the site's dealers.

In another scheme in the last days of their operation, the Driebergen team came up with an idea for how to get the IP addresses of the site's sellers, despite their use of Tor. It involved a sort of Trojan horse. Hansa's administrators announced that they were offering an Excel file to vendors that included codes that would allow them to retrieve their bitcoins stored in escrow on the market, even if the site were taken down. When only a small number of Hansa's dealers took them up on the offer, the police tried adding more helpful information to it, designed to lure vendors, like buyer statistics that would let the sellers track and rank their best customers. When even that feature got lackluster adoption, the Dutch cops pushed their ruse to its extreme: They warned the site's users that they had detected suspicious activity on their servers, and all vendors should download the backup cryptocurrency retrieval file immediately or risk losing their funds.

All the while, of course, the files they were pushing on vendors were functioning as secret digital beacons. The top left of the Excel spreadsheet displayed an image of the Hansa logo, a stylized Viking ship. The police had designed the Excel file to fetch that image from their own server when the spreadsheet was opened. As a result, they could see the IP address of every computer requesting it. Sixty-four sellers on the market took the bait.

In the most involved scheme of all, the Dutch team turned their sights onto the staff of the marketplace itself, the moderators who were directly working for them. They'd found that one moderator in particular was extremely dedicated—very "emotionally involved" in the site, as the team lead, Petra Haandrikman, put it. The Dutch team felt a collective admiration and affection toward this hard worker—while simultaneously hatching a scheme to try to arrest him.

They offered him a promotion. Hansa's two bosses would give him a raise, but only if he agreed to become a third admin of the site. The moderator was overjoyed, immediately accepting. Then they explained that for him to become an admin, they'd have to either arrange a meeting in person or get his mailing address so that they could give him a two-factor authentication token—a physical USB stick plugged into a PC to prove his identity and keep his account secure.

In his next message, the moderator's tone suddenly changed. He explained that he had made a promise to himself that if his bosses at Hansa ever asked for his identifying information or tried to meet him in person, he would immediately quit and wipe all of the devices he had used in his moderator job. Now he planned to abide by that promise. He said goodbye.

That moderator's sudden decision—a very wise one, likely saving him from a prison sentence—meant that the admins now had an opening to fill. So they began advertising that they were taking applications for a new moderator. At the end of a series of questions about qualifications and experience, they would ask "successful" applicants for their address so that they could mail them a two-factor authentication token. Some, eager for the job, handed over the locations of their homes. "Please don't send the cops to this address hahahahahaha just kidding," one would-be moderator wrote, as he, in fact, sent his address to the cops. "I trust you guys because Hansa support was always good and helpful."

Savvier dark web users, of course, never gave out their home addresses. In cases where they needed to receive a package, they sent shippers the address of a "drop"—a location away from their homes where they could, if necessary, deny the package was theirs.

To circumvent that safeguard, the Dutch police went one step further: For moderator applicants who provided a drop address, they shipped them the two-factor token hidden inside the packaging of a teddy bear, a cute stuffed panda with a soft pink nose. To their targets, they intended the panda to appear as an innocuous disguise to hide the authentication token, a sign of their new employers' attention to opsec—and, perhaps, their sense of humor.

The humor part, at least, would be correct. The Dutch cops hoped that their targets would take the stuffed pandas home as a kind of gift or souvenir. Unbeknownst to the recipients, each one also contained, hidden deep in its stuffing, a small GPS tracker.

Aftermath

On July 20, after running Hansa for twenty-seven days, the Dutch prosecutors decided it was finally time to give up their game—over the objections of several members of the Driebergen team controlling the site, who had more ideas for surveillance tricks still up their sleeves.

In a press conference at the Dutch police's national headquarters in The Hague, the head of the agency dramatically pressed a large red plastic button to shut down the site. (In fact, the button was just a prop; an agent sitting nearby with a laptop sent the simultaneous command to the server that finally pulled Hansa off-line.) Simultaneously, the U.S. Justice Department announced the news in a D.C. press conference, in which Attorney General Jeff Sessions himself spoke about the coordinated action against both AlphaBay and Hansa. Sessions used the opportunity to issue a warning to the dark web's users. "You are not safe. You cannot hide," he told them, from a packed room of reporters and cameras. "We will find you, dismantle your organization and network. And we will prosecute you."

Nearly sixteen days after it had inexplicably disappeared, the AlphaBay site rematerialized with a notice covered in law enforcement agency logos and words that would be familiar to any Silk Road user: "THIS HIDDEN SITE HAS BEEN SEIZED."

The Dutch, meanwhile, put up a slightly different message on Hansa: "THIS HIDDEN SITE HAS BEEN SEIZED *and controlled since June 20.*" The Dutch seizure notice linked to another dark web site that the police had created themselves, which listed dark web vendors by pseudonym under three categories: those under investigation, those who had been identified, and those who had been arrested—a list that they suggested was about to grow significantly. "We trace people who are active at Dark Markets and offer illicit goods or services," the site read. "Are you one of them? Then you have our attention."

The Dutch team in Driebergen, even after exposing their operation, still had one last card to play: They decided to try the usernames and passwords they had already collected from Hansa on the largest surviving drug bazaar, known as Dream Market. They found that at least twelve of that site's dealers had reused their Hansa credentials there. They were able to immediately take over those accounts too and lock out the vendors—who promptly posted panicked messages to public forums suggesting that Dream had been compromised as well.

All of that carefully coordinated agitprop and disruption was expressly designed to sow fear and uncertainty across the dark web community—to "damage the trust in this whole system," as the Dutch police's Marinus Boekelo said.

It had its immediate intended effect. "Looks like I'll be sober for a while. Not trusting any markets," wrote one user on Reddit.

"DO NOT MAKE NEW ORDERS ON ANY DNM ANY MORE!" wrote another, using the common abbreviation for "darknet market."

"So it's a wrap for the darknet?" one user asked.

"To everyone who thinks they're screwed and wants to flee the country," another advised, "do so ASAP."

. . .

That all-pervading paranoia was, for many of the dark web's users, warranted. In their nearly four weeks of running Hansa, the Dutch had surveilled twenty-seven thousand transactions. After shutting down the site, they seized 1,200 bitcoins from Hansa, worth tens of millions of dollars as of this writing, thanks in part to silently sabotaging the site's implementation of a Bitcoin feature called multi-signature transactions, designed to make that sort of simple confiscation impossible. They had collected at least some amount of data on a staggering total of 420,000 users, including more than 10,000 home addresses.

In the months following the takeover, Gert Ras, the head of the unit that oversaw the operation, said Dutch police carried out around fifty "knock and talks" in the Netherlands, visiting known buyers to warn them they had been identified and should stop purchasing narcotics online, though he said they arrested only one high-volume customer.

The site's sellers weren't so lucky: Within one year, more than a dozen of Hansa's top dealers had been arrested. Finally, the Dutch police fed the massive corpus of dark web data they'd collected into a database controlled by Europol, who in turn shared it with law enforcement agencies around the world.

The direct ripple effects of that explosion of incriminating data, passed through so many institutions' records, aren't easy to track. But over the following years, Grant Rabenn, who served as custodian of the files the Justice Department had assembled from Operation Bayonet, says he received requests for that information as part of dozens of cases, more times than he bothered to count, that agencies across the United States were still pursuing.

A series of massive, high-profile dark web busts would follow, a collection of operations all carried out by a new group known as JCODE, or Joint Criminal Opioid and Darknet Enforcement, pulling together agents from the FBI, DEA, Department of Homeland Security, U.S. Postal Inspection Service, and half a dozen other federal agencies: in 2018, Operation Disarray; in 2019, Operation SaboTor; in 2020, Operation DisrupTor. In total, according to the FBI, those enforcement campaigns would eventually result in more than 240 arrests, 160 "knock and talks," and the seizure of more than 1,700 pounds of drugs along with $13.5 million in cash and cryptocurrency.

But the Hansa side of the operation was not without its costs. Aside from the vast manpower and resources Operation Bayonet had required, it had demanded that a group of Dutch police become, themselves, dark web kingpins. For nearly a month, they had facilitated the sale of untold quantities of deadly narcotics to unknown buyers across the world. Even as they compromised Hansa, Hansa had compromised them, too.

Did the Dutch police feel that sense of taint—taint that perhaps comes from any undercover work? Some, at least, describe feeling surprisingly unconflicted about their role. "To be honest, it was exciting, mostly," said the team lead, Petra Haandrikman. Dutch prosecutors had, after all, already reviewed the case, weighed its ethics, and given them the green light. After that, the police involved felt they could play their part in the operation to its fullest with a clean conscience.

The Dutch police pointed out that they did ban the especially deadly opiate fentanyl from Hansa while it was under their control, in an effort to minimize the harm they might be responsible for—a move that Hansa's users actually applauded. In truth, however, that ban had come just a few days before the end of their undercover operation. Until then, for more than three weeks, that highly dangerous opioid had continued to be offered on the site, with no guarantee that all of its orders would be intercepted.

And how did the police feel about the decision to oversee those narcotics sales, rather than shut Hansa down and prevent the transactions altogether?

"They would have taken place anyway," the Dutch police's Gert Ras said without hesitation, "but on a different market."

· · ·

In the years since Operation Bayonet, the dark web's observers have tried to determine to what extent the operation actually disrupted that endless interchangeability of markets, the dark web drug trade's constant cycle of raids and renewal. Could that highly coordinated global takedown—or anything else—end or even slow down the eternal shell game that law enforcement agencies had by then been playing for years, with a new market constantly ready to absorb the users of the last?

One study, at least, suggested that the AlphaBay and Hansa busts had lasting effects. The Netherlands Organisation for Applied Scientific Research, which goes by the acronym TNO, found that together the results of that combined takeover-takedown were different from previous dark web busts. When other markets had been seized, like the Silk Road or Silk Road 2, most of their drug vendors soon showed up again on other dark web drug sites. But the TNO study found that vendors who fled Hansa didn't reappear, or if they did, they had been forced to scrub their identities and reputations, re-creating themselves from scratch. "Compared to both the Silk Road takedowns, or even the AlphaBay takedown, the Hansa Market shut down stands out in a positive way," the TNO report read. "We see the first signs of game-changing police intervention."

Carnegie Mellon's Nicolas Christin, the quantitative researcher of the dark web drug markets with perhaps the longest track record, isn't so sure. Based on data he and his fellow researchers assembled by analyzing feedback posted to markets, they conservatively estimated that AlphaBay was generating between $600,000 and $800,000 a day in sales before it was shut down, well over double the Silk Road's peak revenue. But his team found that the next inheritor of the dark web's refugees, Dream Market, eventually grew to become almost as big as, or perhaps even bigger than, AlphaBay, before its administrators disappeared and the market quietly dropped off-line in 2019.

Chainalysis's blockchain-based measurements, by contrast, found that AlphaBay was generating as much as $2 million a day in average sales just before its shutdown—revenue that no other dark web market of its kind has ever rivaled. (The Russian-language dark web site Hydra, which was pulled off-line by German law enforcement in April of 2022, did top those numbers, pulling in more than $1.7 billion in Bitcoin in 2021, according to Chainalysis. But because its black-market contraband sales were difficult to distinguish from its money-laundering services, its inflows of cryptocurrency aren't directly comparable to AlphaBay.) The FBI has estimated that Cazes's site, with more than 369,000 product listings and 400,000 users at its peak, was ten times the size of the Silk Road when it was torn down.

Regardless of who holds the title for the largest dark web market of all time, Christin predicts that this anonymous contraband economic cycle will continue long after the dark web's memory of Operation Bayonet has faded, as long as there are buyers for illegal, lucrative, and often highly addictive products.

"History has taught us that this ecosystem is very, very resilient," he says. "What happened in 2017 was very unique, that one-two punch. But that doesn't seem to have dented the ecosystem in a major way."

Even on the day that the Hansa takedown was announced, in 2017, some users seemed ready to return to the dark web as soon as the chaos had subsided and their insatiable need for another fix began to make itself felt. The very same Reddit user who had posted to the site's darknet market forum that they would be "sober for a while" ended their message with a note of stubborn persistence.

"Things will stabilize, they always do," that anonymous user wrote. "The Great Game of whack-a-mole never ends."

CHAPTER 39

Suvarnabhumi Airport

Tigran Gambaryan had, in helping to develop Chainalysis's "advanced analysis" technique, played a small but pivotal role in the AlphaBay investigation, discovering the Lithuanian IP address that had been core to Operation Bayonet's success. He and his IRS-CI colleagues had traveled all the way to Bangkok to see it through. But when the takedown happened, they had been largely left on the sidelines.

The IRS-CI team had come to Thailand in part to track down and potentially arrest one of Cazes's money-laundering contacts based there, but their lead hadn't panned out. (They declined to reveal more about that dead-ended investigation.) Meanwhile, the FBI and DEA had—in typical fashion, given IRS-CI's place in the interagency pecking order— mostly excluded Gambaryan and his colleagues from Operation Bayonet's inner circle. They hadn't been invited to the Thai NSB headquarters to watch the video stream of Cazes's arrest. They hadn't even stayed at the Athenee along with the other AlphaBay investigators, booking rooms instead at the less glamorous Bangkok Hilton and Marriott across town. The IRS agents in Thailand had gone so far as to name the WhatsApp group they used to coordinate "the Kid's Table."

In the Bangkok Hilton's lounge at the end of each day, often at loose ends, Gambaryan and his colleague on the IRS-CI's new computer crimes unit would talk about what their next case should be. One evening Gambaryan called up Chainalysis's Jonathan Levin while browsing through Reactor to brainstorm ideas. Dark web gambling sites? Illegal online casinos, compared with all the other crime unfolding in the crypto-economy, hardly seemed worth their attention. Another dark web market takedown? Sure, they thought. But the AlphaBay and Hansa takedowns appeared to have already left those markets in a shambles from which they'd take months or even years to recover.

On the way home from Bangkok, Gambaryan and another IRS-CI agent, Chris Janczewski, found that their flight to D.C. was delayed. Stuck in Suvarnabhumi Airport with hours to kill, they wrote to their bosses to see if they could expense a sleep pod in a "capsule hotel" to get a few hours' shut-eye, or even buy access to a first-class lounge. Both requests were denied. So they sat in the terminal, half-awake and bored, literally staring at the wall.

Gambaryan decided to try calling Chainalysis's Levin to talk over next cases again. When Levin picked up the phone, he had news to share. He'd been looking into a website that didn't fit among the IRS's usual targets but that he hoped they'd be willing to check out. It was a dark web market that sold child sexual abuse materials—abbreviated CSAM in law enforcement and child advocacy circles, a class of computer crime that had once been called "child pornography" but had been renamed to better capture the true nature of the abuse recorded in those images and videos.

The site was called Welcome to Video. It appeared to be the largest cryptocurrency-funded CSAM market anyone had ever seen. And Levin had already traced payments from someone who seemed to be the site's administrator to multiple exchanges in South Korea.

By all appearances, the administrator of an enormous collection of videos of the sexual abuse of children—a more secretive, darker echelon of the criminal cryptocurrency economy than any of them had ever before probed—was very likely a couple of countries away from where they sat in Thailand.

"Why don't you hop over to Korea," Levin suggested, only half joking, "and arrest this guy?"

PART IV

WELCOME

TO

VIDEO

Five Characters

A few days before that phone call, while seemingly every dark-web-focused American law enforcement agent was convening in Bangkok, Chainalysis's Jonathan Levin walked into the unassuming brick headquarters of the U.K.'s National Crime Agency on the south bank of the Thames River in London. A friendly agent there led him to the building's second floor and through the office kitchen, offering him a cup of tea. He accepted, as he always did on visits to the NCA, leaving the bag in.

The two men sat, teacups in hand, at the agent's desk in a collection of cubicles. Levin was there on a routine customer visit, to learn what the agent and his colleagues were up to and how Chainalysis could help. After running through a few cases, the agent mentioned a dark web site that had newly come onto his radar. It was called Welcome to Video. At a glance, it seemed to be among the rare child sexual abuse materials sites that sold access to videos for bitcoins.

The site had been spotted by the NCA's child exploitation investigations team, who had come across it in the midst of a particularly horrific case, even by the standards of their usual work. NCA agents had been tracking an offender named Matthew Falder. An academic based in Manchester, England, Falder would pose as a female artist and solicit nude photos from strangers on the internet, then use those images to blackmail them, threatening to share the images of his victims with their family or friends unless they recorded themselves carrying out increasingly demeaning and depraved acts. He'd then use those videos as further blackmail fodder, forcing his victims to commit self-harm and sexually abuse others on camera. By the time he was arrested, he had targeted fifty people, at least three of whom had attempted suicide.

The NCA had found on Falder's computers that he was a registered user of Welcome to Video, a corner of the dark web they hadn't previously encountered. The child exploitation team had passed the lead on to their computer crime team, including the cryptocurrency-focused agent at whose desk Levin now sat. But the computer crime group had barely had time to look at it. Given the steady growth in online black markets, ransomware, and other cybercrime cases, they were constantly drowning in requests for help from other teams less familiar with the digital side of the criminal underworld.

Homing in on one Bitcoin address that the agents had determined to be part of Welcome to Video's financial network, Levin suggested they load it in Chainalysis's Reactor software. He set down his cup of tea, pulled his chair up to the agent's laptop, and began charting out the CSAM site's cluster of addresses on the blockchain.

He was taken aback by what he saw: Many of this child abuse site's users—and, by all appearances, its administrators—had done almost nothing to obscure their cryptocurrency trails. The dark web denizens Levin had traced in the past had often pushed their money through numerous intermediary addresses and sometimes mixers designed to throw off investigators. Levin could see here, within seconds, that these users' bitcoins had flowed from a multitude of cryptocurrency exchanges directly to their wallets, and often from there directly into Welcome to Video's addresses.

The contents of those addresses had themselves been emptied out at just a few exchanges—Bithumb and Coinone in South Korea and Huobi in China—to be converted back into traditional currency. Someone seemed to be continually using large, multi-input transactions to gather up the site's funds and then cash them out. That had made it easy work for Reactor to instantly and automatically cluster thousands of addresses, determining that they all belonged to a single service—which, thanks to the NCA's tip, Levin could now label in the software as Welcome to Video.

What's more, the constellation of exchanges surrounding and connected to that cluster, Levin thought, likely held the data necessary to identify a broad swath of the site's anonymous users—not simply who was cashing out bitcoins from the site, but who was buying bitcoins to put into it.

After spending months analyzing AlphaBay, which had been so careful to avoid centrally collecting its digital bounty in a way that would allow for easy clustering by crypto-tracers, Levin found Welcome to Video's use of cryptocurrency laughably naive. Child sexual abuse sites, perhaps because they hadn't traditionally accepted cryptocurrency or any other form of payment, seemed to be wholly unprepared for the modern state of financial forensics on the blockchain. By the standards of the cat-and-mouse game Levin had by this time lived in for years, Welcome to Video was a hapless rodent that had never encountered a predator. The site's handling of cryptocurrency seemed to be designed by someone who still held the antiquated belief that Bitcoin was magically untraceable—when, in fact, the opposite was often true.

As he sat in front of the NCA agent's laptop, it dawned on Levin, not for the first time but perhaps more clearly than ever before, that he was living in a "golden age," as he later described it—that blockchain analysts like those at Chainalysis had gained a significant lead over those they were targeting. "We've created something extremely powerful, and we're a step ahead of these types of operators," he remembers thinking. "You've got a heinous crime, a terrible thing happening in the world, and in an instant our technology has broken through and revealed in very clear logic who's behind it."

Seeing that someone was cashing out the majority of Welcome to Video's revenues through the two exchanges in South Korea, Levin could already guess that the administrator was very likely located there. Many of the site's users seemed to be paying into the site directly from the addresses where they'd purchased coins on exchanges like Coinbase and Circle, based in the United States. Taking down this global child abuse network might only require getting another law enforcement agency involved, one that could start demanding identifying details from those exchanges.

He thought of the IRS's Tigran Gambaryan and Chris Janczewski, who, as the AlphaBay mission reached its conclusion, had been asking him about new leads.

"I have some people who would be interested," Levin told the NCA agent.

As he prepared to leave, he silently read off the screen the first five characters of the Welcome to Video address that the agent had shown him. Chainalysis's Reactor software had by then included a feature that could autocomplete Bitcoin addresses based on their first few unique numbers or letters. Five would be enough. He committed the characters to memory, a single short password to unlock the living map of a global criminal conspiracy.

. . .

Gambaryan and Janczewski didn't stop in South Korea, as Levin had suggested. But by the time they returned from Thailand to their office in northwest Washington, D.C., Gambaryan's call with Levin had convinced them that Welcome to Video was worth a closer look. Soon they'd enlisted a technical analyst named Aaron Bice from a contract technology firm called Excygent, who had collaborated with Gambaryan on his BTC-e investigation. Together, they charted out Welcome to Video in Reactor and saw how glaringly it presented itself as a target. Its entire financial anatomy was laid before them, thousands of clustered Bitcoin addresses, many with barely concealed pay-ins and cash-outs at exchanges they knew they could squeeze for identifying information. It was indeed, as Levin said, "a slam dunk."

Janczewski brought the case to Zia Faruqui, a prosecutor with whom Janczewski had previously worked to track down a group of Nigerian-prince-style fraudsters who had targeted a member of Congress. Faruqui—the same prosecutor who had been impressed with Gambaryan's enthusiasm at the meeting of the virtual currency strike force back in 2015—was instantly sold on the idea of taking on Welcome to Video and formally opened an investigation.

Gambaryan, Janczewski, Bice, and Faruqui made an unlikely team to be focused on busting a massive child exploitation network. Janczewski was a tall, midwestern agent with a square-jawed look, like a hybrid of Sam Rockwell and Chris Evans, who wore horn-rimmed glasses when looking at computer screens. He'd been recruited to the D.C. computer crimes team from the IRS office in Indiana after proving himself in a grab bag of counterterrorism, drug trafficking, government corruption, and tax evasion cases. Bice was an expert in data analysis and was, as Janczewski described his computer skills, "part robot." Faruqui was a seasoned assistant U.S. attorney with a long history of national security and money-laundering prosecutions. He had an almost manic focus and intensity, spoke in a comically rapid patter, and, it seemed to his colleagues, barely slept. And then there was Gambaryan, who by 2017 had made a name for himself as the IRS's cryptocurrency whisperer and dark web specialist. Faruqui called him "Bitcoin Jesus."

Yet none of the four had ever before worked a child sexual exploitation case. They had no training in handling images and videos of child abuse, whose mere possession, in the hands of normal Americans, represented a felony. They had never even *seen* these sorts of radioactively disturbing materials and had no emotional or psychological preparation for the graphic nature of what they were about to be exposed to.

Gambaryan and his colleagues knew, of course, that CSAM represented a massive undercurrent of the dark web's data. One study a few years earlier by a researcher at the University of Portsmouth in England had found that while dark web drug markets represented the largest single category of dark web sites—about 24 percent of them—dark web traffic was dominated by visits to a far smaller number of child abuse outlets. Those CSAM sites accounted for around 2 percent of the dark web's Tor-protected sites, yet patronage of those sites accounted for as much as 83 percent of the dark web's visits.*

Still, child sexual exploitation investigations had traditionally been the focus of the FBI and Homeland Security Investigations, certainly not the IRS. In part, that was because child sexual abuse images and videos were most often exchanged and shared without money changing hands—what investigators described as a "baseball card trading" system—which put it outside the IRS's domain.

Welcome to Video was different. It had a money trail, and a very clear one. Faruqui, when the two agents showed him what they saw in the blockchain, was undeterred by their collective inexperience in the realm of child exploitation. As a money-laundering prosecutor, he saw no reason why, with the evidence of criminal payments Janczewski and

---

* The Tor Project that develops and maintains Tor, it's worth noting, disputed that study's numbers. The group argued that at least some of those measured "visits" were likely law enforcement undercover agents and "distributed denial of service attacks," in which hackers flood a site with junk traffic to knock it off-line.

Gambaryan had handed him, they couldn't approach Welcome to Video as, fundamentally, a financial investigation.

"We're going to treat this case like we would any other," he said. "We are going to investigate this by following the money."

. . .

Gambaryan had only just returned from his trip to Bangkok for Operation Bayonet, and he had already committed himself to what looked to be another deep-dive dark web case. But even as that new investigation spun up—for a brief interlude between the two—he found he had other unfinished business to attend to.

In mid-July, a tip came in that he'd waited more than a year for. Alexander Vinnik was on the move.

The better part of a decade had passed since Vinnik appeared to have first begun cashing out stolen Mt. Gox bitcoins, as Gambaryan and Michael Gronager had discovered years earlier. For much of that time, Vinnik seemed to also be running BTC-e, a wildly successful, entirely unregulated cryptocurrency exchange that by the end of 2016 had grown to become the third-largest exchange in the world, and a massive nexus of money laundering.

After all that time, it looked like Vinnik finally believed that he'd gotten away with it: He had set foot outside Russia. Agents determined that Vinnik had gone on vacation with his family to Greece, traveling to the Athos peninsula in the north of the country, where he had booked a villa at a luxury resort complete with a Mediterranean garden and optional yacht excursions.

So, one night about three weeks after the AlphaBay takedown, Gambaryan took a carefully timed nap at his desk in the IRS's D.C. office. He woke before dawn to start coordinating his team. There were Secret Service agents in Greece, the prosecutor Alden Pelker on her couch in her home across the Potomac, and Excygent's Aaron Bice, who was inside a data center in New Jersey. Since Gambaryan had first tracked down BTC-e's servers in Virginia, its administrators had moved them to a hosting company a few states north.

Seven time zones away, undercover agents posing as surfers and beachgoers on a stretch of sand facing the Aegean Sea began to close in. Alexander Vinnik suddenly found himself surrounded and then under arrest by Greek police. A few minutes later, a photo appeared on Gambaryan's phone. It showed a man who looked a bit like a young Mikhail Baryshnikov—the same face Gambaryan had seen on a passport photo scanned by a hotel front desk years earlier. He was sitting in a chair in a Greek villa, handcuffed.

Gambaryan later called Michael Gronager to tell him the news: Vinnik had been apprehended and was finally behind bars. Chainalysis's founder received the news with muted pleasure; the gratification of seeing a sort of resolution to the Mt. Gox hacking saga had been delayed so long that he'd largely moved on from it. "It happened and it was super cool," Gronager says of Vinnik's arrest, "and that's nice." Chainalysis never even bothered to write a blog post about the company's work on the case.

For Gambaryan, though, the seized BTC-e server was as much of a prize as Vinnik himself. Back in 2015, his team of investigators had taken a snapshot of the server's data. Now he had a fuller, fresher version of that information, complete with the database of all of BTC-e's users.

Many of the exchange's clients had chosen BTC-e specifically for its no-questions-asked approach to dirty money. They had never expected that their information would end up in the hands of an IRS criminal investigator. Once, BTC-e had been a blank spot on the bitcoin tracer's treasure map. Now its seized data, for a forensic accountant like Gambaryan, was a priceless treasure of its own.

41

"Serach Videos"

When Janczewski and Gambaryan first copied the unwieldy web address mt3plrzdiyqf6jim.onion into their Tor Browsers, they were greeted by a bare-bones site with only the words "Welcome to video" and a log-in prompt, a kind of minimalism Janczewski compares to the Google home page. They each registered a username and password and entered.

Past that first greeting page, the site displayed a vast, seemingly endless collection of video titles and thumbnails, arrayed in squares of four stills per video, seemingly chosen automatically from the files' frames. Those small images were a catalog of horrors: scene after scene of children being sexually abused and raped.

The agents had steeled themselves to see these images. They were nonetheless unprepared for the reality of this hidden, hellish corner of the digital world. "It felt like you had taken a turn down the wrong alley," Gambaryan says, "and you were in the online version of a place you really didn't want to be, but you've always known was there." Janczewski says he found himself attempting to disconnect his eyes from his mind—trying to see the images without really seeing them.

The two agents knew that at some point they would have to actually watch at least some of the advertised videos. But, mercifully, on their first visits to the site they couldn't access them; to do so, they'd have to pay bitcoins to an address the site provided to each registered user, where they could purchase "points" that could then be traded for downloads. And since they weren't undercover agents, they didn't have the authorization to buy those points—nor were they particularly eager to.

Nonetheless, Janczewski remembers the blank shock he felt at the sight of the endless parade of thumbnails alone, the way his brain almost refused to accept what it was seeing. He found that the site had a search page with the misspelled "Serach videos" written at the top of it. Below the search field, it listed popular keywords users had entered. The most popular was an abbreviation for "one-year-old." The second most popular was an abbreviation for "two-year-old."

Janczewski at first thought he must have misunderstood. He had expected to see recordings of the sexual abuse of young teenagers, or perhaps preteens. But as he scrolled, he found, with a kind of mounting revulsion and sadness, that the site was indeed heavily populated with videos of abuse of toddlers and even infants.

"This is a thing, really? No," Janczewski says, numbly recounting his reactions as he first browsed the site. "Oh, there's this many videos on here? No. This can't be real."

At the bottom of several pages of the site was a copyright date: March 13, 2015. Welcome to Video had already been online for more than two years. And even at a glance, it was clear that it had grown into one of the biggest repositories of child sexual abuse videos that law enforcement had ever encountered.

As Janczewski and Gambaryan analyzed the site's mechanics, they saw that users could obtain points not just by purchasing them but also by uploading videos. The more those videos were subsequently downloaded by other users, the more points they would earn. "Do not upload adult porn," the upload page instructed, the last two words highlighted in red for emphasis. The page also warned that uploaded videos would be checked for uniqueness; only new material would be accepted—a feature that, to the agents, seemed expressly designed to encourage more abuse of children.

The element of the site that Gambaryan found most disturbing of all, though, was a kind of real-time chat page, where users could post comments and reactions. The page was filled with posts in all languages, offering a hint at the international reach of the site's network. Most of the messages were spammy requests for free videos or free bitcoins. But others offered a kind of casual discussion of the materials on the site, the sort of banal commentary that might be found in the comments section of a YouTube video.

Gambaryan had hunted criminals of all stripes for years now, from small-time fraudsters, to corrupt federal law enforcement colleagues, to kingpins running sites like BTC-e and AlphaBay. That was his job, after all; the law was the law, as he saw it. But even as he worked to track down and arrest those targets of his investigations, he'd usually felt he could fundamentally understand them. Sometimes, he had even felt sympathy for them—and not just the federal agents. "I've known drug dealers who are probably better human beings than some white-collar tax evaders," he mused. "I could relate to some of these criminals. Their motivation is just greed. I can rationalize that this is their business."

But now he'd entered a world where people were committing atrocities that he didn't understand, driven by motivations that were entirely inaccessible to him. After his childhood in war-torn Armenia and post-Soviet Russia, and a career delving into the criminal underworld, he considered himself familiar with the worst that people were capable of. Now he felt he had been naive: His first look at Welcome to Video exposed and destroyed a hidden remnant of his idealism about humanity.

"I'd seen a lot of stuff, but I had never seen anything like this," Gambaryan says. "It killed a little bit of me."

. . .

As soon as they had seen firsthand what Welcome to Video truly represented, Gambaryan and Janczewski understood that the case warranted an urgency that went beyond that of even a normal dark web investigation. Every day the site spent online, it enabled more child abuse.

Gambaryan and Janczewski knew their best leads still lay in the blockchain. Crucially, the site didn't seem to have any mechanism for its customers to pull money *out* of their accounts. Unlike a dark web market like the Silk Road or AlphaBay, users didn't have Welcome to Video wallets. There was only an address to which they could send bitcoins for credits on the site; there didn't even seem to be anywhere to ask for a refund. That meant that *all* the money they could see flowing out of the site—more than $300,000 worth of bitcoins at the time of the transactions—would almost certainly belong to the site's administrators.

Gambaryan began reaching out to his contacts in the Bitcoin community, looking for staff at exchanges who might know executives at the two Korean exchanges, Bithumb and Coinone, into which most of Welcome to Video's money had been cashed out, as well as one U.S. exchange that had received a small fraction of the funds. He found that the mere mention of child exploitation seemed to evaporate the cryptocurrency industry's usual resistance to government intervention. "As libertarian as you want to be," Gambaryan says, "this is where everybody kind of drew the line." Even before he sent a formal legal request or subpoena, staff at all three exchanges were ready to help: They promised to get him account details for the addresses he had pulled from Reactor as soon as they could.

In the meantime, Gambaryan continued to scour the Welcome to Video site itself. Soon after first registering an account on the site, he thought to try a certain basic check of its security—a long shot, he figured, but it wouldn't cost anything. He right clicked on the page and chose "View page source" from the resulting menu. This would give him a look at the site's raw HTML before it was rendered by the Tor Browser into a graphical web page. Looking at a massive block of illegible code, anyway, certainly beat staring at an infinite scroll of abject human cruelty.

Almost immediately, he spotted what he was looking for: an IP address. In fact, to Gambaryan's surprise, every thumbnail image on the site seemed to display, within the site's HTML, the IP address of the server where it was physically hosted: 121.185.153.64. He copied those eleven digits into his computer's command line and ran a basic traceroute function, following its path across the internet back to the location of that server, just as he had when trying to locate the infrastructure of BTC-e years earlier.

Incredibly, the results showed this computer wasn't a node in the Tor network at all; Gambaryan was looking at the actual, unprotected address of a Welcome to Video server. And, confirming Levin's initial hunch based on where the site's bitcoins had been cashed out, the site was hosted on a residential connection of an internet service provider in South Korea, outside Seoul.

Welcome to Video's administrator seemed to have made a rookie mistake. The site itself was hosted on Tor, but the thumbnail images it assembled on its home page appeared to be pulled from the same computer without routing the connection through Tor, perhaps in a misguided attempt to make the page load faster.

Gambaryan sat in front of his computer screen, laughing in his D.C. cubicle, staring at the revealed location of a website administrator whose arrest he was greatly looking forward to.

. . .

Janczewski was at a firing range in Maryland, waiting for his turn in a marksmanship training exercise, when he got the first response email from an exchange they had subpoenaed. It came from the American exchange that had handled a small sum from the Welcome to Video cluster but that had answered their request faster than any of the Asian exchanges, sending along the identifying information of the suspected Welcome to Video administrator who had cashed out the site's earnings there.

The email's attachments showed a middle-aged Korean man with an address outside Seoul—exactly corroborating the IP address Gambaryan had found. The documents even included a photo of the man holding up his ID, apparently to prove his identity to the American exchange.

For a moment, Janczewski felt as though he were looking at Welcome to Video's administrator face-to-face. But he remembers thinking that something was off: The man in the picture had noticeably dirty hands, with soil under his fingernails. He looked more like a farmworker than the hands-on-keyboard type he'd expected to be running a dark web site.

Over the next days, the answer began to come into focus. One Korean exchange and then the other sent Gambaryan documents on users who controlled Welcome to Video's cash-out addresses. They named not just that one middle-aged man but also a much younger male, twenty-one years old, named Son Jong-woo. The two men listed the same address and shared the same family name. Were they father and son?

The agents believed they were closing in on the site's administrators. But now that they were starting to see the full picture of Welcome to Video, they had come to understand that merely taking down the site or arresting its admins would hardly serve the interests of justice. The constellation of Bitcoin addresses that Welcome to Video had generated on the blockchain laid out a vast, bustling nexus of both consumers and—far more important—*producers* of child sexual abuse materials.

By this point, Faruqui had brought on a team of other prosecutors to help, including Lindsay Suttenberg, a child-exploitation-focused assistant U.S. attorney. She pointed out that even taking the site off-line shouldn't necessarily be their first priority. "You cannot let a child be raped while you go and try to take down a server in South Korea," as Faruqui summed up her argument.

The team began to realize that, as simple as this "slam dunk" case had seemed at first, after the easy identification of the site's admins, it was actually massive in its complexity: They would need to follow the money not to just one or two web administrators in Korea but also from that central point to hundreds of potential suspects—both active abusers and their complicit audience of enablers—around the entire globe.

Gambaryan's right-click IP address discovery and the quick cooperation from crypto exchanges had been lucky breaks. The real work still lay ahead.

42

Octopus

Just two weeks after Levin had passed on his tip, the team of IRS-CI agents and prosecutors knew almost exactly where Welcome to Video was hosted. But they soon realized they'd need help to go further: They had neither connections to the Korean National Police Agency—which had a reputation for formality and impenetrable bureaucracy—nor the resources to potentially make hundreds of arrests of the site's users, an operation that would require far more personnel than the IRS could muster.

Faruqui suggested they bring in Homeland Security Investigations on the case, partnering with a certain field office across the country, in Colorado Springs. He'd chosen that agency and its far-flung outpost because of a specific agent there whom he'd worked with in the past, a national-security-focused investigator named Thomas Tamsi. Faruqui and Tamsi had together unraveled a North Korean arms-trading operation a year earlier, one that had sought to smuggle weapons components through South Korea and China. In the course of that investigation, they'd flown to Seoul to meet with the KNPA, where, after some introductions by an HSI liaison there, they spent an evening with KNPA officers drinking and singing karaoke.

At a particularly memorable point in the night, the KNPA agents had been comparing Korean and American food—ribbing the U.S. team for their alleged hot-dog-and-hamburger diets. One agent mentioned *sannakji,* a kind of small octopus that some Koreans eat not merely raw but alive and writhing. Tamsi had gamely responded that he'd try it.

A few minutes later, a couple of the Korean agents had brought to the table a fist-sized, living octopus wrapped around a chopstick. Tamsi put the entire squirming cephalopod in his mouth, chewed, and swallowed, even as its tentacles wriggled between his lips and black ink dripped from his face onto the table. "It was absolutely disgusting," Faruqui remembers.

The Koreans found this hilarious. Tamsi gained near-legendary status within certain circles of the KNPA, where he was thereafter referred to as Octopus Guy.

Like most of their group, Tamsi had no experience in child exploitation cases. He had never even worked on a cryptocurrency investigation. But Faruqui insisted that to make inroads in Korea, they needed Octopus Guy.

. . .

Not long afterward, Tamsi and a fellow HSI agent authorized for undercover operations flew to Washington, D.C. They rented a conference room in a hotel, and as Janczewski watched, the undercover agent logged on to Welcome to Video, paid a sum of bitcoins, and began downloading gigabytes of videos.

The strange choice of location—a hotel rather than a government office—was designed to better mask the agent's identity, in case Welcome to Video could somehow track its users despite Tor's protection, and also so that, when it came time to prosecute, the D.C. attorney's office would be given jurisdiction. (The HSI agent did, at least, use a Wi-Fi hot spot for his downloading, to avoid siphoning the web's most toxic content over the hotel's network.)

As soon as the undercover agent's work was complete, they shared the files with Janczewski, who, along with Lindsay Suttenberg, would spend the following weeks watching the videos, cataloging any clues they could find of the identities of the people involved, while also saturating their minds with enough images of child abuse to fill anyone's nightmares for the rest of their lives.

Suttenberg's years as a child exploitation prosecutor had left her somewhat desensitized; she would find that other attorneys on the team couldn't stand to even hear her describe the contents of the videos, no less watch them. "They would ask me to stop talking, to put it in writing," she remembers, "and then they'd tell me that was even worse."

Janczewski, as lead agent on the case, was tasked with putting together an affidavit that would be used in whatever charging document they might eventually bring to court. That meant watching dozens of videos, looking for ones that would represent the most egregious material on the site, and then writing technical descriptions of them for a jury or judge. He describes the experience like a scene from *A Clockwork Orange:* an unending montage from which he constantly wanted to avert his gaze but was professionally required not to.

He believes watching those videos altered him, though in ways he could describe only in the abstract—ways even he's not sure he fully understands. "There's no going back," Janczewski said vaguely. "Once you know what you know, you can't unknow it. And everything that you see in the future comes in through that prism of what you now know."

• • •

In the first weeks of the fall of 2017, the growing team investigating the Welcome to Video network began the painstaking process of tracing every possible user of the site on the blockchain and sending out hundreds of legal requests to exchanges around the world. To help with the time-intensive tracing of every tendril of the Welcome to Video cluster in Reactor, they brought on a Chainalysis staffer named Aron Akbiyikian, an Armenian American former police officer from Fresno whom Gambaryan knew from childhood and had recommended to Levin and Gronager.

Akbiyikian's job was to perform what he called a "cluster audit"— squeezing every possible investigative clue out of the site's cryptocurrency trails. Plenty of Welcome to Video's users had made his job easy. "It was a beautiful clustering in Reactor," Akbiyikian says. "It was just so clear." In some cases, he would trace back chains of payments through several hops before the money arrived at an exchange. But for hundreds of users, he says, he could see wallet addresses receive money from exchanges and then put the funds directly into Welcome to Video's cluster, transactions that had created, as Akbiyikian put it, "leads as clean as you could want." With the help of Chainalysis, the investigators' clustering of Welcome to Video and its users on the blockchain would grow from just a few hundred addresses to more than a million.

As responses from exchanges with those users' identity information began to pour in, the team started the process of assembling more complete profiles of their targets: They began to collect the names, faces, and photos of hundreds of men—and they were almost all men—from all walks of life, everywhere in the world. Their descriptions crossed boundaries of race, age, class, and nationality. All these individuals seemed to have in common, in fact, was their gender and their financial connection to a worldwide, hidden haven of child abuse.

By this time, the team felt they'd pinned down the site's Korean administrator. They'd gotten a search warrant for Son Jong-woo's Gmail accounts and many of his exchange records, and they could see that he alone seemed to be receiving the cashed-out proceeds from the site—not his father, who increasingly looked to the investigators like an unwitting participant, a man whose son had hijacked his identity to create cryptocurrency accounts. In Son Jong-woo's emails, they found photos of the younger man for the first time—selfies he'd taken to show friends where he'd chipped a tooth in a car accident, for instance. He was a thin, unremarkable-looking young Korean man with wide-set eyes and a Beatles-style mop top of black hair.

But as their portrait of this administrator took shape, so too did the profiles of the hundreds of other men who had used the site.* A few immediately stuck out to the investigative team: One suspect, to the dismay of Thomas Tamsi and his Homeland Security colleagues, was an HSI agent in Texas. Another, they saw with a different sort of dread, was the assistant principal of a high school in Georgia. The school administrator had posted videos of himself on social media singing duets, karaoke-style, with teenage girls from his school. The videos might otherwise have been seen as innocent. But given what they knew

---

* For several reasons, I've chosen not to identify the defendants in the Welcome to Video case by name, with the exception of the site's administrator. In some instances, at the time of this writing, a defendant's case had not been fully adjudicated. In other cases, I left out names at the request of prosecutors, to avoid providing information that might inadvertently identify victims. I applied the same standard to the rest, to avoid singling out some offenders while others went unnamed.

about the man's suspected Bitcoin payments, more experienced child-exploitation-focused agents warned Janczewski that they might reflect a form of victim grooming.

These were men in privileged positions of power, with potential access to victims. The investigators could immediately see that, as they suspected, they would need to arrest some of Welcome to Video's users as quickly as possible, even before they could arrange the takedown of the site. Child exploitation experts had cautioned them that some offenders had systems in place to warn others if law enforcement had arrested or compromised them—code words or dead man's switches that sent out alerts if they were absent from their computer for a certain period of time. Still, the Welcome to Video investigation team felt they had little choice but to move quickly and take that risk.

Another suspect, around the same time, came on to their radar for a different reason: He lived in Washington, D.C. The man's home, in fact, was just down the street from the U.S. attorney's office, near the capital's Gallery Place neighborhood. He happened to live in the very same apartment building that one of the prosecutors had only recently moved out of.

That location, they realized, might be useful to them. Janczewski and Gambaryan could easily search the man's home and his computers as a test case. If that proved that the man was a Welcome to Video customer, they would be able to charge the entire case in D.C.'s judicial district, overcoming a key legal hurdle.

As they dug deeper, though, they found that the man was a former congressional staffer and held a high-level job at a prestigious environmental organization. Arresting or searching the home of a target with that sort of profile, they worried, might cause him to make a public outcry, sinking their case.

Just as they trained their sights on this suspect in their midst, however, they found that he had gone strangely quiet on social media. Someone on the team had the idea to pull his travel records. They found that he had flown to the Philippines and was about to fly back to D.C. via Detroit.

This discovery led the agents and prosecutors to two thoughts: First, the Philippines was a notorious destination for sex tourism, often of the kind that preyed on children—the HSI office in Manila constantly had its hands full with child exploitation cases. Second, when the man flew back to the United States, Customs and Border Protection could legally detain him and demand access to his devices to search for evidence—a bizarre and controversial carve out in Americans' constitutional protections that, in this case, might come in handy.

Would their D.C.-based suspect sound the alarm and tear the lid off their investigation, just as it was getting started?

"Yes, this all had the potential to blow up our case," Janczewski says. "But we had to act."

Test Cases

In late October, Customs and Border Protection at the Detroit Metropolitan Airport stopped a man disembarking from a plane from the Philippines on his way back to Washington, D.C., asking him to step aside and taking him into a secondary screening room. Despite his vehement protests, the border agents insisted on taking his computer and phone before allowing him to leave.

A few days later, on October 25, one of the prosecutors on the Welcome to Video investigation team in Washington, D.C., saw an email from her old building's management, where she remained on the distribution list despite having moved out. The email noted that the parking garage ramp in an alley at the back of the tower would be closed that morning. An unnamed resident, it explained, had landed there after jumping to their death from the balcony of their apartment.

The prosecutor put two and two together. The jumper was their Welcome to Video "test case." Janczewski and Gambaryan immediately drove to the apartment tower and confirmed with management: The very first target of their investigation had just committed suicide.

Later that day the two IRS-CI agents returned to the scene of the man's death with a search warrant. They rode the elevator up to the eleventh floor with the building's manager, who was deeply puzzled as to why the IRS was involved, but wordlessly unlocked the door for them. Inside they found an upscale, moderately messy apartment with high ceilings. There were suitcases still not fully unpacked from a trip. The man had ordered a pizza the night before, and part of it remained uneaten on the table.

Janczewski remembers feeling the somber stillness of the man's empty home as he imagined the desperate choice he had faced the night before. Looking down eleven floors from the balcony, the agent could see the wet patch in the alley where the pavement had been hosed off.

D.C.'s metropolitan police offered to show the agents a video of the man falling to his death, captured by a security camera. They politely declined. The Customs and Border Protection office in Detroit, meanwhile, confirmed that they had searched the man's computer—some of its storage was encrypted, but other parts were not—and found child exploitation videos along with surreptitiously recorded videos of adult sex. Their decision to target the man had served its purpose: Their test case had come back positive.

The prosecutors in D.C. paused their work briefly to meet and acknowledge the surreal shock of the man's death: Their investigation of a site hosted halfway around the world had already led someone to kill himself, just blocks away. "It was just a reminder of how serious what we were investigating was," Faruqui says.

Still, the group agreed: They couldn't let the suicide distract them from their work. "We've got to focus on the victims here," Faruqui remembers them telling each other. "That provides clarity."

The IRS agents on the team, for their part, didn't dwell for long on the suicide. Janczewski in particular says he took no gratification from it, and would have much preferred that the man be arrested and charged. But he had, by this point, been forced to watch hour after hour of child sexual abuse videos. He had put aside his emotions early in the case, and he had few left to spare for an apparent customer of those materials.

He admits, in fact, that if he felt anything, it was relief, given the time that the suicide had saved him: They still had hundreds more Welcome to Video customers to pursue.

. . .

Next on their list was the high school assistant principal. Just days later, Janczewski flew down to Georgia and joined a tactical team of HSI agents as they carried out their search. For the first time he came face-to-face with an alleged Welcome to Video client, in his own home.

In spite of his stoicism, this second test case affected Janczewski more than the D.C. target had. The tidy, well-kept brick two-story house. The parents questioned in separate rooms. The kids the same age as Janczewski's own, watching *Mickey Mouse Clubhouse.* As he stood in the foyer of that house outside Atlanta, the full toll of the investigation hit him—the fact that every name on their list was a person with human connections and, in many cases, a family. That even accusing suspects of such an unforgivable crime had an irreversible impact on their lives—that it was "a scarlet letter for someone that just cannot be undone," as he put it.

Janczewski and the HSI agents stayed at the home long enough to search it, to question the man, and to seize his devices for analysis. Their target agreed to a polygraph test at the local police station. Janczewski and Faruqui declined to share the results of that test, but Faruqui says that the man acknowledged "inappropriate touching" of students at his school, an admission of hands-on abuse, in addition to the evidence of his payments for material on Welcome to Video. He would later be charged with multiple counts of sexual assault against minors, though he would plead not guilty.

For Janczewski at least, any last doubts he had felt after his first confrontation of a suspect based on cryptocurrency tracing alone were dispelled in a matter of hours. "I would just say, at the end of the day, I felt more confident," he says. "We were correct." The blockchain had not lied.

· · ·

The team was steadily working their way through their short list of high-priority Welcome to Video targets and test cases. But in December 2017, they came upon a different sort of lead—one that would scramble those priorities yet again.

As they followed Welcome to Video's financial trails, investigators had been careful to record the full contents of the site's chat page, where users were still posting a steady stream of comments. Most of it was spam and trolling, the usual garbage that filled any unfiltered, anonymous web forum. The site did seem to be, in fact, entirely unmoderated: There was not so much as an admin email or help contact visible anywhere. But Janczewski would occasionally scan through the chats—using Google Translate for the foreign-language messages—and look for any clues they might offer. He began to notice repeated messages that seemed to be the closest thing the site had to that missing help-desk contact. "Contact the admins," the messages read, "if you want assistance in fixing error."

It included an address on TorBox, a privacy-focused Tor-based email service.

Was this an actual moderator on the site? Or even the administrator himself—the owner of the site they now believed to be Son Jong-woo?

As Janczewski tried to decipher who was behind those messages, he had no blockchain clues to work from. He checked the username before the "@" in the TorBox address, a unique-looking string of six characters, to see if it matched a user on Welcome to Video. Sure enough, he found that someone with that same handle had uploaded more than a hundred videos.

Excygent's Aaron Bice had the idea to run this TorBox email address against IRS-CI's seized BTC-e database, to look for clues in its treasure trove of criminal underworld user data. He found a match: One account on BTC-e had been registered with an email address that included that same unique string of six characters. It wasn't the TorBox email address, but one from a different privacy-focused email service, called Sigaint.

Janczewski knew that TorBox and Sigaint, both dark web services themselves, wouldn't respond to legal requests for their users' information. But the BTC-e data for the user with that Sigaint IP address included IP addresses for ten past log-ins on the exchange. In nine out of ten, the IP address was obscured with a VPN or Tor. But for one single visit to BTC-e, the user had slipped up: They had left their actual home IP address exposed.

"That opened the whole door," says Janczewski. The BTC-e server they'd seized just a few months earlier had immediately proven its worth, allowing them to eke out another lead in the Welcome to Video case.

A traceroute showed that the IP address led to a residential internet connection—not in Korea this time, but in Texas. Was there a second Welcome to Video admin, this one based in the United States? Janczewski and Bice continued pulling the thread with increasing urgency, subpoenaing the user's account information from their internet service provider.

It was a Friday morning in early December, and Janczewski was drinking coffee at his desk in the IRS-CI office when he got back the results of that subpoena: He opened the email to find a name and a home address. The man was an American in his thirties who lived in a town outside San Antonio—an unlikely collaborator for a twenty-one-year-old Korean managing a child exploitation site fifteen time zones away. But the man's employment, when Janczewski looked it up, was even more jarring: He was *another* Department of Homeland Security staffer—this time a Border Patrol agent.

Janczewski quickly began to assemble public information about the agent from his social media accounts; he first found a Facebook page for the man's wife, and later an account for the man himself, with his name written backward to obscure it. Bice dug up his Amazon page, too, where he seemed to leave reviews on hundreds of products and put others on a "wish list"—including external storage devices that could hold terabytes of videos, hidden cameras, and other cameras designed to be snaked through small spaces, like holes drilled in a wall.

Finally, with a creeping sense of dread, Janczewski saw that the Border Patrol agent's wife had a young daughter and that he had created a crowdfunding page on GoFundMe to raise money to legally adopt the girl as his stepdaughter.

"*Fuck,*" Janczewski thought to himself. "Did he upload videos of the daughter?"

Janczewski looked back at Welcome to Video and saw that some of the thumbnails of the videos uploaded by the person with this username showed the sexual assault of a young girl about the daughter's age. He realized he wouldn't be spending that weekend at home—that he now had a duty to separate this Border Patrol agent from his victim as quickly as possible.

For the next ten days, Janczewski barely left his desk. He'd drive home, eat dinner quickly with his family in their small Arlington, Virginia, town house, then drive back to the office to work late, often calling Bice and Faruqui well into the night.

"You are rarely in a situation where your time is zero-sum," Faruqui observed. "Every moment we were not working on that case, a little girl could be getting raped."

Janczewski asked their undercover HSI agent to download the videos that had been uploaded by the Texas agent, and he began the grueling process of watching them one by one. A few videos in, he spotted something that jolted the pattern-matching subroutines of his brain: At one point in the recording, the girl in the video he was watching had a red flannel shirt tied around her waist. He looked back at a photo of the girl posted to the GoFundMe page and saw it: She was wearing the same red flannel.

Was this Border Patrol agent an admin on Welcome to Video? A moderator? It hardly mattered. He now believed he'd found the identity of an active child rapist who lived with his victim and had been recording and sharing his crimes with thousands of other users. The Texas man had earned a place at the very top of their target list.

. . .

Two weeks before Christmas, on the tenth day after he'd identified the Border Patrol agent, Janczewski flew to southern Texas along with HSI's Thomas Tamsi and the team's child-exploitation-focused prosecutor, Lindsay Suttenberg. On a cool, dry evening about a hundred miles from the Mexican border, Tamsi and a group of Texas State Police officers tailed their target as he was driving home from work and pulled him over. Together with a group of FBI agents, they took the man to a nearby hotel for questioning.

Meanwhile, Janczewski and a group of local Homeland Security investigators entered the man's house and began to search for evidence. The two-story home was run-down and messy, Janczewski remembers—with the exception of the man's well-organized home office on the second floor, where they found his computer. Down the hall from that office he came to the girl's bedroom and immediately recognized it as the scene where the videos uploaded by the man had been filmed. He spotted on the wall a poster he'd seen in the recordings and momentarily felt as though he'd fallen through the screen of his own computer into the set of a horror film.

The IRS agent and prosecutor had brought with them an FBI interviewer with child exploitation training to speak to the daughter; the interviewer separated the girl from the agents searching her home and took her to a safer location, where prosecutors say the girl eventually detailed the abuse she'd experienced.

Shortly after the search of the Border Patrol agent's home, Janczewski arrived at the hotel room where other agents were questioning their suspect. He saw, for the first time, the target of his last week and a half's obsession. The man was tall and burly, still in his uniform, with thinning hair. He initially refused to talk about any hands-on abuse he might have committed, Janczewski says, but he eventually confessed to possessing, sharing, and—finally—making child sexual abuse videos.

Janczewski was struck, in fact, by the dispassionate, almost clinical way the man described his actions. He gave his interrogators the password to his home computer, and an agent still at the house began pulling evidence from the machine and sending it to Janczewski. It included detailed spreadsheets of every child sexual exploitation video the man had both amassed on his hard drives and, by all appearances, filmed in his own home.

Another spreadsheet from the man's computer contained a long list of other Welcome to Video users' log-in credentials. Under questioning, the man explained his scheme: He would pose as an administrator in messages he posted to the site's chat page, then ask users who took the bait to send him their usernames and passwords, which he'd use to log in to their accounts and access their videos.

The Border Patrol agent had never been a Welcome to Video administrator or moderator at all, only a particularly devious visitor to the site, willing to scam his fellow users to support his own appetites.

After an intense ten days, they'd identified and arrested another alleged child abuser, and even rescued his victim. But after all of it, Janczewski knew, as he flew back to D.C., that Welcome to Video's vastly larger network of abuse remained very much intact. And until they took the site itself down, it would continue to serve its videos—including the very ones the Border Patrol agent had uploaded from his Texas home office—to an anonymous throng of consumers just like him.

Seoul

In early January 2018, the D.C. investigators got word from Thomas Tamsi that he and the team had arrested the other federal law enforcement customer of Welcome to Video—Tamsi's HSI colleague who'd shown up early in their blockchain tracing and subpoenas. Though seemingly unconnected with the Border Patrol agent case, this second agent had been based in Texas, too, less than an hour away from the home of the man they had just raided.

Aside from that grim coincidence, the news of the HSI agent's arrest also meant that the D.C. team's initial list of high-priority suspects was finally checked off. They could move on to their primary target: Son Jong-woo and the Welcome to Video server under his control.

By February, that Korea-focused operation was coming together. Before the Texas arrests, Janczewski, Gambaryan, Faruqui, and Tamsi had flown to Seoul to meet the Korean National Police Agency. At a dinner set up by the local HSI attaché, the director of the KNPA himself told Tamsi—whose octopus-eating reputation preceded him—that the KNPA director would give them his "best team." Soon they had Son Jong-woo under constant surveillance as he came and went from his home, an apartment building two and a half hours south of Seoul in the province of South Chungcheong.

Now, in the depths of winter on the Korean peninsula, just a week after Korea had hosted the Olympics in Pyeongchang, the U.S. team arrived in Seoul again. Gambaryan had to stay behind for a badly timed conference where the agency's director had volunteered him to speak. But Janczewski and Faruqui brought with them Aaron Bice and Youli

Lee, a Korean American computer crime prosecutor on their team. By this point, too, a growing international force had assembled around the case. The U.K.'s National Crime Agency, which had launched its own investigation into Welcome to Video just after Levin's London visit, sent two agents to Seoul, and the German federal police also joined the coalition. It turned out the Germans had been pursuing the site's administrators independently even before they'd learned about the IRS's investigation, but they'd never been able to secure the KNPA's cooperation.

At one point Faruqui remembers a German official asking him, as they stood in the cold outside the Seoul hotel where they were staying, how the Americans had gotten the Korean police on board so quickly. "Oh, Octopus Guy," Faruqui had explained. "You don't have Octopus Guy. We have Octopus Guy."

. . .

For their first days in Seoul, the takedown team met repeatedly in the KNPA's offices to talk through their plans. Their tracing of the IP address, based on Gambaryan's fortuitous right click, seemed to show that the site's server was located, bizarrely, not in any web-hosting firm's data center but in Son Jong-woo's own apartment. When they seized that server, would they find that its contents were encrypted and inaccessible? Was the hard drive of whatever computer Son used to administer the site set to encrypt itself, too, like the laptops of Ross Ulbricht and Alexandre Cazes? Unlike Cazes, with his tell-all Roosh V posts, Son hadn't leaked information about his computers' configuration anywhere they could find it.

The team decided they couldn't wait for some rare opportunity to grab Son's computer while he was logged in to the site in public, like Ulbricht, or trick him into coming out of his home with the machine unlocked, like Cazes. Perhaps they didn't even need to. They had clear blockchain proof of his receipt of payments from Welcome to Video and a server at the center of a massive child sexual abuse video network *in his home.*

They would keep it simple: arrest him, tear his site off-line, and use that evidence to convict him. The team made a plan to grab him in his apartment early on a Monday morning.

Then, on the Friday before that arrest date, Janczewski got a cold. He spent much of the weekend with the prosecutor Youli Lee, dazedly wandering between markets and stores in Seoul trying to pronounce *gaseubgi,* the Korean word for humidifier. On Sunday evening he took a dose of what he hoped was a Korean equivalent of NyQuil—he couldn't read the label—with the intention of getting some sleep and recovering in time to be at full strength for the arrest.

That's when the KNPA alerted the team that the plan had changed: Son had unexpectedly driven into Seoul for the weekend. Now the team following his whereabouts believed he had begun a late-night drive back to his home south of the city.

If the police could drive down to Son's home that night and stake it out, perhaps they could be there when he returned, ready to arrest him at his door. That way he couldn't destroy evidence or—another looming concern after the deaths of their Washington, D.C., target and Alexandre Cazes—commit suicide. "We had to scramble," Janczewski says.

That evening, Faruqui insisted the group put their hands in for a "Go, team" cheer in their hotel lobby. Then he and Lee went up to their rooms to go to bed. Janczewski, sick, half-asleep from cold medication, and clutching a pillow from his hotel room, walked out into the pouring rain and got in a car with the HSI liaison to start the long night drive south. The HSI agent had begged Janczewski to take the wheel of another car in the caravan, instead of an elderly Korean man on his team who was, the agent said, a notoriously bad driver. But Janczewski insisted he was far too medicated to navigate the dark, wet highways of a country seven thousand miles from his home.

A few hours later, the team arrived in the parking lot of Son's apartment—a ten-story tower with a few small buildings on one side and a vast, empty rural landscape on the other—to begin their long stakeout in the rain.

It was well past midnight before they saw Son's car finally pull in to the parking garage of the complex.

A group of KNPA agents had been waiting there for him. One particularly imposing KNPA officer, whom the HSI agents referred to as Smiley—because he never seemed to smile—led a team of plainclothes police, sidling into the elevator next to Son as he got inside. The agents silently rode the elevator up to Son's floor with him and stepped out when he did. They arrested him, without resistance, just as he reached his front door.

Throughout that arrest and the hours-long search of Son's apartment that followed, Janczewski and the other foreigners remained stuck in their cars in the rain-drenched parking lot: Only the KNPA had authorization to lay hands on Son or enter his home. When the Korean officers had the young Welcome to Video admin handcuffed, they asked him if he'd consent to letting Janczewski or any of the Americans come in as well. Son, unsurprisingly, said no. So Janczewski was limited to a tour via FaceTime of the small and unremarkable apartment that Son shared with his divorced father, the man with the soiled hands in the first photo they'd examined, as the KNPA scoured it for evidence and seized Son's devices.

The KNPA agent showing Janczewski around eventually pointed the phone's camera at a desktop computer on the floor of Son's bedroom, a cheap-looking tower-style PC with its case open on one side. The computer's guts revealed the hard drives that Son had apparently added, one by one, as each drive had filled up with terabytes of child exploitation videos.

This was the Welcome to Video server.

"I was expecting some kind of glowing, ominous thing," Janczewski remembers. "And it was just this dumpy computer. It was just so strange. This dumpy computer, that had caused so much havoc around the world, was sitting on this kid's floor."

. . .

On the return trip, Janczewski learned exactly why the HSI liaison had wanted him to drive the other car. The elderly HSI staffer behind the wheel of the other vehicle in their caravan was somehow so disoriented after a sleepless night that he turned the wrong way down a highway exit ramp, narrowly avoiding a high-speed collision and terrifying his passenger, Aaron Bice.

After barely averting that disaster, as the sun began to rise and the rain let up, the group pulled over at a truck stop along the highway to have a breakfast of gas-station instant ramen. Janczewski, still sick and utterly exhausted, was struck by how anticlimactic it all seemed. His team had located and extricated both the administrator and the machine at the epicenter of the malevolent global network they were investigating. He had been anticipating this moment for more than six months. But he felt no elation.

There were no high fives, no celebration. The agents got back in their cars to continue the long drive back to Seoul.

CHAPTER 45

The Net

The next day, after finally getting some sleep, Janczewski began to see past the dreariness of the previous night's operation to understand just how lucky they had been. He learned from the forensic analysts who had examined Son Jong-woo's computers that Son hadn't encrypted his server. Everything was there: all of Welcome to Video's content, its user database, and the wallets that had handled all of its Bitcoin transactions.

The scale of the video collection, now that they could see it in its entirety, was staggering. There were more than 250,000 videos on the server, more content by volume than in any child sexual abuse materials case in history. When they later shared the collection with the National Center for Missing and Exploited Children, or NCMEC, which helps to catalog, identify, and take down CSAM materials across the internet, NCMEC found that it had never seen 45 percent of the videos before: Welcome to Video's uniqueness check and incentive system for fresh content appeared to serve its purpose, motivating countless new cases of recorded child abuse.

The real prize for the investigators, however, was the site's user information. The KNPA gave the U.S. team a copy of Welcome to Video's databases, and they got to work in a U.S. embassy building in Seoul, reconstructing those data collections on their own machine. Meanwhile, to avoid tipping off the site's users to the takedown, they quickly set up a look-alike Welcome to Video home page on their own server, using the private key pulled from the real server to take over its dark web address. When users visited the site, it now displayed only a message that it was under construction and would be back soon with "upgrades," complete with typos to mimic Son's shoddy English spelling.

Bice spent two days with his head down, rebuilding the site's user data in a form they could easily query—with Janczewski and Faruqui standing behind him, pestering him to see if the system was ready yet. When Bice was finished, the U.S. team had a full directory of the site's pseudonymous users, listed by username. They could now link every Bitcoin payment they had initially mapped out on the blockchain with those usernames and look up exactly what content each of those users had uploaded or downloaded.

By the time the Americans were ready to go home at the end of February, they had integrated the de-anonymized identities from their cryptocurrency exchange subpoenas into a searchable database that mapped out the entire Welcome to Video network, complete with names, photos, and, for those who had paid into the site, the record of those payments and the exact child abuse videos those customers had bought access to. "You could see the whole picture," Janczewski says. "It was like a dictionary, thesaurus, and Wikipedia all put together."

They had, arrayed before them, the fully revealed structure of Welcome to Video's global child exploitation ring—a set of hundreds of exquisitely detailed profiles of consumers, collectors, sharers, producers, and hands-on abusers alike. Now the final phase of the case could begin.

· · ·

Over the weeks that followed, Thomas Tamsi's team in Colorado began sending their Welcome to Video dossiers to HSI agents, local police, and foreign law enforcement agencies around the world. These "targeting packages" included descriptions of the suspects, the record of their transactions, any other evidence they'd assembled about them, and—given that they were being sent out to agents who had in some cases never been involved in a cryptocurrency-related investigation—short primers on how Bitcoin and its blockchain worked.

There would be no coordinated, global takedown, no attempt to create shock and awe with simultaneous arrests. The case's defendants were far too distributed and international for that kind of synchronized operation. Instead, searches, arrests, and interviews began to roll out across the globe—prioritized by those they'd learned might be active abusers, then uploaders, and finally downloaders. Slowly, as Welcome to Video's users were confronted, one by one, the D.C. team began to hear back about the results of their work—with harrowing, sometimes gratifying, often tragic outcomes.

A Kansas IT worker—whose arrest they'd prioritized when they found his wife ran an at-home day care for infants and toddlers—had allegedly deleted all of his child abuse videos from his computer before the agents arrived; prosecutors say he later confessed when remnants of the files in the computer's storage matched their records from the Welcome to Video server.

When the agents came for a twentysomething man in New York, his father blocked the door of their apartment, thinking at first that it was a break-in. But when agents explained what their warrant was for, he turned on his son and let them in. The son, it later turned out, had sexually assaulted the daughter of a family friend and surreptitiously recorded another young girl through her webcam, according to prosecutors.

A repeat offender in Washington, D.C., tried to commit suicide when the HSI team entered his home; he hid in his bathroom and slit his own throat. One of the arresting agents happened to have training as an army medic. He managed to slow the bleeding and keep the man alive. They later found 450,000 hours of child abuse videos on his computers, including recordings of the girl in Texas that had been uploaded by the Border Patrol agent.

As months passed, the stories continued to pile up, a mix of the sordid, sad, and appalling: an elderly man in his seventies who had uploaded more than eighty child abuse videos; a man in his early twenties with traumatic brain damage, deemed to have the same level of cognitive development as the preteens whose abuse he had watched, and whose medication had heightened his sexual appetites and reduced his impulse control; a New Jersey man whose communications, when they were revealed through a search warrant, seemed to show his negotiations to purchase a child for his own sexual exploitation.

Thomas Tamsi, as the lead HSI agent on the case, coordinated more Welcome to Video arrests than anyone else—more than fifty, by his count—and was present for enough of them that they became a blur in which only the most jarring moments remain distinct in his mind:

the mostly nude defendant he found in a basement; the suspect who told him he had been involved in the Boy Scouts and that "children had always been attracted" to him; parents of victims who vehemently denied that a family friend could have done the things Tamsi described, and whose faces then went white as he slid printouts of redacted screenshots across the table.

The cases spanned the globe, well beyond the United States. Dozens of Welcome to Video users were arrested in the Czech Republic, Spain, Brazil, Ireland, France, and Canada. In England, the country's National Crime Agency arrested one twenty-six-year-old who had allegedly abused two children—one of whom they found naked on a bed in his home—and uploaded more than six thousand files to the site. In another international case, a Hungarian ambassador to Peru who downloaded content from Welcome to Video was found to have more than nineteen thousand CSAM images on his computer. He was quietly removed from his South American post, taken to Hungary, charged, and pleaded guilty.

For the D.C. team, many of the international cases fell into a kind of black hole: One Saudi Arabian Welcome to Video user returned to his home country and was captured by Saudi law enforcement. Faruqui and Janczewski say they never heard what happened to the man; he was left to that country's own justice system, which sentences some sex criminals to the Sharia-based punishments of whipping or even beheading. When agents searched the car of a Chinese national living near Seattle with a job at Amazon, they found a teddy bear along with a map of playgrounds in the area, despite the man having no children of his own. The man subsequently fled to China and, as far as the prosecutors know, was never located again.

In each of the hundreds of intelligence packets that the team sent out, Chris Janczewski's contact was listed as the number to call with any questions. Janczewski found himself explaining the blockchain and its central role in the case, again and again, to HSI agents and local police officers around the United States and the world, many of whom had never even heard of Bitcoin or the dark web. "You get this lead sent to you that says, 'Here's this website and this funny internet money,'" Janczewski says, imagining how those on the receiving end of the intelligence packets must have seen it, "and now you need to go arrest this guy because some nerd accountant says so."

In total, Janczewski traveled to six countries and spoke to more than fifty different people to help explain the case, often multiple times each—including one U.S. prosecutor and agent team with whom he had more than twenty conversations. ("Some were a little more high maintenance, respectfully, than others," he says.) Bice, who oversaw the reconstructed server data, says he spoke to even more agents and officers—well over a hundred, by his count.

Ultimately, from the beginning of the case through the year and a half that followed the server seizure, global law enforcement would arrest no fewer than 337 people for their involvement with Welcome to Video. They also removed twenty-three children from sexually exploitative situations.*

Those 337 arrests still represented only a small fraction of Welcome to Video's total registered users. When the U.S. team examined their copy of the server data in Korea, they had found thousands of accounts on the site. But the vast majority of them had never paid any bitcoins into the site's wallets. With no money to follow, the investigators' trail usually went cold.

If not for cryptocurrency, in other words, and the years-long trap set by its purported untraceability, the majority of the 337 pedophiles arrested in the Welcome to Video case—and their rescued victims—likely never would have been found.

---

* With the exception of the girl abused by the Texas Border Patrol agent, the D.C. team refused to tell me anything about the stories of those victims for fear of identifying and retraumatizing them.

Ripples

The IRS and the D.C. U.S. attorney's office had taken an unprecedented approach, treating a massive child sexual abuse materials case as a financial investigation, and it had worked. Just as Faruqui had hoped—and as Gambaryan had first imagined years earlier in the days of the Silk Road—Bitcoin's blockchain had served as a lodestar that had led them through a landmark takedown.

Yes, Son Jong-woo's shoddy opsec and Gambaryan's IP-address discovery had been breakthroughs. But Faruqui argues that they would have found the server anyway via the blockchain's leads, and without those cryptocurrency trails they would never have managed to map out and identify so many of the site's users.

"That was the only path through this darkness," says Faruqui. "The darker the darknet gets, the way that you shine the light is following the money."

Throwing money-laundering investigators into the deep end of the internet's CSAM cesspool, however, had taken its toll. Almost every member of the team had children of their own, and almost all of them say they became far more protective of those children as a result of their work, to the degree that their trust in the people around their family has been significantly damaged.

Janczewski, who after the case moved from D.C. to Grand Rapids, Michigan, won't let his children ride their bikes to school on their own, as he himself did as a child. Even seemingly innocent interactions—like another friendly parent who offers to watch his kids at the other end of a swimming pool—now trigger red alerts in his mind. Youli Lee says she won't allow her nine- and twelve-year-old children to go into public bathrooms by themselves. Nor will she allow them to play at a friend's house unless the friend's parents have top secret security clearances—an admittedly arbitrary rule, but one she says ensures the parents have at least had a background check.

Faruqui says the fifteen or so videos he watched as part of the investigation remain "indelibly seared" into his brain and have permanently heightened his sense of the dangers the world presents to his children. He and his wife argue, he says, about his overprotective tendencies. "You always see the worst of humanity, and so you've lost perspective," he quotes his wife telling him. "And I say, 'You lack perspective, because you don't know what's out there.'"

Gambaryan's wife, Yuki, says that the Welcome to Video case was the only time that her hard-shelled, Soviet-born husband ever discussed a case with her and confessed that it had gotten to him—that he was struggling with it emotionally. Gambaryan says that it was, in particular, the sheer breadth of the cross section of society that participated in the site's abuse that still haunts him.

"I saw that everybody's capable of this: doctors, principals, law enforcement," he reflected. "Whatever you want to call it, evil, or whatever it is: It's in everybody—or it can be in anybody."

. . .

In early July 2020, Son Jong-woo walked out of a Seoul penitentiary wearing a black long-sleeve T-shirt and carrying a green plastic bag of his belongings. He had spent, due to Korea's lenient laws on child sexual abuse, just eighteen months in prison.

U.S. prosecutors, including Faruqui, had argued that he should be extradited to the United States to face charges in the American justice system, but Korea had denied their request. Welcome to Video's convicted creator and administrator was free.

The D.C.-based team that worked the Welcome to Video case remains deeply dissatisfied with Son's mystifyingly light sentence for running, by some measures, the biggest child sexual abuse materials website in history. But Janczewski says he's comforted by the outcry in Korean society over the case. The country's social media exploded in anger over Son's quick release. More than 400,000 people signed a petition to prevent the judge in the case from being considered for a seat on the country's Supreme Court. One Korean lawmaker put forward a bill to allow appeals to extradition judgments, and the country's National Assembly introduced new legislation to strengthen punishments for sexual abuse online and downloading child sexual abuse materials.

In the United States, meanwhile, the ripple effects of the case continued for years. Janczewski, Bice, and Suttenberg say that they still get calls from law enforcement officials following the leads they assembled. On the computer of the D.C. investigators' very first test case—the former congressional staffer who committed suicide—they found evidence in a cryptocurrency exchange account that he'd also paid into a *different* source of dark web sexual materials. They followed those payments to a site called Dark Scandals, what turned out to be a smaller but equally disturbing repository of sexual abuse recordings.

Janczewski, Gambaryan, and the same group of prosecutors pursued that Dark Scandals case in parallel with the tail end of the Welcome to Video investigation, similarly following blockchain leads to trace the site's cash-outs. With the help of the Dutch National Police, they arrested the site's alleged administrator in the Netherlands, a man named Michael Rahim Mohammad, who went by the online handle "Mr. Dark." He faces criminal charges in the United States, and as of this writing his case is ongoing.

From the perspective of Welcome to Video's money-laundering-focused agents and prosecutors, perhaps the most interesting of all those ripple effects of the case stemmed from the fate of the HSI agent they had arrested in Texas, just before their trip to carry out the site takedown in Korea. The Texas man had taken a rare approach to his legal defense: He'd pleaded guilty to possession of child sexual abuse materials, but he also appealed his conviction. He argued that his case should be thrown out because IRS agents had identified him by tracking his Bitcoin payments—without a warrant—which he claimed violated his Fourth Amendment right to privacy and represented an unconstitutional "search."

A panel of appellate judges considered the argument—and rejected it. In a nine-page opinion, they explained their ruling, setting down a precedent that spelled out in glaring terms exactly how far from private they determined Bitcoin's transactions to be.

"Every Bitcoin user has access to the public Bitcoin blockchain and can see every Bitcoin address and its respective transfers. Due to this publicity, it is possible to determine the identities of Bitcoin address owners by analyzing the blockchain," the ruling read. "There is no intrusion into a constitutionally protected area because there is no constitutional privacy interest in the information on the blockchain."

A search requires a warrant, the American judicial system has long held, only if that search enters into a domain where the defendant has a "reasonable expectation of privacy." The judges' ruling argued that no such expectation should have existed here: The HSI agent wasn't caught in the Welcome to Video dragnet because IRS agents had violated his privacy. He was caught, the judges concluded, because he had mistakenly believed his Bitcoin transactions to have ever been private in the first place.

. . .

In 1931, the IRS's Criminal Investigation division carried out a case against the legendary mob boss Al Capone that still holds mythic status within the agency. IRS-CI agents followed the money, proved Capone had evaded taxes, and used that charge to bring down the most notorious and elusive gangster of the era.

IRS-CI agents joke that the agency's director can't give a speech without a reference to the Capone case. Pictures of Capone appear throughout the halls of the agency's headquarters. The case came more than a decade after IRS-CI's initial founding, but still serves almost as an institutional origin story, proof that the most dangerous criminals in the world can be defeated through the unglamorous work of financial accounting.

Chris Janczewski says the full impact of the Welcome to Video investigation didn't hit him until a day in October 2019, when the majority of Welcome to Video's hundreds of arrests were finished, a seizure notice was posted to the site's home page, and the case's results were finally, publicly announced. That morning, Janczewski received a call, unexpectedly, from the IRS commissioner himself, Charles Rettig.

Rettig congratulated Janczewski on his team's good work. He told Janczewski that he'd reviewed the Welcome to Video case and had been receiving messages about it from former commissioners. One of those former commissioners had written, and Rettig agreed, that the case was "this generation's Al Capone"—perhaps the highest compliment that can be bestowed within IRS-CI.

That same day, the Justice Department held a press conference at the U.S. attorney's office to announce the investigation's results. The U.S. attorney Jessie Liu gave a speech to a crowd of reporters about what the case represented—how following the money had allowed agents to score a victory against "one of the worst forms of evil imaginable."

Chainalysis's Jonathan Levin sat in the audience. Afterward, an IRS official named Greg Monahan, who had supervised Gambaryan and Janczewski, came over to thank Levin for his role in the case. It had all started, after all, from Levin's tip to two bored IRS agents in the Bangkok airport. Monahan told Levin that it was the most important investigation of his career, that he could now retire knowing he had worked on something truly worthwhile.

Levin shook the IRS-CI supervisor's hand. As he did, he thought again of the blockchain's bounty of evidence: the countless cases left to crack, the millions of cryptocurrency transactions eternally preserved in amber, and the golden age of criminal forensics it presented to any investigator ready to excavate them.

"There's so much more to do," Levin told Monahan. "We're just getting started."

PART V

THE
NEXT
ROUND

Open Season

For IRS-CI's computer crimes unit, the years that followed the Alpha-Bay and Welcome to Video cases were, just as Jonathan Levin had imagined, a golden age of digital follow-the-money detective work. Tracing cryptocurrency trails, they found leads that carried them from one major operation to the next in a whirlwind, often in such rapid succession that they were overlapping, picking up new investigations as fast as they could track dirty finances to their origins and dismantle the criminal operations behind them.

"It was just one giant case after another," says Matt Price, an agent who had joined the D.C. unit after a stint at the CIA. "We'd do a case that I didn't think we could top. And then we'd just keep blowing stuff up. Welcome to Video was just the start."

Beginning in 2017, even while he was pursuing Welcome to Video, Gambaryan had partnered with his old AlphaBay investigation colleagues Grant Rabenn and Alden Pelker, along with the Los Angeles field office of the FBI, to take down a dark web drug sales site called Wall Street Market. Just as with AlphaBay, the group traced the admins' funds on the blockchain and pinpointed the market's IP addresses using Chainalysis's same ultrasecret "advanced analysis" trick, developed in pursuit of AlphaBay. In the end, they tracked down the site's servers in a five-story underground Cold War military facility in Germany designed to survive a nuclear blast—held by a hosting company that had branded itself CyberBunker. German police arrested the market's three German administrators in the spring of 2019.

As part of the same takedown, Brazilian police arrested another of the dark web market's staffers: a high-level moderator who had once applied for a position on Hansa while it was secretly under the control of the Dutch police—the same man who had written "Please don't send the cops to this address hahahahahaha just kidding." When the cops entered the moderator's home, the man sliced open his own throat with a knife, but he received medical care and survived.

As for Chris Janczewski and Zia Faruqui, they followed the Welcome to Video and Dark Scandals cases by picking up the money trails of two massive heists from Bitcoin exchanges. By the beginning of 2020, they'd traced those two exchange thefts to an increasingly prolific kind of Bitcoin burglar: North Korean state-sponsored hackers.

As international sanctions against North Korea in response to the country's human rights abuses and military threats had limited the dictatorship's access to the global banking system, Kim Jong Un's totalitarian regime was increasingly funding itself with stolen cryptocurrency. By August 2020, Janczewski and Faruqui, working with teams from the FBI and U.S. Cyber Command—the organization within the Department of Defense focused on offensive cyber operations—had managed to trace $300 million worth of bitcoins that North Korean hackers known as the Lazarus Group had siphoned out of the two exchanges. They ultimately identified two Chinese brokers who had helped to cash out $100 million of that stolen loot. Both brokers were indicted in absentia, but they and the Lazarus hackers themselves remained beyond the reach of U.S. law enforcement, and only a few million dollars' worth of the thieves' total haul have been reclaimed.

One summer afternoon in 2020 during that North Korean hacker investigation—in the early months of the COVID-19 pandemic—Twitter suddenly blew up with strange messages, seemingly posted by many of its most high-profile users. Hackers, it soon became clear, had simultaneously taken over the Twitter accounts of Bill Gates, Elon Musk, Jeff Bezos, Barack Obama, Apple, and the then presidential candidate Joe Biden, all to deliver the same message: "I'm feeling generous because of COVID-19. I'll double any BTC payment sent to my BTC address for the next hour. Good luck, and stay safe out there!" The scam netted nearly $120,000 in just minutes before the messages could be deleted. Twitter's staff went so far as to temporarily prevent all verified accounts from posting, a drastic measure to limit the damage from its worst-ever security breach.

Gambaryan and a team of FBI agents jumped on the case, working with Gambaryan's old assistant U.S. attorney partner in San Francisco, Will Frentzen. After a series of feverish twenty-hour days, they had traced the Bitcoin addresses in the scam tweets, as well as other blockchain leads and IP addresses. Many had been found in a leak of user data and messages from a group called OGUsers, frequented by young cybercriminals. They identified three hackers behind the scam—two in Florida and one in the U.K.—who had exploited access to an internal Twitter administration tool. All three were immediately arrested.* The entire investigation took just over two weeks.

. . .

Amid the frenzy of the IRS-CI's back-to-back bombshell cases during those years, two were particularly ironic. They targeted "mixer" services designed, themselves, to protect their customers from precisely these kinds of financial investigations. Helix and Bitcoin Fog both promised to blend together different users' bitcoins and, after taking a commission, send them back with no forensic trail that could be tracked on the blockchain. In the end, IRS-CI busted both—using the very blockchain analysis techniques they were meant to defeat.

Chainalysis had long tracked Helix's cluster of Bitcoin addresses, scoping out its massive hair ball of transactions designed to confound any detective. Many of those transactions were going into and out of AlphaBay; in the market's final months, Cazes had even partnered with Helix and went so far as to advertise its services on the site.

In mid-2017, Chainalysis had tipped off IRS-CI to what appeared to be a pattern of hundreds upon hundreds of small sums of bitcoins, all coming out of that cluster. The payments looked inhuman in their timing, likely the work of an automated program. Were these Helix's commissions?

The IRS-CI computer crime unit's new agent Matt Price picked up

---

* One of the three hackers, a seventeen-year-old named Graham Ivan Clark, pleaded guilty. The cases of the other two men are ongoing.

the thread just after the AlphaBay takedown. He eventually followed one trail out of those hundreds of payments to the service BitPay—the payment processor that offered to let users buy any goods or services with cryptocurrency—and found that the recipient of those apparent commissions had spent some of them to buy a gift card at a hardware store.

A subpoena to BitPay revealed the spender's identity: an Akron, Ohio, man named Larry Harmon. Searching Harmon's Google account revealed an incredible slipup. In 2014, not long after launching Helix, Harmon had taken a picture—perhaps accidentally—of the view of his work space with his Google Glass augmented reality headset, and then uploaded it to his Google Photos account. The photo showed his computer screen. He was logged in to Helix's administrator control panel.

In February 2020, IRS-CI raided Harmon's properties and seized 4,400 bitcoins—worth more than $130 million at today's exchange rates—as well as his mansion in Akron, a second home in Belize, and his Tesla. When Price arrested Harmon in his house in Ohio, he says Harmon initially denied knowing anything about Helix. Price says he showed Harmon his own Google Glass photo of the Helix admin page. "It was probably the most 'oh fuck' expression on his face that I've ever seen from a subject," Price says.

At the same time as that investigation, Gambaryan and Price similarly traced the blockchain trail of Bitcoin Fog, an even older bitcoin-obfuscating service, founded in 2011. Bitcoin Fog by then had laundered hundreds of millions of dollars' worth of cryptocurrency, much of it from dark web markets. The IRS-CI agents identified a Russian-Swedish man named Roman Sterlingov, who they believed to be the site's administrator and—since the United States had no extradition agreement with Sweden that applied to money laundering—patiently waited for an opportunity to lay hands on him. (During that years-long wait, they also carried out undercover transactions with the site in which they explicitly told Bitcoin Fog's staff they were laundering drug money, which, according to Price, proves that the service was aware of its criminal customers.)

Finally, in April 2021, IRS-CI learned that Sterlingov was traveling to Los Angeles. Gambaryan had by this point finished a stint at Europol in The Hague and moved his family back to his hometown of Fresno, to be closer to his aging parents. He and Price asked Customs and Border Protection to detain Sterlingov at LAX Airport and rushed to L.A. to catch him there. Price cuffed Bitcoin Fog's alleged admin in a CBP secondary screening room while Gambaryan explained to him in Russian that he was being arrested by the IRS. Sterlingov responded in an offended tone that he spoke English perfectly well.

While Helix's founder Harmon pleaded guilty in August 2021, Sterlingov has continued to protest his innocence. His lawyer, the veteran hacker defense attorney Tor Ekeland, vowed to fight the case. "Our review of the blockchain analysis tells a different story," he said. "I'm convinced Mr. Sterlingov has been unjustly accused, and we look forward to taking this matter to trial as soon as possible."

Unlike in Harmon's case, the clearest financial trail pointing to Sterlingov wasn't from the years after he allegedly founded Bitcoin Fog. Instead, prosecutors argue his fateful mistake was made *before* the service was even created: He had bought bitcoins on Mt. Gox and traded them for another early, soon-to-be-defunct virtual currency called Liberty Reserve, then used that currency to rent Bitcoin Fog's servers from a hosting company. Sterlingov's very first Bitcoin transactions to allegedly launch the business, along with the BTC-e and Mt. Gox databases of customers, were enough for IRS-CI to identify him.

The financial trail that pointed to Sterlingov, in other words, came from financial records and blockchain evidence created fully a decade earlier—perhaps the oldest Bitcoin transaction records to have ever put someone in jail. As the Berkeley researcher Nick Weaver had warned, and as cryptocurrency users around the world were finally learning, "The blockchain is forever."

. . .

Throughout that period, Price says, Tigran Gambaryan always seemed to be at the center of IRS-CI's most impactful investigations. He would somehow have every IP address or blockchain tip that led to the next major case. He had the best sources within the cryptocurrency industry. He was the one who would drive through the night from Fresno to get to LAX in time to assist Price in the Sterlingov arrest. "He was just a shit magnet," Price remembers. "He was just always somehow connected to these things."

Amid the avalanche of cases during those manic few years, it was the BTC-e investigation, Gambaryan found, that had perhaps the longest-lasting resonance of all. After Vinnik's arrest, the Russian remained detained in a Greek jail, caught in legal limbo for years as the United States, Russia, and, strangely, France fought over his extradition. In the meantime, as it became clear just how central BTC-e had been to so many criminal schemes, hundreds of requests for access to the exchange's seized database began to pour in from other agents and prosecutors.

BTC-e, it turned out, had been used to source and cash out bitcoins by everyone from the Russian military intelligence spies who hacked the Democratic National Committee and the Hillary Clinton Campaign in 2016, to the vast majority of ransomware groups increasingly plaguing the internet. Before it was torn off-line, a study by Chainalysis, along with Google's security researchers, UCSD, and NYU, had found that BTC-e was the destination for 95 percent of the extortion payments those ransomware gangs collected, a growing online scourge disrupting everything from major corporations to government agencies.

BTC-e's data also provided Gambaryan with a key clue in an investigation of his own—one that would result in, by some measures, the biggest win of his career. That case had begun, just as in his first crypto-tracing case against Force and Bridges, with a loose thread trailing off from the Silk Road.

After the BTC-e server seizure in the summer of 2017, in a moment of downtime before the Welcome to Video investigation began heating up, Gambaryan had been on the phone with Chainalysis's Levin once again. Gambaryan was, as had become his habit, "shaking the tree to see what fruit comes out," as Levin put it, restlessly querying Chainalysis's co-founder for new leads to pursue.

Levin pointed him toward a Bitcoin address that had long been on his mind: It held 69,370 bitcoins, worth close to $200 million at exchange rates at the time. The coins seemed to be connected to the Silk Road, but they had sat almost entirely untouched for three years. Chainalysis's tracing of the coins showed that they had come out of the Silk Road's cluster in fifty-four transactions over the course of 2012 and 2013, and those payments hadn't been included in the Silk Road's internal accounting. Was this, as in the case of Mt. Gox, the work of a hacker thief? Could this pile of coins actually be an enormous cache of Silk Road profits stolen from Ross Ulbricht?

Gambaryan and an IRS-CI colleague named Jeremy Haynie began

examining that mysterious treasure trove. They found that weeks after Ulbricht was arrested and in jail, 101 of the coins had been moved into a BTC-e account. That gave them two clues: First, it confirmed that the money almost certainly wasn't still controlled by Ulbricht, who wouldn't have been able to transfer the 101 coins from a jail cell. And second, they could dig into BTC-e's seized database to look for hints of the real owner.

As with all BTC-e data, there was no identifying information associated with the 101 coins moved from the Silk Road into the Russian exchange. But when Gambaryan and Haynie checked the same user's BTC-e account for other transactions, they found a payment that had come *out* of BTC-e. After a few hops through addresses on the blockchain, the money had been deposited into a different exchange—one that responded to their subpoena for account information.

In a matter of days, with the results of that subpoena in hand, Gambaryan and Haynie had identified the mysterious owner of the nearly 70,000 bitcoins—or at least someone they knew must have received money from that person. Neither the IRS nor the Department of Justice has ever publicly named that individual. They refer to them, even in court documents, only by the pseudonym Individual X.

Over the next years, Gambaryan and Haynie patiently waited for the opportunity to knock on Individual X's door and pressure them to explain their connection to such an enormous haul of the Silk Road's drug money. "You can't always force people to talk," Gambaryan explains vaguely. "It takes some convincing sometimes."

By the fall of 2020, as the value of Bitcoin steadily ascended, the collection of coins that Levin had first pointed out to Gambaryan had grown to a towering value of more than $1 billion. Among bitcoiners, it had become a subject of widespread curiosity: one of the largest sums of mystery money ever seen on the blockchain.

Then, one day in early November 2020, blockchain watchers noticed that this massive money pile had suddenly moved. Some guessed that it had belonged to an early investor and had finally been cracked by hackers. Others managed to tie it to the Silk Road, speculating that perhaps it belonged to a Silk Road vendor or, somehow, the Dread Pirate Roberts himself.

In fact, that same afternoon in November, Jonathan Levin received a

photo via text message from Tigran Gambaryan. It showed the IRS-CI
agent wearing a suit, a smile on his face, sitting behind a laptop showing
blockchain records, giving two thumbs up on either side of the screen.

"I just moved a bilion," Gambaryan wrote, not bothering to correct
his typo.

Somehow—Gambaryan refused to share any details that might help
identify Individual X—he and Haynie had finally made contact with
that pseudonymous Bitcoin mogul and confirmed that they had, in fact,
hacked the Silk Road and stolen the 69,370 bitcoins from the site. Ross
Ulbricht, they wrote in an affidavit, had even gone so far as to threaten
the hacker in 2013, trying to coerce them to return the money. Instead,
Individual X had held on to the sum for more than seven years as it slowly
ballooned in value—perhaps fearing that moving the money or cashing
it out at an exchange would draw the attention of law enforcement.

At last, however, Gambaryan and Haynie had come calling. In a November 2020 meeting at the San Francisco U.S. attorney's office, Individual X had typed out the private key that controlled that gargantuan
fortune, character by character, on Gambaryan's laptop. The hacker had
agreed to turn over the money, almost certainly as an alternative to jail.

Over the year that followed—before the federal government had a
chance to finish the seizure process, put those 69,370 bitcoins up for
auction, and add the proceeds to the U.S. Treasury, as it typically does
with property seized in criminal investigations—Bitcoin spiked again in
value. Thanks to the vagaries of cryptocurrency's appreciation and the
long-term restraint of one still-unnamed hacker, the sum of stolen Silk
Road coins had grown, based on Bitcoin's volatile exchange rate around
the time of this writing, to be worth more than $2 billion.

Gambaryan and his IRS-CI colleagues had pulled off the largest seizure of cryptocurrency ever carried out by American law enforcement.
It was also, for that matter, the biggest criminal seizure of *any* currency
in U.S. history.

Limits

Just before 5:00 a.m. on May 7, 2021, an employee in the control room of Colonial Pipeline, a gasoline and jet fuel distribution company based in the Atlanta suburb of Alpharetta, Georgia, was the first to discover a deeply unnerving message posted on one of the firm's computer screens. The note explained that Colonial had been catastrophically hacked, that its IT network was being held ransom, and that control of it would be returned only in exchange for millions of dollars in cryptocurrency.

Colonial owns and manages a fifty-five-hundred-mile-long pipeline that runs from Houston to New Jersey, a colossal artery providing nearly half the gas supply of the entire East Coast of the United States. That massive operation had been brought to its knees by a cybercriminal group, widely believed to be based in Russia, known as DarkSide.

Colonial has never publicly released the text of the ransom note it received from that hacker gang. But by that May, DarkSide's extortion messages had become all too familiar to the cybersecurity industry, which had tracked its six-month rampage across dozens of victim organizations in the finance, health-care, construction, and energy industries. "Welcome to Dark," a typical message from the group read. "What happend? Your computers and servers are encrypted, backups are deleted. We use strong encryption algorithms, so you cannot recover your data. But you can restore everything by purchasing a special program from us."

Within less than an hour on that May morning, Colonial Pipeline's staff could see that its digital operations were irrevocably crippled. Before encrypting the hard drives of key systems across the network, the hackers had, the day before, stealthily stolen nearly a hundred gigabytes of the company's data, too, and now warned Colonial that they would dump it all on their dark web site if the firm didn't pay. Engineers feared that the hackers' access could still spread to the systems overseeing and safe-guarding the roughly 2.5 million gallons of petroleum products Colonial siphoned across the country daily, potentially leading to changes in the pipeline's pressure or even triggering disastrous spills.

Just before 6:00 a.m., the company's executives made the call: For the first time in Colonial's nearly sixty-year history, it would shut down its pipeline entirely.

Soon, Colonial hired three different security firms to scour its net-work, assessing the damage, finding and eradicating the hackers' foot-holds, and working to rebuild the company's IT systems. One of those firms alone, Mandiant, had dozens of staffers working on the case in shifts. "There was a clock we were up against. We knew the pipeline's operations had to come back online as soon as possible," says Charles Carmakal, who led Mandiant's team. "We all recognized the impact that this was going to have on our economy and our society."

Within five days, 30 percent of gas stations in Atlanta and 31 percent of stations in Raleigh had run out of fuel. Gas prices in the southeastern United States rose to their highest average in seven years. Secretary of Energy Jennifer Granholm reported a supply crunch in states across the region and urged consumers there not to panic buy or hoard gas. Colo-nial's ransomware meltdown had become, by some measures, the most high-profile cyberattack on U.S. critical infrastructure of all time.

Only on the sixth day after Colonial's shutdown, however, did report-ers at Bloomberg News reveal the full story: The widespread mayhem wasn't a result of the company's principled refusal to pay a ransom. Colonial had, in fact, secretly given the hackers $4.4 million in bitcoins, almost immediately upon receiving their demands. All of the subsequent chaos was due to Colonial's slow process of recovering its data, using a decryptor tool DarkSide itself had provided in exchange for the payment.

"The attack forced us to make difficult decisions in real time that no company ever wants to face," the company's CEO, Joseph Blount, later told a congressional hearing, wearing a pained expression. "It was the hardest decision I've ever made in my 39 years in the energy industry."

DarkSide, like countless other ransomware gangs plaguing the inter-net, had no doubt chosen to extract its ransoms in Bitcoin because of its cash-like properties. Cryptocurrency remained the digital world's closest equivalent to a briefcase of bills, ready to be handed off in an alley in exchange for a kidnapping victim's release. But thanks to the unlikely properties of that currency as a medium for extortion, the 75 bitcoins that Colonial paid could be followed directly into the criminals' coffers. The blockchain analysis firm Elliptic, a Chainalysis competitor, quickly published a blog post that showed how Colonial's extortion payoff had been collected in a wallet that had already received fifty-seven other payments over just the previous two months, all presumably the fruits of DarkSide's ransomware.

In fact, another $4.4 million payment from the German chemical firm Brenntag—another DarkSide ransomware victim—had gone into the same wallet just days after Colonial's. In all, the wallet had amassed $17.5 million. And it was only one of several such caches of payoffs tied to a single group, which was itself merely one out of dozens of ransomware gangs. Just days after Colonial and Brenntag, it was revealed that the insurance company CNA Financial had paid a staggering $40 million to another cybercriminal group called Phoenix CryptoLocker that was holding its IT systems hostage.

Chainalysis, too, was tracking the ransomware economy as it exploded beyond a silent, digital epidemic into a full-blown—if sporadic and unevenly distributed—societal crisis. In 2020, Chainalysis's staff had tracked no less than $350 million in total ransomware payments. Ransomware payouts in 2021 looked to be on pace to break that record. And even as companies like Chainalysis and Elliptic followed the path of those ransoms, often in exacting detail, the scourge was only growing.

Somehow, all of this was occurring in the very midst of Jonathan Levin's "golden age" of digital follow-the-money investigations. Law enforcement continued to exploit blockchain analysis in its years-long, climactic crackdown on dark web markets, digital thieves, money launderers, and child exploitation networks—a crackdown that showed no signs of abating. Yet the numbers spoke for themselves: Ransomware seemed somehow immune.

Even as bitcoin tracing's investigative power reached its zenith, the tracers had found a form of crime they couldn't control.

. . .

How were ransomware gangs defying law enforcement's efforts at tracing cryptocurrency transactions? Had the cleverest cyber extortionists somehow finally figured out how to skirt blockchain analysis somewhere along the paths to their bank accounts? Or, perhaps, to cash out their profits faster than Chainalysis and its federal-agent customers could track them?

Part of the answer, it seemed, might be the rise of a new class of cryptocurrency sometimes referred to as "privacy coins," expressly designed to thwart blockchain analysis. As bitcoin tracing had become a standard tool within law enforcement agencies, ransomware operators had by 2021 increasingly begun demanding that victims pay not in that decade-old cryptocurrency but in another digital coin called Monero. Designed by a pseudonymous cryptographer in 2013 and launched in 2014, Monero promised to integrate an arsenal of modern privacy and anonymity features that Bitcoin lacked. Using a collection of cryptographic tricks, Monero mixes every payment with a group of other transactions by default. It also hides the amount of every transaction from blockchain snoops and creates unique "stealth addresses" for every recipient—all of which makes it vastly more difficult to cluster addresses or identify the owner of a wallet.

Another, newer cryptocurrency called Zcash had taken those privacy improvements even further. Zcash doesn't simply tangle up its blockchain as Monero does, but instead renders it fully opaque. Launched by a group of cryptographers in 2016, Zcash offers a feature called "shielded transactions" designed to ensure true anonymity—by implementing an improved version of the zero-knowledge proofs used in the eCash system Sarah Meiklejohn had worked on so many years before.

Zero-knowledge proofs' semi-magical, mathematical sleight-of-hand means that, like bitcoins, Zcash coins can't in theory be forged or spent twice. But Zcash creates those assurances with a blockchain whose "shielded transactions" are entirely encrypted and thus don't reveal any information about who owns any particular sum of money, the amount in any wallet, or where its funds move. That data isn't merely obscured but *provably* inaccessible. Zcash's shielded transactions serve as a true black box, guaranteed to offer no information at all to any would-be snoop.

These privacy coins seemed to signal a new challenge to anyone attempting blockchain analysis, one that went well beyond the problem of ransomware. Even in the years before that crisis came to a head, the online criminal underworld had been slowly migrating from Bitcoin to Monero and Zcash. Money launderers had begun "chain-hopping," trading their bitcoins for other currencies and back again, to cut off the forensic trail. (AlphaBay had begun accepting Monero payments as an option as early as 2016, and it announced that it would add Zcash, too, just days before the site's takedown.) By 2019, a handful of dark web markets had begun allowing their vendors to accept Zcash, and two markets had switched exclusively to Monero, banning all Bitcoin payments.

It all seemed to add up to a massive, looming brick wall facing Chainalysis—and law enforcement—in their incredible spree of blockchain investigations.

Michael Gronager, the optimist, said he wasn't concerned.

Both Zcash and Monero, he pointed out, aren't nearly as widely adopted as Bitcoin—even years after their invention—and have only a tiny sliver of its value. Only a single-digit percentage of Zcash's transactions even use its "shielded transactions" feature. Most of its owners seem to have bought it as a speculative investment rather than a way to move money with true secrecy. And if Monero and Zcash do start to seriously catch on among criminals and pose a real threat for law enforcement, Gronager argued, the few exchanges that offer to let people buy and sell those currencies will likely come under enormous regulatory pressure to cut them off.

As Gronager put it, Monero and Zcash still live in the pre-Chainalysis period of 2014, when banks were too wary of the potential criminal use of Bitcoin to partner with his exchange, Kraken. "They're stuck in that era," he said.

Gronager even cast doubts—albeit vague ones—on whether Zcash's and Monero's privacy guarantees will stand up to scrutiny for years to come. "Any of these systems, anything that's developed, you always see a couple of years later, someone finds something," Gronager said. In fact, a 2017 study by one group of Carnegie Mellon, Princeton, and other university researchers discovered that in as many as 80 percent of cases, they could use clues like the age of coins in a Monero transaction to carry out a process of elimination and deduce who moved which coins. (Monero subsequently upgraded its privacy features to foil those techniques. Chainalysis, for its part, hired one of the paper's authors.)

Another group of researchers, including Sarah Meiklejohn, had found in 2018 that Zcash wasn't quite as anonymous as it appeared either—largely just because the number of users turning on "shielded transactions" was so small. "And that's only the stuff that's being printed in public, right? So I just don't believe in anything being safe," Gronager said. After all, he deadpanned, wasn't Bitcoin once understood to be anonymous?

"There is always a cat-and-mouse game," Chainalysis's CEO concluded.

Did that mean that Chainalysis had in fact found ways to trace Monero and Zcash? Gronager, unsurprisingly, declined to answer. "We are not really interested in revealing capabilities," he said slyly. "Even if we did say something, it's likely people wouldn't believe it."

Yet at the same time, neither Chainalysis nor any other blockchain analysis firm seemed able to solve the growing ransomware epidemic. The company could point to occasional wins: In the case of the ransomware group NetWalker, Chainalysis had helped the FBI trace and seize half a million dollars of ransoms. The bureau had arrested a Canadian man who worked as one of NetWalker's "affiliates"—a kind of partner who rents and deploys its ransomware in exchange for a cut of profits. But a single half-million-dollar seizure and one arrest represented only the tiniest disruption of the nine-figure annual ransomware economy.

In fact, Gronager himself conceded that Chainalysis has no silver bullet for ransomware investigations. The truth was that for most of those extortion cases, visibility wasn't enough. Many of the cybercriminals involved—and the money-laundering services and exchanges they used to cash out their profits—were simply based in countries beyond the grasp of Western law enforcement. Particularly Russia.

Gronager pointed to the 2018 charges against a group of twelve Russian military intelligence agents accused of hacking Democratic targets to interfere in the 2016 presidential election. The indictment detailed exactly how they paid Bitcoin to rent servers for the phishing sites they used to steal their victims' passwords and to host the documents they leaked after stealing them from those victims. But like Alexander Vinnik, those Russian agents remain out of reach from U.S. law enforcement—until they someday make the mistake of leaving the safety of their home soil.

"You have the names of people who did this. But does that matter?" Gronager asked. "It means that they're not going on vacation outside of Russia."

When it comes to the global affliction of ransomware, he made clear, privacy coins or any other tool designed to defy tracing methods aren't the problem. The real problem remains rogue countries like Russia and North Korea—countries whose governments allow their citizens to defy global law enforcement action even when their activities are fully visible on the blockchain.

When a transaction goes behind that political barrier, he concluded, even the cleverest crypto-tracing rarely helps to retrieve it. "When you send a Bitcoin ransom payment to Moscow," Gronager said, "the money is still gone."

. . .

Close to a month after the Colonial Pipeline shutdown, the Justice Department made a surprising announcement: It had recovered 63.7 of the 75 bitcoins Colonial had paid to DarkSide. The FBI had, in fact, followed the money to DarkSide's wallet and clawed back the majority of the profits from the group's most disruptive score.

The bureau declined to reveal details of that investigation. Gronager and other Chainalysis staffers confirmed the company was involved, but refused to share details of how the funds were reclaimed. The Justice Department would say only that U.S. law enforcement had somehow obtained the private keys for that portion of DarkSide's extortion loot and used those keys to move the money back into U.S. control. ("You'll have to write another book in five years," Gronager said with a laugh when I asked about the investigation.)

In June 2021, *The New York Times* put the headline "Pipeline Investigation Upends Idea That Bitcoin Is Untraceable" on an article about the announcement—a reflection of just how many years it had taken to finally, fully debunk the myth of Bitcoin's anonymity.

Yet when I asked Tigran Gambaryan about the outcome of the Colonial case, he said he had no illusions that the ransomware problem was under control—or, at least, that cryptocurrency tracing would offer the solution. To him, a few million dollars seized out of the hundreds of millions flowing into cybercriminal wallets represented a rare exception to ransomware operators' general impunity.

In fact, Gambaryan said he generally avoided taking on ransomware cases for just that reason: He knew all too well how untouchable most of the key criminal players in Russia remained, and he had no interest in futile indictments in absentia or seizures of money that represented mere drops from the fire hose of extortion payments. "Don't work a case if you can't get a body," Gambaryan said, describing a maxim he'd first heard formulated by Will Frentzen and had since tried to use as a filter to choose which investigations to pursue among all of the blockchain's available leads. "Those guys don't travel to places that extradite," he said of ransomware's Russian kingpins. "They know the game."

"You might get a name-and-shame out of it," Gambaryan concluded dismissively. "You're not going to get a body."

In the months that followed, though, signs began to appear that the federal government was throwing new heft and resources behind its efforts to eradicate ransomware—or at least, as cybersecurity policy wonks put it, to "impose cost" on its operators, to push them into less disruptive forms of crime. President Joe Biden himself brought up the subject with Russia's president, Vladimir Putin, in a July 2021 phone call, pressuring him to stop harboring hackers who were wreaking havoc across the world. The U.S. State Department announced a $10 million bounty for information about the cybercriminals responsible for the Colonial shutdown. DarkSide, for its part, had posted a public note explaining that it hadn't intended to cause the pipeline's disruption; the group apparently disbanded not long after the incident. The U.S. Treasury imposed new sanctions on two cryptocurrency exchanges, Chatex and Suex, believed to have been used by ransomware operators, cutting them off from the global financial system.

By November 2021, Europol had announced the arrest of seven affiliates of two ransomware gangs—REvil and GandCrab—in South Korea, Romania, Kuwait, and Poland. The U.S. Justice Department had indicted two hackers, who it said had been responsible for a widespread REvil ransomware campaign that exploited a vulnerability in IT automation software to hit more than a thousand companies just ahead of the Fourth of July that year. The FBI recovered $6.1 million of those hackers' profits. "Today, and now for the second time in five months, we announce the seizure of digital proceeds of ransomware deployed by a transnational criminal group," Attorney General Merrick Garland said in a speech to announce the rare win. "This will not be the last time."

In an even more shocking turn of events, Russia's FSB law enforcement agency in January 2022 announced that it had arrested no fewer than fourteen members of the REvil ransomware gang—a dramatic exception to its years-long policy of allowing ransomware crews to operate without consequence. That group, according to one U.S. official's comments to *The Wall Street Journal,* included a hacker responsible for the Colonial Pipeline breach—but only one. By all appearances, DarkSide's other members seemed to escape into Russia's shadows. Putin's full-scale invasion of Ukraine the next month, and the crippling new U.S. and European sanctions imposed in response, make it less likely than ever that those cybercriminals will face justice.

The long-overdue, global ransomware crackdown may nonetheless continue. But Gambaryan's point stands: The prognosis for that epidemic will depend not on which coins can be traced, but on which bodies can be got—and which never will be.

Gray Zones

On a crisp autumn morning in 2021, Michael Gronager walked onto a stage in front of a small crowd at a private event space in a midtown high-rise, towering over a corner of New York's Times Square. Chainalysis's CEO wore a slim gray suit and an untucked white dress shirt with black buttons. The only real hint of his crypto-eccentricity was his shoes, a pair of green and blue sneakers covered in the Chainalysis logo, a set of chain links intersecting a bright orange letter *C*. Gronager's entrance was met with applause from the audience, a mix of dresses and suits—both the boxier, firearm-obscuring kind worn by federal agents and the sleeker formal wear of Wall Street.

In Gronager's short speech, the opening remarks of Chainalysis's annual customer conference, called Links, he quickly made clear that the second of those two categories of customers was his focus that day—and, perhaps, the real source of his company's stratospheric growth. "I'm very, very delighted to welcome many new customers from the banking sector," Gronager told the crowd. "Crypto is about how we, as an industry, change the course of finance."

He began rattling off numbers about exactly how much the cryptocurrency industry had changed since just 2019, the last time Chainalysis held its conference, before the COVID-19 pandemic. Two years earlier, a bitcoin had been worth just over $8,000. On the day of Gronager's speech, it was worth more than $66,000, a new record. The total value of all bitcoins had grown from being measured in billions of dollars to rocketing past $3 *trillion*. "Virtually any single metric in crypto has 10x-ed over the last two years," he said. "Amazing industry."

Within that booming crypto economy, the criminal transactions that Chainalysis tracked were growing too—from $7.8 billion in total in 2020 to a record $14 billion in 2021. But the growth of those illicit transactions hadn't kept up with the far faster expansion of the legitimate cryptocurrency world. By Chainalysis's measure, they accounted for a tiny 0.15 percent of all crypto transactions in 2021, perhaps a sign of how relatively civilized the overall industry had become.

Gronager went on to list Chainalysis's own growth statistics, which paralleled the industry's heady numbers: more than four hundred employees in sixty countries around the world; more than six hundred customer organizations. He left unsaid the growth in Chainalysis's financial valuation: A few months earlier it had taken another round of investment that put the company's value on paper at more than $4.2 billion—an absurd, dizzying explosion of wealth. (Just six months later, Chainalysis would announce yet *another* injection of capital that this time put the company's valuation at $8.6 billion, more than doubling its worth again.)

"I'd like to give a huge thanks to all of you for coming here today," Gronager concluded to another round of applause, "for trusting us with your data and trusting us to help you make crypto a safer place to be."

. . .

Given the warm reception of Gronager's words in that room, it might be hard to imagine that within the Bitcoin community there were those who saw things otherwise—who had, in fact, come to see Chainalysis as an entirely malignant force.

"I think they're digital mercenaries," an activist named Alex Gladstein said flatly, "and I think they're contributing to the warrantless spying on Americans—and on others. I think they're terribly bad people and they should be doing something else with their lives."

For fifteen years, Gladstein has worked for the Human Rights Foundation, a global civil-liberties nonprofit that has always taken a tech-friendly bent to human rights around the world. He's supported Iranian activists building censorship-resistant podcast apps, Eritrean exiled dissidents beaming radio shows into that East African country, and North Korean defectors smuggling contraband movies and TV shows back into the Hermit Kingdom on USB drives and tablet computers. But for the past several years, Gladstein has been obsessed with Bitcoin's potential—as a permissionless digital currency—for financing human freedom around the world.

"I've seen democracies erode and dictatorships persist based on the technological ability to surveil and control people," Gladstein said. "So I firmly believe that it's not just encrypted communications that we need to protect ourselves and to protect our democracy, but also private money."

Gladstein spoke about a group he'd been working with in Belarus called the Belarus Solidarity Foundation, which had collected donations in Bitcoin and sent them to striking workers in that country opposing the dictatorial regime of Alexander Lukashenko. When Russia launched its invasion of Ukraine in February 2022, Ukrainian resistance groups and the country's government itself had raised tens of millions of dollars in international cryptocurrency donations, even as payment services like PayPal and Patreon froze their accounts. Gladstein pointed to the potential for cryptocurrency in Xinjiang, China, where ethnic Uyghurs have been made to live in a panopticon, and Hong Kong, where protesters line up to buy subway tokens in cash for fear that Xi Jinping's government will track their credit card or digital payments. And he argued that even the Kim regime's use of cryptocurrency in North Korea would backfire, that the country's citizens would eventually figure out that cryptocurrency is not merely a hacking target and a means to evade sanctions but also a way to defy their own government's economic controls.

"Regardless of where you are, the elites, the people who control the society, they will use their power over the banking system to try and shut down opposition," Gladstein said. "And you're watching that happen, whether it's in Hong Kong or Nigeria or Belarus or Russia."

In the context of that global struggle against surveillance, including financial surveillance, Gladstein said he sees Chainalysis and the rest of the budding, worldwide industry of blockchain analysis as a tool of oppression. Everywhere in the world that Chainalysis sells its services, he argued, its coin tracing will consolidate centralized power and serve the status quo.

The United States is no exception, he suggests. "They try to claim that they're on some high horse and helping people. No, you're protecting the establishment and you're participating in this propaganda that the

U.S. government will use to prevent the spread of privacy technology," Gladstein said. "Call me when Chainalysis helps put a Wall Street banker in prison."

The company's role in tracing the funds of opposition activists, including in the United States, is more than theoretical. In January 2021, Chainalysis described in a blog post how it had tracked more than half a million dollars' worth of bitcoins to right-wing protesters who had participated in or attended the January 6 storming of the U.S. Capitol, in which five people died. The money trail led back to a French computer programmer who had written far-right messages about the decline of "Western civilization," before committing suicide. "Chainalysis is actively looking to identify any additional extremist payments and activity and will keep our customers updated," the blog post read.

Gladstein describes himself as a progressive, but he nonetheless pointed to that tracing after January 6 as evidence of Chainalysis's capabilities to surveil social movements. "I have no doubt that if Trump continued for a second term that Black Lives Matter protesters would absolutely be using Bitcoin to raise money and their bank accounts would be frozen," Gladstein said. Would Chainalysis be used to follow racial justice protesters' cryptocurrency, just as it was used to follow the money of the January 6 rioters?

And what did Gladstein make of Chainalysis's unequivocally good work, like in child sexual abuse cases? He didn't deny that bitcoin tracing had been effectively used to stop serious crimes. But he stood by his stance that governments need to find other ways to fight the threats of extremist violence or child exploitation, and not succumb to the decades-old call from law enforcement to use those dangers as an excuse to undermine privacy and anonymity.

"I think it is ultimately *really bad* to go down the route of trying to expand and grow a surveillance state, whether it's in the name of fighting terrorism or child porn or whatever horrible thing you can think of," Gladstein concluded. "I truly believe that we should not. I think that spying on people is the tactic of tyrants. And I think that democratic societies should find other ways of solving crime that don't involve warrantless surveillance."

. . .

Even as activists like Gladstein made that argument for financial privacy, the U.S. justice system was moving in the other direction. The trillion-dollar infrastructure funding bill signed by President Joe Biden in November 2021 included two provisions—designed, in theory, to help pay for the bill's spending—that passed despite their radioactive unpopularity in the cryptocurrency world. These new rules require vaguely defined cryptocurrency "brokers"—or, for that matter, any cryptocurrency business doing a transaction worth more than $10,000—to report the Social Security number of the person on the other side of the transaction to the IRS. "It basically makes it effectively impossible to transact anonymously," says Marta Belcher, a cryptocurrency-focused attorney and special counsel to the Electronic Frontier Foundation. "It's a total disaster for civil liberties."[*]

Then in March of 2022, President Biden signed an executive order on "Ensuring Responsible Development of Digital Assets" that also—with little specificity—called for new rules to prevent the use of cryptocurrency for illicit purposes, from human trafficking to terrorism. At the same time, U.S. lawmakers on both sides of the partisan aisle issued public warnings that cryptocurrency could be used to evade the strict new sanctions Western governments imposed on Russia in response to its Ukraine invasion. If that renewed focus on regulating digital money continues to sharpen, Chainalysis may soon be far from the biggest problem for any American seeking to use cryptocurrency anonymously.

Even one of the creators of Zcash, a Johns Hopkins computer scientist and cryptographer named Matthew Green, argued that Chainalysis

---

[*] Belcher also wrote an article following the Welcome to Video investigation criticizing the appellate ruling in the case of the HSI agent caught paying for child sexual abuse videos. She sided with the man's defense that the IRS's tracing of his bitcoins represented a breach of his Fourth Amendment rights—not because IRS-CI had searched Bitcoin's public blockchain, but because they had gotten his exchange records without using a warrant. Instead, investigators had obtained those records with only a subpoena, a legal request that doesn't require a judge's sign-off. That subpoena held up under appeal because of a precedent in U.S. law called the "third-party doctrine," which states that if you share your data with a third party—be it Google, Verizon, or Coinbase—you no longer have an expectation that it will remain private. Belcher believes, very reasonably, that this is nonsense.

can't really be blamed for cryptocurrency's real privacy woes, regulatory or otherwise. Green spent his twenties working at AT&T Labs, reading cryptography papers and the Cypherpunks Mailing List, and imagining—like all cypherpunks—a future of truly private money. But from his first look at Bitcoin in 2011, Green says he understood that its pseudonymous blockchain was bound to serve as a kind of trap for users seeking real anonymity.

"The privacy is not there," he said. "You know like, you're buying an ice cream cone, and then it turns out not to be an ice cream cone but the exact *opposite* of an ice cream cone? That's how I think about Bitcoin."

Despite devoting years of his career to building encryption systems that can resist surveillance, and specifically a cryptocurrency that could foil blockchain analysis, he doesn't fault any agency or company for taking advantage of Bitcoin's inherent traceability. "I have nothing bad to say about Chainalysis, as a business," Green said, "aside from the fact that I don't like the existence of their technology."

For his part, Alex Gladstein refuses to let Chainalysis off so easily—or to believe that the fight for Bitcoin's privacy is really so futile. He's placing his hopes in a feature developers have discussed adding to Bitcoin called Cross-Input Signature Aggregation, designed to allow users to combine their transactions while reducing fees. Exchanges in particular, Gladstein argues, will use that feature to bundle up users' transactions as a cost-saving mechanism. The result will be that those exchanges might, almost as a side effect, render it nearly impossible to definitively identify any individual user in connection to a certain amount of Bitcoin.

That upgrade, Gladstein acknowledged, is still years away. But he warned that Chainalysis's success stories—the stories in this book—represent an "epitaph for an era," when a blockchain analysis firm could wield enormous surveillance powers. "I don't think that's permanent," he insisted. "I think that we are at the beginning of the end for that."

Green, the co-creator of Zcash, disagrees. Looming regulation aside, he says he's seen too many claims before of future Bitcoin upgrades or add-ons that would solve its anonymity issues but that were, in the end, defeated by yet another innovation in blockchain analysis.

"Privacy is a really hard problem," Green said in summation.

He remains hopeful about Zcash, which he helped to design from the ground up to preserve that sort of anonymity and untraceability.

But Bitcoin adoption dwarfs Zcash by every measure. It seems likely to continue to do so. And Bitcoin, by its very nature, practically invites the sort of tracking that Chainalysis has spent years perfecting.

"Once you set up the conditions that make a thing like Chainalysis possible, it's going to exist," Green concluded. "Chainalysis is inevitable."

. . .

Amid all his criticisms of Chainalysis, Gladstein told me he had repeatedly called on the company to name the list of its client countries and had never gotten a straight answer. So I thought I'd ask Chainalysis's CEO myself: Who are his customers?

I put the question to Michael Gronager when we met one afternoon in the back room of a café in Chelsea, not far from the New York office space he was scoping out for his company's new headquarters. Gronager, accompanied by Chainalysis's head of communications, Maddie Kennedy, had been walking me through the details of the company's origin story, from his Danish seaside walks with Jan Møller to his first sales visits. He had just finished describing to me how law enforcement agencies, at least in the company's early days, made up the majority of its customers.

So, which countries' law enforcement agencies? Any country that can pay?

"No. No, we can't do that," Gronager said. "We are a U.S.-based company. And that means that certain countries we can't work with and we don't want to work with." He cited China, North Korea, and Russia.

But what about the Middle East? "The Middle East is a big mix, right?" Gronager responded. "Like, Israel, it's fine. Let's take Abu Dhabi, it's another."

At Gronager's mention of Israel, I could have asked about whether the country is using blockchain analysis to surveil the finances of people in the occupied territories of the West Bank and Gaza. Instead, at the mention of Abu Dhabi, the capital of the United Arab Emirates, my thoughts jumped to the case of Ahmed Mansoor, the Emirati human rights activist and father of four whose phone was targeted by the U.A.E. government using tools from the Israeli hacking contractor NSO. Following that surveillance, Mansoor was arrested and sentenced to ten years in prison, then held in isolation ever since. Despite its close ties to the U.S. and the global economy, the U.A.E. has an abysmal human rights record, of which Mansoor is just one tragic example.

So, I asked, is the U.A.E. a customer? "We can't say that," Kennedy cut in, with the recognizable tone of a PR person who has identified a red flag.

"No, we can't say that," Gronager agreed, sounding almost disappointed, as though he wished he could share more. "The Middle East—there's a lot of things that are important there and good activity. And some of it is gray zones. That's just how it is."

Those gray zones, Gronager tried to explain, don't just break down cleanly across national borders, but also cover different uses within a single government. "We want to understand how our products are being used, right? What is the use case here?" Gronager said. "We have a pretty high bar. There has never been a problem."

I pointed to Chainalysis's tracing of the January 6 protesters' funds and asked how Chainalysis would handle a situation where the U.A.E. used its tools to trace the funding of opposition movements in the country. Gronager seemed almost to read my mind, to detect that I was thinking about Ahmed Mansoor. "There are companies selling solutions to governments to hack people's computers, and we are not doing that, right?" Gronager said. "Absolutely not."

Chainalysis isn't a hacking tool, but it is a tracking tool, I pointed out—and a powerful one. "It is," Gronager agreed.

Here Kennedy intervened again. "We have an internal framework and a board internally that discusses and analyzes different opportunities," she said coolly. "And we take all sorts of things into account, like human rights records, to determine if we might want to work with someone and also understand how they're going to use our tools to determine if it would be an appropriate customer. And we're constantly reevaluating, and we'll fire customers if we feel like it's an irresponsible use, and we have done that."

"Yes, we've done that more than once," Gronager interjected.

"We don't come out and give a list of the countries or make public all of our criteria, because people are just going to pick it apart," Kennedy continued.

"This can't be a policy that we go out with publicly," Gronager agreed, sounding slightly pained. "It doesn't work. Things are not black and white that way."

I told Gronager and Kennedy that I'd talked to Alex Gladstein and that he'd called Chainalysis "mercenaries" and "terribly bad people." I explained Gladstein's point that Chainalysis warrantlessly de-anonymizes private citizens.

Gronager smiled, unfazed and seemingly unoffended. "Crypto is the most transparent value transfer system that's ever been created," he said. "So if anyone says the word 'de-anonymizing,' they missed the whole point. I'm not de-anonymizing, because it was never anonymous."

Then he threw in a darker point. "Another company can build a product that can do some of the things we can do. And that will be built in China and that will be built in Russia, and elsewhere. It will happen," Gronager said. "*Of course* it will happen."

Gronager added that he has nothing against Gladstein or anyone else opposed to blockchain analysis. He just sees them as Don Quixote figures, fighting their own illusory battles in a different, imaginary universe. "If you want another world, go create a revolutionary army and make it happen," Gronager quipped, smiling. I was reminded of his comments on Bitcointalk—"I am Danish, I don't believe in revolutions"—in response to Chainalysis's first privacy blowup so many years earlier.

"We have a world that's put together in a certain way today, and you can agree with it or disagree with it, but it's a fact," Gronager said. "That is the nature of the world."

Rumker

In early August 2021, just as I was reporting out the final details of Alpha-Bay's downfall for this book, something unexpected happened: It rose from the dead.

"AlphaBay is back," read a message posted to Ghostbin, a site for publishing anonymous text-based messages. "You read that right, AlphaBay is back."

The message appeared to be authored by DeSnake, AlphaBay's former number two administrator and security specialist. To prove his identity, DeSnake had cryptographically signed the message with his PGP key—a method to show that the writer of the message possessed the long, secret series of characters that only DeSnake had access to, like a king stamping a letter with a personal signet ring. Multiple security researchers privately confirmed that the signature matched the one from DeSnake's messages as an AlphaBay administrator years earlier. The author seemed to be AlphaBay's real, long-lost lieutenant—or, at the very least, someone who'd gotten ahold of his key.

"I welcome you to the re-opening of our professionally-run, anonymous, secure marketplace AlphaBay to buy or sell products and services," DeSnake's message began. The staff of this new AlphaBay, he wrote, had "20 years of experience in computer security alone, underground businesses, darknet market management, customer support and most importantly evading Law Enforcement."

Sure enough, when I entered the site's address into a Tor Browser, a reincarnated AlphaBay appeared—albeit, a newly launched one. It was the same market as the one last seen in 2017, but restarted from scratch, with none of AlphaBay's many thousands of vendors.

Now that he had taken over from Alpha02, DeSnake had made some changes: First, the new market allowed transactions only in Monero, not Bitcoin, to prevent blockchain analysis, the tool that had played such a central role in AlphaBay's takedown. In addition to Tor, it offered users the option to connect via an alternative dark web anonymity system, known as I2P; DeSnake explained that he didn't trust Tor's security. He had also imposed new restrictions on the market's sales. In addition to the old prohibitions on child pornography, murder for hire, or the hacked data of any citizens of former Soviet countries, he had banned—without explanation—sales of fentanyl and any data or services related to ransomware.

Just as I had with the Dread Pirate Roberts eight years earlier, I reached out to DeSnake for an interview, writing to his account on the Tor-protected web forum Dread. Within twenty-four hours, I found myself exchanging encrypted instant messages with the newly resurfaced, would-be kingpin of the dark web.

DeSnake quickly explained why he had reappeared only now—fully four years after the original AlphaBay had been torn off-line, after Cazes had died in jail, and after the rest of AlphaBay's staff had scattered. He had intended, he wrote, to retire after AlphaBay was seized, but his plans had changed after he saw the news that an FBI agent involved in the AlphaBay takedown had shown a video of Cazes's arrest at the 2018 Fordham International Conference on Cyber Security and had spoken about Cazes in a way that DeSnake deemed disrespectful.

"The biggest reason I am returning is to make the AlphaBay name be remembered as more than the marketplace which got busted and the founder made out to have committed suicide," DeSnake wrote, in his slightly foreign-inflected English. "AlphaBay name was put in bad light after the raids. I am here to make amends to that."

DeSnake repeated the claim I'd heard before: that Cazes was murdered. He offered no real evidence, but said that he and Alpha02 had developed a contingency plan in case of his arrest—a kind of automated mechanism that would reveal Alpha02's identity to DeSnake if he disappeared for a certain amount of time, so that AlphaBay's number two could help him in jail. (Whether that help would have come in the form of a legal defense fund or the "helicopter gunship" Cazes had mentioned to Jen Sanchez, DeSnake refused to say.)

Cazes would never have committed suicide before their plan could even go into effect, DeSnake argued. "He was a fighter," DeSnake wrote. "Me and him had backup plan, I guarantee you that a good and working one, backed by funds etc. However he got killed."

DeSnake described countermeasures he'd since perfected for practically every tactic that had been used to capture Cazes and take down the original AlphaBay. DeSnake never stepped away from his computer when it was unlocked, he wrote, not even to use the bathroom. He claimed to use an "amnesiac" operating system to avoid storing incriminating data, as well as "kill switches" to destroy any remaining information that law enforcement might find on his machines, should they leave his control. He even wrote that he'd designed a system called AlphaGuard that will automatically set up new servers if it detects that the ones that run the site are being seized.

But the biggest factor protecting DeSnake was almost certainly geographic: He wrote that he was based in a former U.S.S.R. country where he's beyond Western governments' reach. While he acknowledged that Cazes had used fake clues of a Russian nationality to throw off investigators, he claimed that AlphaBay's ban on victimizing people from that part of the world was genuine and designed to protect him and other actual post-Soviet AlphaBay staffers from local law enforcement.

"You do not shit where you sleep. We did that for security of other staff members," DeSnake wrote. Cazes then "decided to embrace it as a way to secure himself."

Even so, DeSnake claimed that he had traveled multiple times through countries with U.S. extradition treaties and had never been caught. He credited that track record in part to his careful money laundering, though aside from his preference for Monero, he declined to detail his methods.

"Anyone who believed any currency method or cryptocurrency is safe is a fool or at the very least very ignorant. Everything is tracked," he wrote. "You have to go through certain methods to be able to enjoy the fruits of your work . . . it costs to do what you do. If you are a legit business you pay taxes. If you are doing this you pay taxes in forms of obfuscating your money."

DeSnake said he was shocked when he learned of Alpha02's early slipup that first revealed his email address to the DEA. "I am still in disbelief to this day that he had put his personal email on there," DeSnake wrote. "He was a good carder and he knew better opsec."

But he added that Cazes's failure to hide his money trails to the degree DeSnake recommended was a more willful mistake. DeSnake had warned the previous AlphaBay boss about the need to take more measures against financial surveillance, he said. Alpha02 hadn't listened.

"Some advice he took, other he disgarded as 'overkill,'" DeSnake wrote. "In this game there is no overkill."

. . .

One afternoon, at the end of several weeks of on-and-off chats with DeSnake about how he planned to win this next round of the dark web's cat-and-mouse game, he shared some news: The mice had scored another small victory.

DeSnake sent me a series of links to Tor-protected websites that he described as "DarkLeaks." Someone, it seems, had hacked the Italian police agency responsible for investigating a pair of dark web drug sites, known as Deep Sea and Berlusconi Market. Now that hacker had published a broad collection of stolen documents that offered an inside view into law enforcement's secret work to take down those sites.

Within the DarkLeaks collection, one slide deck immediately caught my eye. It was a presentation from Chainalysis. It described, in Italian, a remarkable set of surveillance capabilities and tricks that Chainalysis offered to law enforcement but that had never before been publicly revealed.

Chainalysis claimed in one slide of the presentation, for instance, that it could track Monero, the "privacy coin," in a shockingly high number of instances, despite its anonymizing properties. "In many cases, the results can be proven far beyond reasonable doubt," the presentation read in Italian, though it conceded that "the analysis is of a statistical nature and as such any result has a confidence level associated with it."

The company claimed to be able to provide a "usable lead" in no less than 65 percent of cases involving Monero. In 20 percent of cases, it could determine a transaction's sender but not a recipient, and in only 15 percent of cases did it fail to produce any leads. For another tool called

Wasabi, a wallet that promised to mix users' Bitcoin transactions to foil tracking, Chainalysis said it could still follow the money in 60 percent of cases.

Another slide delivered a different surprise: Since Chainalysis had acquired WalletExplorer, the pre-Reactor, free rudimentary blockchain analysis tool that Tigran Gambaryan had used to track Shaun Bridges's bitcoins back in 2014, it had turned that service into a kind of honeypot. When someone checked a Bitcoin address of interest, WalletExplorer would record their IP address. "We collect this data," the slide reads. "Using this dataset we were able to provide law enforcement with meaningful leads to the IP data associated with a relevant cryptocurrency address."

Nervous criminal suspects, in other words, had used WalletExplorer to check how traceable their transactions were on the blockchain. And all the while, WalletExplorer had been informing on those users' checks to the very agencies hunting them.

But amid all these revelations, it was another slide that finally offered the most elusive answer I'd been looking for: a possible solution to the mystery of the "advanced analysis" trick that Chainalysis had used to locate the AlphaBay server in Lithuania.

The Italian presentation confirmed that Chainalysis can, in fact, identify the IP addresses of some wallets on the blockchain. It did so by running its own Bitcoin nodes, which quietly monitored transaction messages—the very practice that had led to the blowup on Bitcointalk in the company's earliest days.

First, the slide explained, some wallets that use tools called Simple Payment Verification or Electrum—designed to avoid storing the entire blockchain—leak certain information with every transaction. Nodes that receive a transaction message from those wallets can see not only the user's IP address but all of their blockchain addresses and even their wallet's software version, a tidy bundle of identifying information. Chainalysis had code-named the tool they use to collect that wallet data Orlando.

The next slide was even more revealing. It described a tool called Rumker, explaining that Chainalysis could use its surreptitious Bitcoin nodes for identifying IP addresses not only of individual users' wallets but also those of unknown services—including dark web markets. "Although many illegal services run on the Tor network, suspects are often negligent and run their bitcoin node on clearnet," the slide read, using a term for the traditional internet not protected by Tor.

Had AlphaBay made this mistake? Rumker sounded very much like the secret weapon that had pinpointed that dark web giant's IP address, as well as that of Wall Street Market—and likely others, too.

I wrote to Michael Gronager to ask about the slides and specifically about Rumker. He didn't deny their legitimacy. Instead, he sent me a statement that read like a kind of summation of Chainalysis's philosophy on privacy questions: "Open protocols are openly monitored—to keep the space safe—and to enable a permission-less value transfer network to flourish."

Gronager was reiterating the argument that he'd made for years: Chainalysis doesn't violate privacy; it analyzes public information. But the DarkLeaks slides had shown just how far that analysis goes: If a cryptocurrency, its tools, or its users ever slip up and reveal a shred of sensitive information, Chainalysis will be there to find it.

Rumker, if it was in fact the tool that located AlphaBay, had likely been "burned," just as Gambaryan had feared it might be. Whoever leaked it had, in doing so, exposed the vulnerabilities of the Bitcoin protocol it exploits. Dark web administrators like DeSnake will no doubt take more care in the future to prevent their cryptocurrency wallets from revealing their IP addresses to snooping Bitcoin nodes.

But there will be other vulnerabilities, and other secret weapons to exploit them. The cat-and-mouse game continues.

EPILOGUE

In early 2016, in the midst of Michael Gronager's investigation into Mt. Gox and BTC-e—years before Chainalysis would swell to a multibillion-dollar start-up—Gronager paid a visit to Sarah Meiklejohn. He wanted to offer her a job.

By that time, Meiklejohn had become a computer science professor at University College London. She and Gronager met in her cramped, shared office on campus. The university's computer science building was, by Meiklejohn's own description, one of UCL's least attractive pieces of architecture, a modern block of stone whose interior was, on her side, almost lightless. Her office at the time resembled a storage closet, barely more inhabitable than the one at UC San Diego that had once contained her collection of random Bitcoin test purchases back in 2013.

Gronager, affable as always, told Meiklejohn that his tiny company, Chainalysis, was looking for talent and asked her if she might be interested in becoming the "head of something or other," as she remembers it. He showed her a demo of Reactor; she was impressed with how Gronager had managed to refine and scale up her group's techniques, assembling a vast collection of known Bitcoin clusters and integrating several of the ideas she'd first demonstrated into a powerful and highly responsive tool.

The position that Gronager was proposing to Meiklejohn would make her one of the first ten employees of Chainalysis, and it would come with equity in the company. Unbeknownst to either of them at the time—given the start-up's exponential growth in the years that followed—Gronager was offering her a stake that would soon be worth a life-changing fortune.

Meiklejohn found Gronager charming. She was intrigued by what he'd created. But she politely explained that she didn't want the job. She told Gronager that she had just started her tenure-track university position and wasn't ready to leave academia; at best, she suggested she could consult for Chainalysis on the side. Gronager wasn't interested in a consultant or adviser; he was looking for a fully engaged "operator" who would throw themselves into the work as completely as he and his co-founders had. The two parted on friendly terms.

In truth, Meiklejohn said years later, her reasons for turning Gronager down were more complex than she had let on. It wasn't that she had come to regret her "Men with No Names" paper. She considered it, among other things, a kind of "public service announcement" to anyone who believed that they could use Bitcoin anonymously, warning them about the objective limits of that imagined privacy.

Nor did she feel that Chainalysis's work was unethical, exactly. Like Zcash's Matt Green, she had come to believe that a company like Chainalysis—or even an entire industry of companies in its image—was inevitable, thanks to the public nature of the blockchain's data.

But rather than throw her lot in with the predators in the blockchain analysis cat-and-mouse game, Meiklejohn wanted to maintain a position somewhere in the middle of that game—or rather, outside it. She wanted to continue her blockchain research, but also to be free to build privacy technologies, or to publicly call out privacy vulnerabilities in cryptocurrencies when she found them, rather than help to exploit them in secret.

During her meeting with Gronager, her old adviser's joke about her being a "cyber narc" had popped back into her head. That was one job description to which she did not intend to devote her career.

"I don't think what Chainalysis does is morally wrong. It's just not how I wanted to make my living," Meiklejohn explained years later. "I don't want to be a cyber narc, in any form."

. . .

On a winter day nearly five years after that meeting, Meiklejohn and I sit on a bench in Central Park, not far from the Upper West Side apartment where she grew up, drinking coffee and watching cyclists and runners circle the park loop as a birthday party of rambunctious schoolgirls assembles on a lawn in front of us.

I've caught Meiklejohn during this visit back to her hometown to try a strange exercise: Instead of asking her to tell me more stories of her life and work, as I'd been doing for nearly a year, I want to tell her the stories I've learned over the course of my reporting on the world of crypto-tracing—to see how she feels about the years-long law enforcement feeding frenzy, the golden age of follow-the-money cybercriminal investigations that had all started with the blockchain analysis techniques she'd been the first to describe.

I walk Meiklejohn through the entire timeline of this book, from the tracing of Force's and Bridges's Silk Road money, to the Mt. Gox and BTC-e investigations, to AlphaBay. She mostly listens silently, taking the stories in. I tell her how the FBI analysts Ali and Erin traced Alexandre Cazes's funds to confirm his identity ("Cool," she responds), how the blockchain led to hundreds of arrests in the Welcome to Video case, as well as the rescue of twenty-three children ("That's nice," Meiklejohn says quietly), and to at least one suicide ("Jesus," she whispers). Then I give her a brief list of the last year's bounty of Bitcoin busts, from the Twitter hack arrests to the North Korean exchange theft case, to the Bitcoin mixer takedowns to the multibillion-dollar Silk Road seizure.

"That's about it," I conclude.

"That's a lot," she says.

Meiklejohn considers it all for a moment, looking out over the children's birthday party toward the Jackie Onassis Reservoir beyond. She explains that not all of it came as a surprise to her; she had read the Justice Department's press releases on some of the cases and spotted that they included a thanks to Chainalysis.

"These are, I think, objectively bad things," she says of the crimes IRS-CI targeted. "So I guess it's nice to see this is being used to help in these investigations. I feel good about that."

Then she launches into an explanation of why it's not nearly so simple. Companies like Chainalysis in the budding blockchain analysis industry will make their *real* money, she speculates, not from contracts with the IRS or the Justice Department but from banks and exchanges who are using their services to "de-risk" their transactions, ranking a certain sum of money's cleanliness and regulatory liability based on algorithms the public will never see. "Then it gets much sketchier, right?" she says. "That looks much more like surveillance. Your bank is basically spying on you and judging you based on where your money came from. That stuff is not as nice, and it's not going to make headlines."

Blockchain analysis will help trace dark web market deals, ransomware revenue, and crypto heists, but there's no reason it will stop there, she says. Like Gladstein, she points to the same potential for dictatorships to abuse Chainalysis-like services, tracing the finances of protesters, for instance.

She argues that the slippery slope could start in more insidious ways: She imagines that the same Western banks and exchanges will use Chainalysis-style tools to spot sex workers who accept payment in cryptocurrency, for example, automatically cutting off their accounts or even filing reports about them with law enforcement, just as they do with clearer-cut cases of black-market money. "It's very easy for there to be that kind of mission creep," Meiklejohn suggests.

Over the years since Meiklejohn first became interested in questions of mass surveillance, following Snowden's revelations in 2013, her interest in privacy has only grown. She's adopted measures others might consider paranoid: She encrypts her communications and stays off social media. She avoids using Google whenever possible, opting for the more private alternative search engine DuckDuckGo. She doesn't use ride-sharing services or food delivery apps. She turns off the GPS on her phone, or leaves it at home whenever she can.

When it comes to cryptocurrency, though, Meiklejohn makes clear that her position is more nuanced than a simple moral opposition to "surveillance" of the blockchain. She's concerned about a world of total, granular financial tracking, where governments and corporations can see every individual purchase and payment that a person makes. But she frets, too, about a future where a technology like Zcash actually catches on and makes truly untraceable and anonymous finances possible, enabling the sort of perfect money laundering and untouchable black markets that some crypto-anarchists once believed Bitcoin heralded.

"We haven't seen that extreme yet," she says. "And yeah, I definitely worry about what could happen there."

So instead of taking either side, she remains perched between them, trying to maintain her position as an impartial researcher. She hasn't stopped working on blockchain analysis: She and her UCL colleagues, after all, published findings on privacy vulnerabilities in Zcash in 2018, for instance. She's even hoping, she tells me, to publish a paper in 2022 about new methods to track Bitcoin peel chains, using the fingerprints of how different wallets create change addresses to better follow those forking paths on the blockchain.

But she considers that body of work to be, like the "Men with No Names" paper that started it all, a public service announcement—not a tool designed to empower either side of the conflict.

And, I ask, how would she sum up that public service announcement?

"If you really care about privacy," Meiklejohn says, "don't use Bitcoin."

.   .   .

My first meeting with Tigran Gambaryan after the end of his government career comes on a sunbaked summer day in 2021, at a small salad and poké restaurant in a strip mall not far from his home in Fresno. Following his stints in Oakland, D.C., and The Hague, he's finally back in California, where he's agreed to drive me around and show me some sights in his hometown.

Gambaryan's appearance has transformed from his days as a junior investigator chasing Force and Bridges. He's wearing a gray T-shirt from his kickboxing ring. He's let his hair and beard grow out, and he has a few days' stubble around its formerly clean edges. He's also dropped his stone-faced federal-agent expression and looks more relaxed.

In fact, he's on vacation. After ten years, Gambaryan has just left the IRS. After a brief break, he plans to take a job leading the investigations division at Binance, the world's largest cryptocurrency exchange, founded in China.

Binance, Gambaryan tells me, handles a "ridiculous" amount of cryptocurrency transactions—as much as $100 billion worth on some days. (The giant exchange, it's worth noting, has come under increasing scrutiny from European regulators for suspected laundering of criminal funds. Hiring Gambaryan, several of his colleagues told me, was part of the exchange's belated cleanup effort.) "It's a chance to make a big impact," Gambaryan says of his new job there.

Gambaryan's departure from the IRS, even after a decade, comes as little surprise: Most of the federal agents and prosecutors in this book have given in to the pull of the booming cryptocurrency industry. Grant Rabenn has taken a position as in-house counsel at Coinbase. Kathryn Haun, Gambaryan's old boss, became a high-flying crypto start-up investor at the venture capital firm Andreessen Horowitz, then went off to start her own fund. The IRS's Matt Price and the Dutch police's Nils Andersen-Röed are joining Gambaryan's team at Binance. Chris Janczewski would later leave the IRS to lead the investigations team at Chainalysis competitor TRM Labs. Even the DEA's Jen Sanchez, who had never touched a cryptocurrency case before AlphaBay, now works at the cryptocurrency exchange Luno.

I ask Gambaryan if this exodus is in part because savvy agents like him are realizing that the golden era of cryptocurrency tracing is coming to a close—that changes in technology like Monero, Zcash, or other privacy tools will finally end his years-long hot streak of cybercriminal busts.

"Monero is a huge issue," he concedes. "People are out there talking about how they can trace Monero. They can't. Not to a level where you can actually convict somebody in a criminal court without other evidence."

But he's still not convinced the golden era of crypto-tracing is over. Not just yet, Gambaryan says. Even if Zcash and Monero were to somehow take over the cryptocurrency market—and regulators will likely do their best to prevent that, he argues—he says the limiting factor in bitcoin-tracing cases has never been the number of leads to follow. It's been the time and resources of the federal agencies taking them on.

That means that even after the IRS's epic run of the last several years, there are still countless leads left to dig up from the blockchain's archive—a largely untapped bounty of incriminating clues, still preserved in amber, that agents will be harvesting for years to come.

"Maybe the era is going to end, but we're at least two years behind it," he says. "There's still a ton of unsolved cases out there." He warns me to expect another major indictment or two in the near future. (Just six months later, in fact, Gambaryan's old partner Chris Janczewski would arrest two alleged money launderers in New York for their role in the 2016 theft of nearly 120,000 bitcoins from the cryptocurrency exchange Bitfinex. In that case, the Justice Department would seize $3.6 billion in cryptocurrency—breaking Gambaryan's record for the biggest financial seizure in U.S. history.)

Looking back on Gambaryan's years at IRS-CI, I bring up Alexander Vinnik, one of the biggest indictments to come out of his work. Gambaryan tells me that he's heard about two attempts by fellow inmates to murder Vinnik while he was in jail in Greece, and that Vinnik's wife has since died while he was incarcerated. "Cancer," Gambaryan says grimly. By that summer, Vinnik had been convicted of money laundering in France but was still appealing his case to the country's supreme court.

I'd later reach out to Vinnik's French lawyer, Frédéric Bélot, who described his client as entirely innocent of the scale of crime that Gambaryan and the U.S. Justice Department had accused him of. According to Bélot, Vinnik had no connection to the Mt. Gox theft and wasn't even a founder or administrator of BTC-e, just one of its low-level staffers who never even knew the real admins' identities. "He is a poor simple Russian citizen working for people he doesn't know," Bélot told me. "He is not the big fish they pretend he is."

Bélot went on to relay my written questions to Vinnik in a French prison, and then share the Russian's responses: Vinnik wrote that he never had any knowledge of dirty money flowing into BTC-e—a difficult assertion to swallow, given the many public reports of its criminal users—and claimed that he had never even used the handle WME. In fact, he said the post on Bitcointalk linking him to WME must have been created by the real BTC-e administrators to set him up. "I am convinced of it, I have been used," Vinnik wrote. "They used my name and personal data. I am their victim as well!"

When I'd later share all this with Gambaryan, he would respond—after a long silence filled with things he was restraining himself from saying—that Vinnik would "have his day in a U.S. court."

But on the day of our meeting in Fresno, I focus on a pair of Gambaryan's cases with tidier resolutions. I point out to Gambaryan that his first two crypto-tracing cases, the ones that started it all, have reached an interesting milestone: Both Carl Mark Force and Shaun Bridges, as of our meeting in Fresno, are now out of prison. I'd reached out to both men via their lawyers, and neither of them responded. But I had gotten a strange email shortly afterward, and I was eager to show it to Gambaryan.

The message came from an anonymous source, sent from the encrypted email provider ProtonMail. "Mr. Bridges has not authorized me to speak on his case and thus I am violating certain ethical duties I am bound by in conversing with you," the email reads. "However, I have certain personal feelings concerning the case and possibly could point you in the right direction regarding some matters."

The message went on to emphasize, just as Bridges had done in his sentencing hearing, that the case against Force—and against Bridges— had arisen only because Bridges had told Bitstamp to issue a suspicious activity report on Force to FinCEN. In other words, the message cast Shaun Bridges as a kind of whistleblower in the case, rather than an unwitting partner in Force's corruption.

"Mr. Bridges had every opportunity to conceal Mr. Force's suspicious actions but chose not to," the note reads, "and instead put his name in the spot light by directing the filing of a SAR against Mr. Force."

Gambaryan smiles as he reads the message off my phone. He tells me, without hesitation, that the email was written by Bridges himself. "It was 100 percent Shaun," he says.

Regardless of its author, I tell Gambaryan I'm most interested in the last paragraph of the email, which includes a remarkable statement: "On a side note, it is ironic that Mr. Bridges' incarceration may have inadvertently made him one of the richest bitcoin investors."

That bold claim echoes something I heard from Carl Force's lawyer, too, I tell Gambaryan. Despite the IRS seizing all the bitcoins known to be associated with his crimes, Force's lawyer told me in a phone call, Force still held other stashes of coins that the government didn't know about, or couldn't prove were the proceeds of illegal activity. Given that Bitcoin has appreciated nearly a hundredfold since Force went to prison, "I have no doubt he's a millionaire," Force's lawyer suggested.

The anonymous email about—or written by—Bridges ended on a similar note. "Due to his inability to trade from within prison he has been forced to accompany the meteoric rise in the price of bitcoin originating from his lawful investments dating back to 2011," it read. "As a result I have no concerns over his future after his release."

Gambaryan finishes reading the mysterious email and hands my phone back to me.

"All I can say is," the former IRS agent tells me with a smile and a raised eyebrow, "they'd better pay their taxes."

ACKNOWLEDGMENTS

The people most responsible for making this book possible, as in so many works of nonfiction, were its central subjects and sources who spent countless hours telling me their stories. In many cases they did so without any direct benefit to themselves, and often with the understanding they would not be named in the book. I remain grateful that there are such people, motivated to take the time—and in some cases, the risk—to tell these stories simply because events are too significant to leave untold, or because they want to see them told accurately.

I owe a huge thanks to the two translators and fixers whom I worked with on this book, Vijitra "Aum" Duangdee and James Yoo. Maura Fox, as the book's fact-checker, spent months diligently and painstakingly retracing my steps and reinterviewing the book's subjects. Whatever mistakes remain in the text after her careful work are mine.

Once again, my *Wired* colleagues generously adjusted their lives to give me the time and freedom to write this book in the midst of the always-busy cybersecurity beat. My *Wired* web editor Brian Barrett and my security reporting colleague Lily Hay Newman both stepped up their productivity to fill in for me—in particular during one truly harrowing week, when news of Russia's SolarWinds hacking campaign hit while I was on leave and trying to meet a book proposal deadline. Thank you both for covering for me that week and so many others. Thank you, as well, to everyone else at *Wired* who supported this book in so many ways, including Matt Burgess, Andrew Couts, Megan Greenwell, Maria Streshinsky, Nick Thompson, Hemal Jhaveri, Gideon Litchfield, Zak Jason, and Michelle Legro among others. I'm particularly grateful to John Gravois, who so thoughtfully and skillfully edited the two excerpts of the book that were published in *Wired*.

Among all my *Wired* colleagues, Lily deserves another, more specific thank-you for her especially close reading of the book in draft form, which resulted in a hundred fixes, big and small. Other early readers, many of whom offered invaluable corrections and advice, include Nicolas Christin, Cory Doctorow, Garrett Graff, Dan Goodin, Caitlin Kelly, Robert McMillan, Nicole Perlroth, and Nick Weaver.

My agent Eric Lupfer once again instantly believed in the potential for this book when it was still a germ of an idea, and deftly managed the deal to make it possible—all despite my inveigling him in a failed, years-earlier attempt to get any interest from publishers on this topic. Thank you to Kristina Moore for your early work exploring the film and television possibilities of the book, and to Gideon Yago for showing me how to distill the most exciting narrative from it in a hundred Zoom calls.

At Doubleday, my editor Yaniv Soha once again served as the best guide and partner through the fraught book-writing process that any author could ask for, and I appreciated his careful and patient editorial judgment on this work more than ever. Thanks to Dan Novack, once again, for detailing to me all the various people who might sue me—and how to avoid those outcomes—in the most fun and encouraging tone imaginable. I'm very grateful to Michael Windsor for creating a striking and perfectly crafted cover. Additional thanks to all those at Doubleday for their work to make this book a success go to Milena Brown, Tricia Cave, Michael Goldsmith, Kate Hughes, Serena Lehman, Betty Lew, Maria Massey, Cara Reilly, Suzanne Smith, Bill Thomas, and Sean Yule.

Other heartfelt thanks for countless favors, tips, advice, and acts of support go out to Angela Bell, Sabrina Bezerra, Brett Callow, Ryan Carr, Roman Dobrokhotov, Ian Gray, Maddie Kennedy, Veronica Kyriakides, Rob Lee, Alan Liska, Sarah Maxwell, Michael Miller, Nicole Navas, Minh Nguyen, Apiradee "Gop" Pleekam, Ari Redbord, Alethea Smock, Riccardo Spagni, Gina Swankie, Jason Wool, Steve Worrall, Naima Zouhali, and Brandon Zwagerman. Special thanks also to Bertha Auquilla, Adam Kurnitz, Julie Hazan, Jill and Bob Kail, Barbara Kellman, Nazzie Noel, and Jamila Wignot.

Finally, thanks to Bilal Greenberg for modeling the persistence in demanding answers to all questions that any journalist should aspire to. And again, the last, immeasurable thank-you goes to my wife, Malika Zouhali-Worrall, my partner in this work as in everything.

SOURCE NOTES

The following notes are intended to credit prior reporting, suggest further reading, and, where possible, point readers to publicly available documents and records that serve as the basis for this book. *Tracers in the Dark* is, however, based primarily on hundreds of hours of my own interviews (and follow-up interviews conducted by the book's fact-checker, Maura Fox) with the agents, analysts, researchers, prosecutors, investigators, criminal suspects, and other sources whose stories are told here—along with nonpublic documents, photos, videos, and other records that many of those sources shared with me, which I haven't documented here.

In many cases, sources asked that I not include their names or that I omit the identities of others from the book, such as certain defendants whose names might also help to identify their victims. In some cases, particularly in the "Welcome to Video" section of the book, I've thus omitted citations of other reporting where I might have otherwise included them, and instead expressed my thanks to the reporters and publications whose work informed mine in the text introduction to that section below.

Otherwise, with the exception of any stray facts reported by others that I mistakenly failed to cite—apologies in advance for any such omissions—anything not included in the endnotes below can be attributed to my own firsthand reporting.

NOTES

PART I: MEN WITH NO NAMES

As I delved into the criminal cases of Carl Mark Force and Shaun Bridges, I had an invaluable guide in Cyrus Farivar and Joe Mullin's excellent 2016 feature for *Ars Technica,* "Stealing Bitcoins with Badges: How Silk Road's Dirty Cops Got Caught," which first untangled that winding rabbit hole of a story.

Situating that tale and others in this book in their historical context required partially retelling the story of the Silk Road and Ross Ulbricht. For some details of that story, I relied on the excellent reporting of Joshuah Bearman in his two-part *Wired* magazine feature on the Silk Road, "The Untold Story of Silk Road," and Nick Bilton's definitive book on the Silk Road investigation, *American Kingpin.*

Aside from interviewing the Dread Pirate Roberts for *Forbes* in 2013, much of my own Silk Road reporting came from attending Ross Ulbricht's trial, and my stories from that trial are linked on a page of Wired.com titled "The Silk Road Trial: WIRED's Gavel-to-Gavel Coverage." For further reading on the history, culture, and community of the Silk Road, as well as dark web markets in general, I'd recommend the work of Eileen Ormsby, including her books *Silk Road* and *The Darkest Web.*

CHAPTER 1: ELADIO GUZMAN FUENTES

9 sent them to 1AJGTi3i2tPUg3ojwoHndDN1DYhJTWKSAA: Bitcoin address 15T7SagsD2JqWUpBsiifcVuvyrQwX3Lq1e in blockchain records, blockchain.com.

12 "I utilize TOR for privacy": Criminal Complaint, *United States of America v. Carl Mark Force IV et al.,* Justice Department, filed March 25, 2015, justice .gov.

12 "through my investigation of DREAD PIRATE ROBERTS": Ibid.

13 Agents had swarmed into: Joshuah Bearman, "The Untold Story of Silk Road, Part II: The Fall," *Wired*, May 2015, wired.com.

CHAPTER 2: NOB

16 the IRS's Gary Alford: Nathaniel Popper, "The Tax Sleuth Who Took Down a Drug Lord," *New York Times*, Dec. 25, 2015, nytimes.com.

18 When the New York team arrested: Indictment, *United States of America v. Ross William Ulbricht*, Justice Department, filed Feb. 4, 2014, justice.gov.

18 had helped Ulbricht to carry out: Indictment, *United States of America v. Ross William Ulbricht*, U.S. Immigration and Customs Enforcement, filed Oct. 1, 2013, ice.gov.

19 He'd gotten in too deep: Nick Bilton, *American Kingpin* (New York: Penguin, 2018), 160.

19 "Could you please delete": Cyrus Farivar and Joe Mullin, "Stealing Bitcoins with Badges: How Silk Road's Dirty Cops Got Caught," *Ars Technica*, Aug. 27, 2016, arstechnica.com.

CHAPTER 3: THE AUDITOR

21 none fared worse than Armenia: Margaret Shapiro, "Armenia's 'Good Life' Lost to Misery, Darkness, Cold," *Washington Post*, Jan. 30, 1993, washingtonpost.com.

24 "Participants can be anonymous": Satoshi Nakamoto, email with subject line "Bitcoin P2P e-cash paper," Oct. 31, 2008, archived by Satoshi Nakamoto Institute, nakamotoinstitute.org.

CHAPTER 4: CRYPTOANARCHY

26 Gavin Andresen giving a talk: Amherst Media, "Making Money—Gavin Andresen @ Ignite Amherst," Feb. 17, 2011, youtube.com.

28 chronicled the cypherpunk movement: Andy Greenberg, *This Machine Kills Secrets* (New York: Dutton, 2012).

28 the archives of the Cypherpunks Mailing List: "Cypherpunks Mailing List Archive," mailing-list-archive.cryptoanarchy.wiki/.

29 In a semi-satirical essay: Timothy May, email with subject line "no subject (file transmission)," Aug. 18, 1993, Cypherpunks Mailing List Archive, venona.org, archived at archive.is/otyLu.

29 In his most famous essay: Timothy May, "The Crypto Anarchist Manifesto," June 1988, groups.csail.mit.edu, archived at archive.is/ZYpoA.

CHAPTER 5: SILK ROAD

31 April 2011 issue of *Forbes*: Andy Greenberg, "Crypto Currency," *Forbes*, April 20, 2011, forbes.com.

31 With an estimated million-plus bitcoins: Sergio Demian Lerner, "The Well Deserved Fortune of Satoshi Nakamoto, Bitcoin Creator, Visionary, and Genius," Bitslog, April 17, 2013, bitslog.com.

32 Tor worked by triple encrypting: "Tor: Onion Service Protocol," Tor Project, torproject.org.

33 "It's a certifiable one-stop shop": "Schumer Pushes to Shut Down Online Drug Marketplace," Associated Press, June 5, 2011, nbcnewyork.com.

33 "It kind of felt like": Adrian Chen, "The Underground Website Where You Can Buy Any Drug Imaginable," *Gawker,* June 1, 2011, gawker.com, archived at archive.is/dtvE9.

34 "Attempting major illicit transactions": Ibid.

34 "take immediate action and shut down": Brett Wolf, "Senators Seek Crackdown on 'Bitcoin' Currency," Reuters, June 8, 2011, reuters.com.

CHAPTER 6: THE DREAD PIRATE

35 Its number of user accounts: Gwern, "Silk Road 1: Theory & Practice," Sept. 29, 2018, gwern.net, archived at archive.is/NPLlZ.

36 Ratings and reviews allowed customers: Nicolas Christin, "Traveling the Silk Road: A Measurement Analysis of a Large Anonymous Online Marketplace," Carnegie Mellon University Cylab, May 4, 2012, cmu.edu.

36 "Silk Road doesn't really sell drugs": Andy Greenberg, "Meet the Dread Pirate Roberts, the Man Behind Booming Black Market Drug Website Silk Road," *Forbes,* Aug. 14, 2013, forbes.com.

36 "Dread Pirate Roberts": Joshuah Bearman, "The Untold Story of Silk Road, Part I," *Wired,* April 2015, wired.com.

37 "swallowed by the nightmare reality": Andy Greenberg, "Collected Quotations of the Dread Pirate Roberts, Founder of Underground Drug Site Silk Road and Radical Libertarian," *Forbes,* April 29, 2013, forbes.com.

38 "our own Che Guevara": Greenberg, "Meet the Dread Pirate Roberts."

38 $15 million in narcotics annually: Christin, "Traveling the Silk Road."

39 "What inspired you to start": Andy Greenberg, "An Interview with a Digital Drug Lord: The Silk Road's Dread Pirate Roberts (Q&A)," *Forbes,* Aug. 14, 2013, forbes.com.

CHAPTER 7: THE PUZZLE

41 In early 2013, the shelves: Sarah Meiklejohn et al., "A Fistful of Bitcoins: Characterizing Payments Among Men with No Names," University of California, San Diego, Aug. 2013, ucsd.edu.

44 Linear B had been deciphered: Alex Gallafent, "Alice Kober: Unsung Heroine Who Helped Decode Linear B," *The World,* Public Radio International, June 6, 2013.

46 allow people to pay road tolls: Sarah Meiklejohn et al., "The Phantom Toll-booth: Privacy-Preserving Electronic Toll Collection in the Presence of Driver Collusion," University of California, San Diego, Aug. 2011, ucsd.edu.

46 thermal camera technique: Keyton Mowery et al., "Heat of the Moment: Characterizing the Efficacy of Thermal Camera-Based Attacks," University of California, San Diego, Aug. 2011, ucsd.edu.

CHAPTER 8: MEN WITH NO NAMES

48 After downloading the entire blockchain: Meiklejohn et al., "Fistful of Bitcoins."

48 Bitcoin developer Hal Finney: Andy Greenberg, "Nakamoto's Neighbor: My Hunt for Bitcoin's Creator Led to a Paralyzed Crypto Genius," *Forbes,* March 25, 2014, forbes.com.

48 the first payment with real value: Galen Moore, "10 Years After Laszlo Hanyecz Bought Pizza with 10K Bitcoin, He Has No Regrets," *CoinDesk,* May 22, 2020, coindesk.com.

49 "Some linking is still unavoidable": Satoshi Nakamoto, "Bitcoin: A Peer-to-Peer Electronic Cash System," Oct. 31, 2008, archived by Satoshi Nakamoto Institute, nakamotoinstitute.org.

50 called a "change" address: For the Swiss and German researchers, see Elli Androulaki et al., "Evaluating User Privacy in Bitcoin," in *Financial Cryptography and Data Security,* ed. Ahmad-Reza Sadeghi (Berlin: Springer, 2013), eprint.iacr.org; for the Israeli team, see Dorit Ron and Adi Shamir, "Quantitative Analysis of the Full Bitcoin Transaction Graph," in ibid.; and for the Irish team, see Fergal Reid and Martin Harrigan, "An Analysis of Anonymity in the Bitcoin System," *Security and Privacy in Social Networks,* July 13, 2012, arxiv.org.

52 He had been one of the lead advisers: Andy Greenberg, "GM Took 5 Years to Fix a Full-Takeover Hack in Millions of OnStar Cars," *Wired,* Sept. 10, 2015, wired.com.

52 Savage had helped lead a group: Kirill Levchenko et al., "Click Trajectories: End-to-End Analysis of the Spam Value Chain," University of California, San Diego, May 2011, ucsd.edu.

53 With just a few hundred tags: Meiklejohn et al., "Fistful of Bitcoins."

54 613,326 bitcoins—5 percent of all the coins: Ibid.

55 Another theft of 18,500 bitcoins: Ibid.

55 "Even our relatively small experiment": Ibid.

CHAPTER 9: CYBER NARC

57 Each one contained a teaspoon: Brian Krebs, "Mail from the (Velvet) Cyber-crime Underground," Krebs on Security, July 30, 2013, krebsonsecurity.com.

58 "(I like having them nipping": Greenberg, "Interview with a Digital Drug Lord."

59 I'd ordered one gram of pot: Andy Greenberg, "Here's What It's Like to Buy Drugs on Three Anonymous Online Black Markets," *Forbes,* Aug. 14, 2013, forbes.com.

59 Immediately, Meiklejohn's findings were covered: Robert McMillan, "Sure, You Can Steal Bitcoins. But Good Luck Laundering Them," *Wired,* Aug. 27, 2013, wired.com; Meghan Neal, "Bitcoin Isn't the Criminal Safe Haven People Think It Is," *Vice Motherboard,* Aug. 27, 2013, vice.com; G. F., "Following the Bitcoin Trail," *Economist,* Aug. 28, 2013, economist.com; Joshua Brustein, "Bitcoin May Not Be So Anonymous After All," *Bloomberg Businessweek,* Aug. 27, 2013, bloomberg.com.

60 For my two deposits: Andy Greenberg, "Follow the Bitcoins: How We Got Busted Buying Drugs on Silk Road's Black Market," *Forbes,* Sept. 5, 2013, forbes.com.

61 "There have been a number of papers": "Building Collaborations Between Developers and Researchers," Bitcoin and Cryptocurrency Research Conference, March 27, 2014, video recording downloaded from Princeton website, princeton.edu.

CHAPTER 10: GLEN PARK

63 twenty-nine-year-old named Ross Ulbricht: Bilton, *American Kingpin,* 285.

63 Just at that moment, a disheveled couple: Ibid., 290.

64 Before he was even aware: Ibid., 291.

64 On the Silk Road's forums: Andy Greenberg, "End of the Silk Road: FBI Says It's Busted the Web's Biggest Anonymous Drug Black Market," *Forbes,* Oct. 2, 2013.

65 The FBI, meanwhile, had tracked down: See Andy Greenberg, "Feds 'Hacked' Silk Road Without a Warrant? Perfectly Legal, Prosecutors Argue," *Wired,* Oct. 7, 2014, wired.com.

CHAPTER 11: THE DOUBLE AGENT

66 Working in his office on an upper floor: Criminal Complaint, *United States of America v. Carl Mark Force IV et al.,* Justice Department, filed March 25, 2015, justice.gov.

67 "What is a federal prosecutor": Farivar and Mullin, "Stealing Bitcoins with Badges."

68 Force had first approached DPR: Bearman, "Untold Story of Silk Road, Part I."

70 After gaining DPR's trust: Criminal Complaint, *United States of America v. Carl Mark Force IV et al.,* Justice Department, filed March 25, 2015, justice.gov.

CHAPTER 12: RECEIPTS

73 "since Bitcoin does not have": FBI, "Bitcoin Virtual Currency: Unique Features Present Distinct Challenges for Deterring Illicit Activity," April 24, 2012, hosted at cryptome.org, archived at archive.is/Vegqf.

CHAPTER 13: FRENCHMAID, DEATHFROMABOVE

78 Gambaryan had once observed: Criminal Complaint, *United States of America v. Carl Mark Force IV et al.*, Justice Department, filed March 25, 2015, justice.gov.

79 The message Force had written: Ibid.

CHAPTER 14: THE TRIAL

83 In the defense's opening statement: Andy Greenberg, "Silk Road Defense Says Ulbricht Was Framed by the 'Real' Dread Pirate Roberts," *Wired,* Jan. 13, 2015, wired.com.

84 After that seizure announcement: Nick Weaver, "How I Traced 20% of Ross Ulbricht's Bitcoin to the Silk Road," *Forbes,* Jan. 20, 2015, forbes.com.

85 Yum presented a bombshell revelation: Andy Greenberg, "Prosecutors Trace $13.4M in Bitcoins from the Silk Road to Ulbricht's Laptop," *Wired,* Jan. 29, 2015, wired.com.

85 A would-be contract killer: Andy Greenberg, "Read the Transcript of Silk Road's Boss Ordering 5 Assassinations," *Wired,* Feb. 2, 2015, wired.com.

85 Bitcoin's permanent ledger: Bitcoin transaction e7db5246a810cb76e 53314fe51d2a60f5609bb51d37a4df105356efc286c6c67 in blockchain records, blockchain.com.

86 The evidence stacked against him: Andy Greenberg, "The Silk Road Trial: WIRED's Gavel-to-Gavel Coverage," *Wired,* Feb. 2, 2015, wired.com.

86 Three months later, Ulbricht reappeared: Kari Paul, "Unsealed Transcript Shows How a Judge Justified Ross Ulbricht's Life Sentence," *Vice Motherboard,* Oct. 5, 2015, vice.com.

87 she sentenced Ulbricht to two life sentences: Andy Greenberg, "Silk Road Creator Ross Ulbricht Sentenced to Life in Prison," *Wired,* May 29, 2015, wired.com.

PART II: TRACER FOR HIRE

Telling the story of Chainalysis's early days required setting the stage for the company's first investigation with the 2014 collapse of Mt. Gox. I was guided through that recent history by the work of my former *Wired* colleagues Robert McMillan and Cade Metz in their stories from 2013 and 2014 titled "The Rise and Fall of the World's Largest Bitcoin Exchange" and "The Inside Story of Mt. Gox, Bitcoin's $460 Million Disaster." For a magazine-style narrative of the story of Mt. Gox and Mark Karpelès, I also recommend Jen Wieczner's *Fortune* feature "Mt. Gox and the Surprising Redemption of Bitcoin's Biggest Villain."

For the resolution of the Shaun Bridges investigation, I'm once again indebted to the reporting of Cyrus Farivar and Joe Mullin in *Ars Technica,* and in particular Mullin's detailed news coverage of events in Bridges's case.

CHAPTER 15: COLLAPSE

91 Mt. Gox had abruptly collapsed: Yoshifumi Takemoto and Sophie Knight, "Mt. Gox Files for Bankruptcy, Hit with Lawsuit," Reuters, Feb. 28, 2014, reuters.com.

92 The signs of illness: David Gilson, "Mt. Gox Temporarily Suspends USD Withdrawals," *CoinDesk,* June 20, 2013, coindesk.com.

93 In May and June 2013, the Department: Robert McMillan and Cade Metz, "The Rise and Fall of the World's Largest Bitcoin Exchange," *Wired,* Nov. 6, 2013, wired.com.

93 As the crises mounted: Robert McMillan and Cade Metz, "The Inside Story of Mt. Gox, Bitcoin's $460 Million Disaster," *Wired,* March 3, 2014, wired .com.

93 The exchange was insolvent: Kashmir Hill, "Mt. Gox CEO Says All the Bitcoin Is Gone in Bankruptcy Filing," *Forbes,* Feb. 28, 2014, forbes.com.

93 One aggrieved Mt. Gox user: Sam Byford, "'Mt. Gox, Where Is Our Money?,'" *Verge,* Feb. 19, 2014, theverge.com.

93 A YouTube video of Karpelès: Patrick Nsabimana, "MtGox CEO Mark Karpales Interrupted by Protester at MtGox Headquarters," YouTube, Feb. 15, 2014, youtube.com.

94 A central pillar of the Bitcoin economy: Matthew Kimmell, "Mt. Gox," *CoinDesk,* July 22, 2021, coindesk.com.

96 the Large Hadron Collider's search: "Storage," CERN, home.cern.

97 The 2011 Prague conference: "European Bitcoin Conference 2011, Prague Nov. 25–27," forum thread on Bitcointalk, Aug. 30, 2011, bitcointalk.org.

97 programmer named Amir Taaki: Andy Greenberg, "How an Anarchist Bitcoin Coder Found Himself Fighting ISIS in Syria," *Wired,* March 29, 2017, wired.com.

97 "If Bitcoin means anything": Andy Greenberg, "Waiting for Dark: Inside Two Anarchists' Quest for Untraceable Money," *Wired,* July 11, 2014, wired .com.

CHAPTER 16: DIRTY MONEY

99 Bitcoin's exchange rate plummeted: Alex Hern, "Bitcoin Is the Worst Investment of 2014. But Can It Recover?," *Guardian,* Dec. 17, 2014, theguardian .com.

CHAPTER 17: NOISE

104 A report from the Japanese newspaper: Tim Hornyak, "Police Suspect Fraud Took Most of Mt. Gox's Missing Bitcoins," IDG News Service, Dec. 31, 2014, networkworld.com.

105 Mt. Gox's CEO had discovered: Jen Wieczner, "Mt. Gox and the Surprising Redemption of Bitcoin's Biggest Villain," *Fortune,* April 19, 2018, fortune .com.

107 Gregory Maxwell, the Bitcoin developer: "Is Someone Monitoring Large Parts of the Network? (Evidence+Firwall Rules)," Forum thread, Bitcoin-talk, March 6, 2015, bitcointalk.org.

CHAPTER 18: THE SECOND AGENT

112 Alford had spotted an email: Farivar and Mullin, "Stealing Bitcoins with Badges."

112 Bridges had complied, sending: Criminal Complaint, *United States of America v. Carl Mark Force IV et al.,* Justice Department, filed March 25, 2015, justice.gov.

115 In late March 2015, Gambaryan signed: Ibid.

CHAPTER 19: A HOLE IN THE VAULT

119 until Trade Hill shut down: Timothy Lee, "Major Bitcoin Exchange Shuts Down, Blaming Regulation and Loss of Funds," *Ars Technica,* Feb. 15, 2012, arstechnica.com.

CHAPTER 20: BTC-E

122 "conferred with an individual": Criminal Complaint, *United States of America v. Carl Mark Force IV et al.,* Justice Department, filed March 25, 2015, justice.gov.

123 The managing entity behind BTC-e: Superseding Indictment, *United States of America v. BTC-E, A/K/A Canton Business Corporation and Alexander Vinnik,* June 17, 2017, justice.gov.

123 a "Silk Road 2" had popped up: Andy Greenberg, " 'Silk Road 2.0' Launches, Promising a Resurrected Black Market for the Dark Web," *Forbes,* Nov. 6, 2013, forbes.com.

123 In all, more than two dozen: Greenberg, "Waiting for Dark."

123 known as Operation Onymous: Andy Greenberg, "Global Web Crackdown Arrests 17, Seizes Hundreds of Dark Net Domains," *Wired,* Nov. 7, 2014, wired.com.

123 vulnerability in Tor: Phobos, "Thoughts and Concerns About Operation Onymous," *Tor Blog,* Nov. 9, 2014, torproject.org.

123 who had joined Silk Road 2: Joseph Cox, "Silk Road 2 Founder Dread Pirate

Roberts 2 Caught, Jailed for 5 Years," *Vice Motherboard,* April 12, 2019, vice
.com.

123 this one called Evolution: Andy Greenberg, "The Dark Web Gets Darker
with Rise of the 'Evolution' Drug Market," *Wired,* Sept. 10, 2014, wired
.com.

123 When Evolution's administrators disappeared: Nicky Woolf, "Bitcoin 'Exit
Scam': Deep-Web Market Operators Disappear with $12M," *Guardian,*
March 18, 2015, theguardian.com.

124 another market called Agora: Andy Greenberg, "Agora, the Dark Web's
Biggest Drug Market, Is Going Offline," *Wired,* Aug. 26, 2015, wired.com.

124 A study by Nicolas Christin's research group: Andy Greenberg, "Crack-
downs Haven't Stopped the Dark Web's $100M Yearly Drug Sales," *Wired,*
Aug. 12, 2015, wired.com.

CHAPTER 21: WME

129 He'd traced the 650,000 stolen coins: Kim Nilsson, "The Missing MtGox
Bitcoins," *WizSec* (blog), April 29, 2015, blog.wizsec.jp, archived at archive
.is/oDn3o.

129 Nilsson had shared those results: Justin Scheck and Bradley Hope, "The
Man Who Solved Bitcoin's Most Notorious Heist," *Wall Street Journal,*
Aug. 10, 2018, wsj.com.

CHAPTER 22: VINNIK

132 Whoever used the WME pseudonym: WME, posts on Bitcointalk forum,
bitcointalk.org, archived at archive.is/sySzm.

132 "Demand for the release": WME, "Re: Scam Report Against Crypto-
Xchange $100K USD," post on Bitcointalk, July 18, 2012, bitcointalk.org,
archived at bit.ly/33EiufE.

CHAPTER 23: CONSOLATION PRIZES

135 In October 2015, not long after: Joe Mullin, "Corrupt Silk Road Agent Carl
Force Sentenced to 78 Months," *Ars Technica,* Oct. 19, 2015, arstechnica
.com.

135 Two months later, Shaun Bridges: "Former Secret Service Agent Sentenced
to 71 Months in Scheme Related to Silk Road Investigation," Dec. 7, 2015,
Justice Department, justice.gov.

135 A panel of judges: Andy Greenberg, "Silk Road Creator Ross Ulbricht Loses
His Life Sentence Appeal," *Wired,* May 31, 2017, wired.com.

135 He apologized and added: Farivar and Mullin, "Stealing Bitcoins with
Badges."

136 That decision went against: Joe Mullin, "Corrupt Agent Who Investigated

Silk Road Is Suspected of Another $700K Heist," *Ars Technica,* July 3, 2016, arstechnica.com.

136 Nonetheless, the former Secret Service agent: Justin Fenton, "Silk Road Administrator Sentenced, Corrupt Agent Rearrested," *Baltimore Sun,* Jan. 30, 2016, baltimoresun.com.

136 He learned that the agency: Application for a Search Warrant, Jan. 27, 2016, hosted at arstechnica.com, archived at bit.ly/3IsQDCq.

137 When the agents searched the house: Motion to Terminate Defendant's Motion for Selfsurrender and Motion to Unseal Arrest Warrant and [Proposed] Order, Jan. 28, 2016, hosted at archive.org, archived at bit.ly/3qOwhOj.

137 Meanwhile, Kim Nilsson, the Swedish: Nilsson, "Missing MtGox Bitcoins."

137 Nilsson was profiled: Scheck and Hope, "Man Who Solved Bitcoin's Most Notorious Heist."

137 credited with cracking the case: Wieczner, "Mt. Gox and the Surprising Redemption of Bitcoin's Biggest Villain."

138 By the end of 2015, Chainalysis: Daniel Palmer, "Chainalysis Raises $1.6 Million, Signs Cybercrime Deal with Europol," *CoinDesk,* Feb. 19, 2016, coindesk.com.

PART III: ALPHABAY

As I pieced together the early criminal cases that served as the foundation for the Fresno-based law enforcement team's probe of AlphaBay, the beat reporting of Cyrus Farivar in *Ars Technica* was once again an invaluable guide. The story of AlphaBay's takedown was also previously told in narrative form by Jack Rhysider in his podcast, *Darknet Diaries,* in the episode titled "Operation Bayonet." Rhysider's audio piece drew in part from my *Wired* feature on the Dutch police takeover of Hansa, "Operation Bayonet: Inside the Sting That Hijacked an Entire Dark Web Drug Market," but I also found it helpful to hear his weaving together of the Hansa and AlphaBay investigations as I approached the larger story myself.

Many of my descriptions of the dark web landscape—both quantitative and qualitative—leading up to AlphaBay's rise would not have been possible without the research and guidance of Nicolas Christin and his fellow researchers at Carnegie Mellon.

CHAPTER 24: ALPHA02

145 "University of Carding Guide": Alpha02, "Carding Guide, All My Knowledge," May 17, 2014, archived at archive.md/enMww.

146 "Be safe, brothers": Patrick Howell O'Neill, "How AlphaBay Has Quietly Become the King of Dark Web Marketplaces," CyberScoop, April 5, 2017, cyberscoop.com.

146 "I am absolutely certain my opsec": new_dww, "Interview with AlphaBay Market Admin," DeepDotWeb, republished at theonionweb.com, archived at archive.md/Xcsxf.

146 "goal is to become the largest": Forfeiture Complaint, *United States of America v. Alexandre Cazes,* Justice Department, July 19, 2017, justice.gov.

147 "We want to have every imaginable": Ibid.

147 A study in *The British Journal:* Isak Ladegaard, "We Know Where You Are, What You Are Doing, and We Will Catch You: Testing Deterrence Theory in Digital Drug Markets," *British Journal of Criminology* 58, no. 2 (March 2018), oup.com.

147 The study's author, trying: Andy Greenberg, "The Silk Road Creator's Life Sentence Actually Boosted Dark Web Drug Sales," *Wired,* May 23, 2017, wired.com.

147 "Courts can stop a man": Joseph Cox, "Dark Web Market Admins React to Silk Road Life Sentence," *Vice Motherboard,* June 1, 2015, vice.com.

148 Agora's administrators had taken their site: Greenberg, "Agora, the Dark Web's Biggest Drug Market, Is Going Offline."

148 Shortly before AlphaBay took over: Forfeiture Complaint, *United States of America v. Alexandre Cazes,* Justice Department, July 19, 2017, justice.gov.

148 AlphaBay had more than 200,000 users: Jack Rhysider, "Ep. 24: Operation Bayonet," *Darknet Diaries* podcast, darknetdiaries.com.

148 more than 21,000 product listings: "AlphaBay, the Largest Online 'Dark Market,' Shut Down," Justice Department, July 20, 2017, justice.gov.

CHAPTER 26: CAZES

158 On that site, someone named "Alex": Alex, profile page on Skyrock, June 28, 2008, skyrock.com, archived at bit.ly/3FRDy45.

159 The words on his shirt: Raptr, blog on Skyrock, June 11, 2008, skyrock.com, archived at archive.md/EUfvn.

159 He had signed his messages: Forfeiture Complaint, *United States of America v. Alexandre Cazes,* Justice Department, July 19, 2017, justice.gov.

159 His photo on the site: "Canadian Found Dead in Thai Cell Wanted for Running 'Dark Web' Market," Agence France-Presse, July 15, 2017, image hosted at gulfnews.com.

160 On Comment Ça Marche: Forfeiture Complaint, *United States of America v. Alexandre Cazes,* Justice Department, July 19, 2017, justice.gov.

CHAPTER 27: THAILAND

162 For more than half a century: Department of Justice Office of the Inspector General Audit Division, "The Drug Enforcement Administration's International Operations," Office of the Inspector General, Feb. 2007, justice.gov.

162 In the late 1950s that triangle: Alfred W. McCoy, *The Politics of Heroin in Southeast Asia,* with Cathleen B. Read and Leonard P. Adams II (New York: Harper Colophon, 1972), hosted at renincorp.org.

162 an epidemic of addicted U.S. soldiers: Lauren Aguirre, "Lessons Learned—and Lost—from a Vietnam-Era Study of Addiction," *Stat,* July 19, 2021, statnews.com.

164 One RTP official named Thitisan Utthanaphon: Jonathan Head, "Joe Ferrari: The High-Rolling Life of Thailand's Controversial Ex–Police Chief," BBC, Sept. 6, 2021, bbc.com.

166 highest "alfresco" dining in the world: Sirocco website, lebua.com.

166 The American opioid crisis: Bureau of International Narcotics and Law Enforcement Affairs, "Addressing the Opioid Crisis," U.S. State Department, state.gov.

CHAPTER 28: TUNAFISH

169 "No level of blockchain analysis": Forfeiture Complaint, *United States of America v. Alexandre Cazes,* Justice Department, July 19, 2017, justice.gov.

CHAPTER 29: RAWMEO

178 Founded by the blogger Daryush "Roosh" Valizadeh: "Daryush 'Roosh' Valizadeh," Southern Poverty Law Center, splcenter.org.

CHAPTER 30: HANSA

186 The Dutch investigation into Hansa: Andy Greenberg, "Operation Bayonet: Inside the Sting That Hijacked an Entire Dark Web Drug Market," *Wired,* March 3, 2018, wired.com.

188 "We could use that arrest": Ibid.

191 the Australian Federal Police had run a site: Michael Safi, "The Takeover: How Police Ended Up Running a Paedophile Site," *Guardian,* July 12, 2016, theguardian.com.

191 Journalists and legal scholars: Håkon F. Høydal, Einar Otto Stangvik, and Natalie Remøe Hansen, "Breaking the Dark Net: Why the Police Share Abuse Pics to Save Children," *Verdens Gang,* Oct. 17, 2017, vg.no.

CHAPTER 31: TAKEOVER

197 "The quality really went up": Greenberg, "Operation Bayonet."

CHAPTER 33: THE ATHENEE

204 the Athenee, a five-star luxury hotel: Hotel Athenee Bangkok website, marriott.com.

CHAPTER 35: CAPTIVITY

217 "using only the world's strongest gear": SiamBeast, "Project 'Blue Pearl'—a Computer Using Only the Strongest Hardware," thread on forum Overclock .net, Feb. 25, 2017, overclock.net.

CHAPTER 36: POSTMORTEM

226 Looking into the medical research: See Michael Armstrong Jr. and Gael B. Strack, "Recognition and Documentation of Strangulation Crimes," *Journal of the American Medical Association Otolaryngology—Head and Neck Surgery,* Sept. 2016, jamanetwork.com; Anny Sauvageau et al., "Agonal Sequences in 14 Filmed Hangings with Comments on the Role of the Type of Suspension, Ischemic Habituation, and Ethanol Intoxication on the Timing of Agonal Responses," *American Journal of Forensic Medicine and Pathology* 32, no. 2 (2011), nih.gov.

CHAPTER 37: THE TRAP

228 Rumors had begun to swirl: Benjamin Vitaris, "AlphaBay Went Down a Week Ago: Customers Looking for Alternatives," *Bitcoin Magazine,* July 11, 2017, bitcoinmagazine.com.

229 *The Wall Street Journal* broke the news: Robert McMillan and Aruna Viswanatha, "Illegal-Goods Website AlphaBay Shut Following Law-Enforcement Action," *Wall Street Journal,* July 13, 2017, wsj.com.

232 "Please don't send the cops": Criminal Complaint, *United States of America v. Marcos Paulo de Oliveira-Annibale,* U.S. Justice Department, May 2, 2019, justice.gov.

CHAPTER 38: AFTERMATH

233 "You are not safe": Andy Greenberg, "Global Police Spring a Trap on Thousands of Dark Web Users," *Wired,* July 20, 2017, wired.com.

234 "We trace people who are active": Ibid.

234 "damage the trust in this whole system": Greenberg, "Operation Bayonet."

234 "Looks like I'll be sober": Greenberg, "Global Police Spring a Trap on Thousands of Dark Web Users."

234 "DO NOT MAKE NEW ORDERS": Nathaniel Popper and Rebecca R. Ruiz, "2 Leading Online Black Markets Are Shut Down by Authorities," *New York Times,* July 20, 2017, nytimes.com.

235 in 2018, Operation Disarray: "Operation Disarray: Shining a Light on the Dark Web," FBI, April 3, 2018, fbi.gov.

235 in 2019, Operation SaboTor: "J-CODE Announces 61 Arrests in Its Second Coordinated Law Enforcement Operation Targeting Opioid Trafficking on the Darknet," FBI, March 6, 2019, fbi.gov.

235 in 2020, Operation DisrupTor: "Operation DisrupTor," FBI, Sept. 22, 2020, fbi.gov.

236 The Dutch police pointed out: Nathaniel Popper, "Hansa Market, a Dark Web Marketplace, Bans the Sale of Fentanyl," *New York Times,* July 18, 2017, nytimes.com.

236 "They would have taken place": Greenberg, "Operation Bayonet."

236 "Compared to both the Silk Road takedowns": Rolf van Wegberg et al., "AlphaBay Exit, Hansa-Down: Dream On?," *Dark Web Solutions,* Netherlands Organization for Applied Scientific Research, Aug. 2017, tno.nl.

237 Based on data he and his fellow researchers: Nicolas Christin and Jeremy Thomas, "Analysis of the Supply of Drugs and New Psychoactive Substances by Europe-Based Vendors via Darknet Markets in 2017–18," European Monitoring Centre for Drugs and Drug Addiction, Nov. 26, 2019, europa.eu.

237 The FBI has estimated: Popper and Ruiz, "2 Leading Online Black Markets Are Shut Down by Authorities."

237 "History has taught us": Andy Greenberg, "Feds Dismantled the Dark-Web Drug Trade—but It's Already Rebuilding," *Wired,* May 9, 2019, wired.com.

237 "Things will stabilize": Greenberg, "Operation Bayonet."

PART IV: WELCOME TO VIDEO

I first learned about the Welcome to Video investigation from the excellent reporting of my *Wired* colleague Lily Hay Newman, who nailed the coverage of the news the day the case became public in October 2019 with the headline "How a Bitcoin Trail Led to a Massive Dark Web Child-Porn Site Takedown." The story of the case was also told in newspaper feature format the next month by Aruna Viswanatha in *The Wall Street Journal,* in her piece "How Investigators Busted a Huge Online Child-Porn Site."

As I considered how to approach the difficult and sensitive subject of child sexual abuse materials in a longer, narrative format, I found it extremely valuable to read and listen to the joint work done by the Norwegian newspaper *VG* and CBC Radio on the investigation of a similar child sexual abuse dark web site, Childs Play. The *VG* feature that resulted from that reporting partnership, written by Håkon F. Høydal, Einar Otto Stangvik, and Natalie Remøe Hansen, is titled "Breaking the Dark Net: Why the Police Share Abuse Pics to Save Children," and the podcast series based on their reporting along with that of CBC Radio is called "Hunting Warhead."

I'm additionally grateful to the following reporters for their work on Welcome to Video–related cases, all of which I relied on: Raisa Habersham of *The Atlanta Journal-Constitution,* Berny Torre of the *Daily Mirror,* and András Dezső of *Index.*

CHAPTER 40: FIVE CHARACTERS

243 NCA agents had been tracking: Josh Halliday, "Cambridge Graduate Admits 137 Online Sexual Abuse Crimes," *Guardian,* Oct. 16, 2017, theguardian.com.

247 Those CSAM sites accounted for: Andy Greenberg, "Over 80 Percent of Dark-Web Visits Relate to Pedophilia, Study Finds," *Wired,* Dec. 30, 2014, wired.com.

248 The better part of a decade: Global Witness, " 'Do You Know Alexander Vinnik?,' " Global Witness, Nov. 18, 2019, globalwitness.org.

248 Agents determined that Vinnik: Avaton Luxury Hotel & Villas website, avaton.com.

248 Alexander Vinnik suddenly found himself: Andrei Zakharov, "Hunting the Missing Millions from Collapsed Cryptocurrency," BBC News, Dec. 30, 2019.

CHAPTER 41: "SERACH VIDEOS"

250 When Janczewski and Gambaryan first copied: Welcome to Video screenshots, Justice Department, Oct. 16, 2019, justice.gov, archived at archive.is/YK1CW.

CHAPTER 46: RIPPLES

280 In early July 2020, Son Jong-woo walked out: "U.S. Regrets Korean Child Porn King Walking Free," *Korean JoongAng Daily,* July 8, 2020, joins.com.

281 He faces criminal charges: "Dutch National Charged in Takedown of Obscene Website Selling over 2,000 'Real Rape' and Child Pornography Videos, Funded by Cryptocurrency," U.S. Immigration and Customs Enforcement, March 12, 2020, ice.gov.

283 "one of the worst forms of evil": Lily Hay Newman, "How a Bitcoin Trail Led to a Massive Dark Web Child-Porn Site Takedown," *Wired,* Oct. 16, 2019, wired.com.

PART V: THE NEXT ROUND

As I retold the Colonial Pipeline breach case as an illustration of the power and limits of bitcoin tracing in ransomware cases, I relied on the detailed news reporting of William Turton and Kartikay Mehrotra at Bloomberg, as well as David Sanger, Nicole Perlroth, and others at *The New York Times.* My *Wired* colleague Lily Hay Newman's news coverage of the ransomware beat and the insights she shared in conversation also helped to inform this chapter.

As I sought to verify the authenticity and contextualize the history of Alpha-Bay's new administrator, DeSnake, in the summer of 2021, both Carnegie Mellon's Nicolas Christin and Flashpoint's Ian Gray served as invaluable sources of analysis and archival information.

CHAPTER 47: OPEN SEASON

287 Just as with AlphaBay, the group traced: Ed Caesar, "The Cold War Bunker That Became Home to a Dark-Web Empire," *New Yorker,* July 27, 2020, newyorker.com.

288 They ultimately identified two Chinese brokers: "Two Chinese Nationals Charged with Laundering over $100 Million in Cryptocurrency from Exchange Hack," Justice Department, March 2, 2020, justice.gov.

288 "I'm feeling generous": Nick Statt, "Twitter's Massive Attack: What We Know After Apple, Biden, Obama, Musk, and Others Tweeted a Bitcoin Scam," *Verge,* July 16, 2020, theverge.com.

289 Many had been found in a leak: Nicholas Thompson and Brian Barrett, "How Twitter Survived Its Biggest Hack—and Plans to Stop the Next One," *Wired,* Sept. 24, 2020, wired.com.

289 They identified three hackers: Criminal Complaint, *United States of America v. Nima Fazeli,* July 31, 2020, justice.gov.

290 A subpoena to BitPay revealed: "Ohio Resident Charged with Operating Darknet-Based Bitcoin 'Mixer,' Which Laundered over $300 Million," Justice Department, Feb. 13, 2020, justice.gov.

290 Bitcoin Fog by then had laundered: Andy Greenberg, "Feds Arrest an Alleged $336M Bitcoin-Laundering Kingpin," *Wired,* April 27, 2021, wired .com.

290 The IRS-CI agents identified: "Individual Arrested and Charged with Operating Notorious Darknet Cryptocurrency 'Mixer,' " Justice Department, April 28, 2020, justice.gov.

291 Sterlingov's very first Bitcoin transactions: Greenberg, "Feds Arrest an Alleged $336M Bitcoin-Laundering Kingpin."

292 BTC-e, it turned out, had been used: Timothy Lloyd, "US and Russia Spar over Accused Crypto-launderer," Organized Crime and Corruption Reporting Project, Jan. 24, 2019, occrp.org.

292 Before it was torn off-line: Catalin Cimpanu, "BTC-e Founder Sentenced to Five Years in Prison for Laundering Ransomware Funds," *ZDNet,* Dec. 7, 2020, zdnet.com.

293 They refer to them: "United States Files a Civil Action to Forfeit Cryptocurrency Valued at over One Billion U.S. Dollars," Justice Department, Nov. 5, 2020, justice.gov.

293 By the fall of 2020, as the value: Andy Greenberg, "The Feds Seized $1 Billion in Stolen Silk Road Bitcoins," *Wired,* Nov. 5, 2020, wired.com.

CHAPTER 48: LIMITS

295 Just before 5:00 a.m. on May 7, 2021: William Turton and Kartikay Mehrotra, "Hackers Breached Colonial Pipeline Using Compromised Password," Bloomberg, June 4, 2021, bloomberg.com.

295 Colonial owns and manages a fifty-five-hundred-mile-long pipeline: Chris Bing and Stephanie Kelly, "Cyber Attack Shuts Down U.S. Fuel Pipeline 'Jugular,' Biden Briefed," Reuters, May 8, 2021, reuters.com.

295 known as DarkSide: Turton and Mehrotra, "Hackers Breached Colonial Pipeline Using Compromised Password."

295 DarkSide's extortion messages: Trend Micro Research, "What We Know About the DarkSide Ransomware and the US Pipeline Attack," Trend Micro, May 12, 2021, trendmicro.com.

295 Before encrypting the hard drives: Turton and Mehrotra, "Hackers Breached Colonial Pipeline Using Compromised Password."

296 Within five days, 30 percent of gas stations: Devika Krishna Kumar and Laura Sanicola, "Pipeline Outage Causes U.S. Gasoline Supply Crunch, Panic Buying," Reuters, May 11, 2021, reuters.com.

296 Secretary of Energy Jennifer Granholm: Cecelia Smith-Schoenwalder, "Energy Secretary: Don't Hoard Gasoline as Pipeline Shutdown Creates Supply Crunch," U.S. News & World Report, May 11, 2021, usnews.com.

296 Colonial had, in fact, secretly given: William Turton, Michael Riley, and Jennifer Jacobs, "Colonial Pipeline Paid Hackers Nearly $5 Million in Ransom," Bloomberg, May 13, 2021, bloomberg.com.

296 All of the subsequent chaos: David E. Sanger and Nicole Perlroth, "Pipeline Attack Yields Urgent Lessons About U.S. Cybersecurity," New York Times, May 14, 2021, nytimes.com.

296 "The attack forced us": "House Homeland Security Committee Hearing on the Colonial Pipeline Cyber Attack," C-SPAN, June 9, 2021, c-span.org.

297 The blockchain analysis firm Elliptic: Tom Robinson, "Elliptic Follows the Bitcoin Ransoms Paid by Colonial Pipeline and Other DarkSide Ransomware Victims," Elliptic, May 14, 2021, elliptic.co.

297 CNA Financial had paid a staggering: Kartikay Mehrotra and William Turton, "CNA Financial Paid $40 Million in Ransom After March Cyberattack," Bloomberg, May 20, 2021, bloomberg.com.

297 Chainalysis's staff had tracked: Chainalysis Team, "Ransomware Skyrocketed in 2020, but There May Be Fewer Culprits Than You Think," Chainalysis, Jan. 26, 2021, chainalysis.com.

297 Ransomware payouts in 2021: Nathaniel Lee, "As the U.S. Faces a Flurry of Ransomware Attacks, Experts Warn the Peak Is Likely Still to Come," CNBC, June 10, 2021, cnbc.com.

298 Designed by a pseudonymous cryptographer: Andy Greenberg, "Monero,

the Drug Dealer's Cryptocurrency of Choice, Is on Fire," *Wired,* Jan. 27, 2017, wired.com.

298 Another, newer cryptocurrency called Zcash: Andy Greenberg, "Zcash, an Untraceable Bitcoin Alternative, Launches in Alpha," *Wired,* Jan. 20, 2016, wired.com.

299 In fact, a 2017 study by one group: Malte Möser et al., "An Empirical Analysis of Traceability in the Monero Blockchain," *Proceedings on Privacy Enhancing Technologies,* April 23, 2018, arxiv.org.

300 Another group of researchers: George Kappos et al., "An Empirical Analysis of Anonymity in Zcash," Usenix Security '18, May 8, 2018, arxiv.org.

300 In the case of the ransomware group NetWalker: Chainalysis Team, "Chainalysis in Action: U.S. Authorities Disrupt NetWalker Ransomware," Chainalysis, Jan. 27, 2021, chainalysis.com.

300 The bureau had arrested: "Department of Justice Launches Global Action Against NetWalker Ransomware," Justice Department, Jan. 27, 2021, justice.gov.

300 Gronager pointed to the 2018 charges: Indictment, *United States of America v. Viktor Borisovich Netyksho et al.,* Justice Department, July 13, 2018, justice.gov.

301 It had recovered 63.7 of the 75 bitcoins: "Department of Justice Seizes $2.3 Million in Cryptocurrency Paid to the Ransomware Extortionists Darkside," Justice Department, June 7, 2021, justice.gov.

301 In June 2021, *The New York Times:* Nicole Perlroth, Erin Griffith, and Katie Benner, "Pipeline Investigation Upends Idea That Bitcoin Is Untraceable," *New York Times,* June 9, 2021, nytimes.com.

302 President Joe Biden himself brought up: Steve Holland and Andrea Shalal, "Biden Presses Putin to Act on Ransomware Attacks, Hints at Retaliation," Reuters, July 10, 2021, reuters.com.

302 The U.S. State Department announced: Ned Price, "Reward Offers for Information to Bring DarkSide Ransomware Variant Co-conspirators to Justice," State Department, Nov. 4, 2021, state.gov.

302 DarkSide, for its part, had posted: Michael Schwirtz and Nicole Perlroth, "DarkSide, Blamed for Gas Pipeline Attack, Says It Is Shutting Down," *New York Times,* May 14, 2021, nytimes.com.

302 The U.S. Treasury imposed new sanctions: "Treasury Continues to Counter Ransomware as Part of Whole-of-Government Effort; Sanctions Ransomware Operators and Virtual Currency Exchange," State Department, Nov. 8, 2021, state.gov.

302 By November 2021, Europol had announced: "Five Affiliates to Sodinokibi/REvil Unplugged," Europol, Nov. 18, 2021, europa.eu.

303 The FBI recovered $6.1 million: "Ukrainian Arrested and Charged with Ransomware Attack on Kaseya," Justice Department, Nov. 8, 2021, justice .gov.

303 "Today, and now for the second time": "Attorney General Merrick B. Garland, Deputy Attorney General Lisa O. Monaco, and FBI Director Christopher Wray Deliver Remarks on Sodinokibi/REvil Ransomware Arrest," Justice Department, Nov. 8, 2021, justice.gov.

303 In an even more shocking turn: Dustin Volz and Robert McMillan, "Russia Arrests Hackers Tied to Major U.S. Ransomware Attacks, Including Colonial Pipeline Disruption," *Wall Street Journal,* Jan. 14, 2022, wsj.com.

CHAPTER 49: GRAY ZONES

305 By Chainalysis's measure, they accounted: Chainalysis Team, "Crypto Crime Trends for 2022: Illicit Transaction Activity Reaches All-Time High in Value, All-Time Low in Share of All Cryptocurrency Activity," Chainalysis, Jan. 6, 2022, chainalysis.com.

305 A few months earlier it had taken: Chainalysis, "Chainalysis Raises $100 Million at a $4.2 Billion Valuation to Execute Vision as the Blockchain Data Platform," press release, June 24, 2021, prnewswire.com.

306 the potential for cryptocurrency in Xinjiang, China: Ross Andersen, "The Panopticon Is Already Here," *Atlantic,* Sept. 2020, atlantic.com.

306 Hong Kong, where protesters line up: Mary Hui, "Why Hong Kong's Protesters Were Afraid to Use Their Metro Cards," *Quartz,* June 17, 2019, quartz .com.

307 "Chainalysis is actively looking": Chainalysis Team, "Alt-Right Groups and Personalities Involved in the January 2021 Capitol Riot Received over $500K in Bitcoin from French Donor One Month Prior," Chainalysis, Jan. 14, 2021, chainalysis.com.

308 These new rules require: Scott Ikeda, "Crypto Regulation Tucked into Infrastructure Bill Raises Surveillance Concerns; Receivers Would Have to Collect Tax IDs on Transactions over $10,000," *CPO Magazine,* Nov. 18, 2021, cpomagazine.com.

310 Following that surveillance, Mansoor: "The Persecution of Ahmed Mansoor," Human Rights Watch, Jan. 27, 2021, hrw.org.

CHAPTER 50: RUMKER

313 "AlphaBay is back": DeSnake, "AlphaBay Is Back," post on Ghostbin, Aug. 2021, ghostbin.com, archived at archive.is/vWT3U.

314 I reached out to DeSnake: Andy Greenberg, "He Escaped the Dark Web's Biggest Bust. Now He's Back," *Wired,* Sept. 23, 2021.

314 the 2018 Fordham International Conference: Lorenzo Franceschi-Bicchierai, "FBI Shows Arrest Video of Dark Web Kingpin Who Died by Suicide in Police Custody," *Vice Motherboard,* Jan. 10, 2018, vice.com.

317 Since Chainalysis had acquired WalletExplorer: Danny Nelson and Marc Hochstein, "Leaked Slides Show How Chainalysis Flags Crypto Suspects for Cops," *CoinDesk,* Sept. 21, 2021, coindesk.com.

EPILOGUE

323 (The giant exchange, it's worth noting: Angus Berwick and Tom Wilson, "Crypto Giant Binance Kept Weak Money-Laundering Checks Even as It Promised Tougher Compliance, Documents Show," Reuters, Jan. 21, 2022, reuters.com.

324 Kathryn Haun, Gambaryan's old boss: Kate Rooney, "Crypto Investor Katie Haun Is Leaving Andreessen Horowitz to Launch Her Own Fund," CNBC, Dec. 15, 2021, cnbc.com.

INDEX